Du Bois

Du Bois

A Critical Introduction

Reiland Rabaka

polity

First published in 2021 by Polity Press

Polity Press
65 Bridge Street
Cambridge CB2 1UR, UK

Polity Press
101 Station Landing
Suite 300
Medford, MA 02155, USA

ISBN-13: 978-1-5095-1924-8
ISBN-13: 978-1-5095-1925-5 (pb)

A catalogue record for this book is available from the British Library.

Library of Congress Cataloging-in-Publication Data
Names: Rabaka, Reiland, 1972- author.
Title: Du Bois : a critical introduction / Reiland Rabaka.
Description: Cambridge, UK ; Medford, MA, USA : Polity Press, 2021. |
   Series: Key Contemporary Thinkers | Includes bibliographical references
   and index. | Summary: "The pioneering work of America's greatest black
   nineteenth-century thinker explained"-- Provided by publisher.
Identifiers: LCCN 2020041247 (print) | LCCN 2020041248 (ebook) | ISBN
   9781509519248 (hardback) | ISBN 9781509519255 (paperback) | ISBN
   9781509519262 (pdf) | ISBN 9781509519286 (epub)
Subjects: LCSH: Du Bois, W. E. B. (William Edward Burghardt), 1868-1963. |
   African Americans--Study and teaching. | African American educators. |
   Critical theory. | Racism--United States. | United States--Race
   relations. | African Americans--Politics and government.
Classification: LCC E185.97.D73 R3225 2021 (print) | LCC E185.97.D73
   (ebook) | DDC 323.092--dc23
LC record available at https://lccn.loc.gov/2020041247
LC ebook record available at https://lccn.loc.gov/2020041248

Typeset in 10.5 on 12pt Palatino
by Fakenham Prepress Solutions, Fakenham, Norfolk NR21 8NL
Printed and bound in Great Britain by Short Run Press

The publisher has used its best endeavors to ensure that the URLs for external websites referred to in this book are correct and active at the time of going to press. However, the publisher has no responsibility for the websites and can make no guarantee that a site will remain live or that the content is or will remain appropriate.

Every effort has been made to trace all copyright holders, but if any have been overlooked the publisher will be pleased to include any necessary credits in any subsequent reprint or edition.

For further information on Polity, visit our website:
politybooks.com

For my family – both my biological family and my radical political family

Contents

Acknowledgments

In this book, I have attempted to guide readers through W. E. B. Du Bois's life and legacy in a way that is clear, accurate, and critical. Although the focus of the book is on the key issues Du Bois addressed, the historical and cultural context in which he developed his social, political, and economic thought has not been neglected. *Du Bois: A Critical Introduction* is not an intellectual biography of Du Bois, but instead an introduction to his discourse and its most distinctive features. This book also seeks to demonstrate why Du Bois and his discourse remain relevant in the twenty-first century.

I am grateful to students, colleagues, and comrades throughout the years who have contributed in important ways to the research, writing, and revision of this book. I would be remiss if I did not offer my sincere gratitude to the editorial team at Polity Press, especially George Owers and Julia Davies, who supported my vision for an accessible but *critical* introduction to Du Bois's sprawling oeuvre. Lastly, I thank my friends and family for their support during the many years it took me to research, write, and revise this book. If I were to sincerely say thank you a thousand times (*asante sana, na gode sosai, daalu nke ukwuu, ke leboha haholo, ndokutenda zvikuru, aad ayaad u mahadsantahay, hatur nuhun pisan, enkosi kakhulu, o şeun pupọ, ngibona kakhulu,* etc.), I would not have thanked each of you enough. *Ubuntu* – I am because we are.

In the spirit of W. E. B. Du Bois …

Reiland Rabaka
Boulder, Colorado
July 2020

Introduction: Du Bois's Lifework

W. E. B. Du Bois's life was bookended by the Civil War and the Civil Rights Movement. In the period between the aftermath of the Civil War known as the Reconstruction era (1865–77) and the Civil Rights Movement years (1954–68), Du Bois altered American history – and, indeed, world history – by aligning himself with many of the most cutting-edge and controversial causes of his epoch.[1] Yet the public view of Du Bois is often that of an elitist advocate of "racial uplift" via a "Talented Tenth," and, of course, the author of the 1903 classic *The Souls of Black Folk*, a collection of essays that ingeniously captured the complexities of African Americans' past, present, and future.[2] After the publication of *The Souls of Black Folk*, Du Bois took a hard-activist turn that ultimately culminated in the founding of the National Association for the Advancement of Colored People (NAACP) in 1909. The next year, 1910, he inaugurated *The Crisis: A Record of the Darker Races*, the monthly magazine of the NAACP. Du Bois edited *The Crisis* for nearly a quarter of a century, from 1910 to 1934. Under his editorship, *The Crisis* touched on an array of topics dealing with black history, culture, politics, economics, and the arts. Although it began with a monthly circulation of 1,000 copies, by its peak period (*circa* 1917–27) *The Crisis* reached more than 100,000 readers monthly.[3]

After his break with the NAACP in 1934, because he felt the organization wanted to mute his increasing militancy and commitment to Marxism, Du Bois published his radical revisionist history of African American enslavement, the Civil War, and Reconstruction, *Black Reconstruction*, in 1935.[4] *Black Reconstruction* explored the aftermath of the Civil War from the bottom-up points of view of the freedmen and freedwomen, black workers and white workers. The book revealed Du Bois's serious study of Marxism and the shedding of many elements of his early elitist leadership model. As a result of the Great Depression, Du Bois ramped up his search for alternatives to the racism and capitalism he believed were deeply embedded in, and deforming, US democracy. This search led him back to Pan-Africanism – essentially the commitment to continental and diasporan African unification, decolonization, and liberation – which he first embraced at the Pan-African Conference held in London in 1900. Du Bois gradually evolved from reformist to radical internationalist who traveled to, and openly supported, revolutions and anti-colonial movements in Russia, Japan, China, India, Africa, and the Caribbean. He spent roughly half of his life committed to what the Communist International (Comintern) called "world revolution" – the goal of fomenting socialist-oriented revolutions internationally.

After the publication of *Black Reconstruction*, a combination of anti-racism, anti-colonialism, and Marxist internationalism dominated Du Bois's thought. As a consequence of the Cold War and his many political misjudgments surrounding Marxism, it was Du Bois's search for a democratic socialist model for Africa and its diaspora that got him into the most trouble during the last decades of his long life. For example, Du Bois was duped into supporting despotic and deformed versions of communism in Russia under Joseph Stalin (i.e., Stalinism) and China under Mao Tse-tung (i.e., Maoism). Even after the horrors of Stalinism were revealed in the wake of Stalin's death in 1953 – such as the famines it caused and the brutal repression of Russian workers – Du Bois refused to publicly denounce and distance himself from Stalinism, stubbornly stating that he would not give in to anti-communism. Du Bois's Marxism made him an easy target in the midst of the widespread anti-communist panic known as the "Second Red Scare" (*circa* 1945–55). Although he lived through the "First Red Scare," which materialized in the aftermath of World War I and which marked the rampant fear of Bolshevism and anarchism, Du Bois's increasing commitment to Marxism in the 1930s, 1940s, and 1950s brought his work to the attention of the notorious Cold War anti-communist Senator Joseph McCarthy, and Du Bois fell victim to McCarthyism. Consequently, in 1951, Du Bois was indicted by the US federal government as an agent of a foreign state as a result of his work with the Peace Information Center, an organization committed to peace activism and nuclear disarmament. As detailed in his 1952 book, *In Battle for Peace*, the then 82-year-old Du Bois was arrested, handcuffed, searched for concealed weapons, fingerprinted, briefly jailed, and subsequently released on bail.[5] However, his passport was immediately revoked and remained canceled until 1958. Du Bois's misguided support for dictatorial leaders such as Joseph Stalin and Mao Tse-tung, who claimed to be communist and committed to Marxist principles, has caused many scholars to disregard or even lampoon his late-life work and instead focus almost exclusively on his early and middle years up to his resignation from the editorship of *The Crisis* in 1934.

Considering the complex nature of his life, scholarship, and activism, this volume's primary objective is to provide a brief introduction to Du Bois's discourse and chart his inimitable development from reformist social scientist to radical internationalist. Along the way, Du Bois innovatively synthesized the study and critique of race and racism, gender and sexism, class and capitalism, and colonialism and anti-colonialism. Indeed, his work can be characterized as an interesting combination of anti-racism, anti-colonialism, male feminism, and Marxism. Consequently, *Du Bois: A Critical Introduction* explores Du Bois's solutions to the "problems" of racism, sexism, capitalism, and colonialism. Most scholarship on Du Bois seems to isolate one period or aspect of his polymathic thought. There is also a tendency to de-radicalize and domesticate his discourse by sanitizing it of its radical and internationalist elements, especially in his later socialist-cum-communist years. *Du Bois: A Critical Introduction* will instead examine the strengths and weaknesses in Du Bois's development from reformist to radical to late-life revolutionary.

Abbreviated biography, embryonic intersectionality, and early interdisciplinarity

William Edward Burghardt Du Bois (pronounced "Due-Boyss") was born five years after the Emancipation Proclamation on February 23, 1868, in Great Barrington, Massachusetts. In his lifetime, Great Barrington was a tiny mill town in the Berkshire Mountains, about 140 miles west of Boston. The few African Americans in the area worked as domestics in homes or servants at summer resorts, while the Irish, German, and Czech folk worked in the town's factories. Du Bois was raised solely by his mother, Mary Silvina Burghardt

Du Bois, who he described as "a dark shining bronze, with smooth skin and lovely eyes."[6] His debonair but delinquent absentee father, Alfred Du Bois, a "Franco-Haitian" "light mulatto" war veteran of "indeterminate color," went missing before his toddling son turned 2 years old.[7] Mary Silvina was a domestic worker and washerwoman, and supported her precocious son through other odd jobs and outright charity from the well-to-do white town residents. Du Bois's father's absence greatly affected him, although perhaps not as much as his mother's paralytic stroke, which, his biographer David Levering Lewis reported, "impaired her left leg or arm, or both."[8]

Du Bois's early life, Lewis lamented, was "a milieu circumscribed by immiseration, dementia, and deformity."[9] As with so many African American children born within the shameful shadow of American slavery, Du Bois grew up very poor and, consequently, developed a consciousness of his lower-class status before he was aware of his race and American racism, even though he was the only black child in his all-white school. It was not long, however, before race and racism unforgivingly crept into his life, and from his first unforgettable and life-altering experience of anti-black racism he defiantly decided to "prove to the world that Negroes were just like other people."[10]

After his mother's untimely death on March 23, 1885, when he was only 16 years old, a forlorn Du Bois was determined to make something of himself, solemnly keeping a promise he made to his beloved mother.[11] Hence, after high school, an orphaned Du Bois sought every scholarship he could find to fund his studies at Fisk University, Harvard University, and the University of Berlin (where he came into contact with Max Weber) before returning to Harvard to become the first African American to be conferred a Ph.D. from that eminent institution in 1895.[12] Tellingly, his doctoral dissertation, entitled *The Suppression of the African Slave Trade to the United States of America, 1638–1870*, was the first social scientific engagement of African American enslavement, according to Lewis.[13] Duly recognizing Du Bois's monumental achievement, Harvard quickly published the dissertation as the first volume of its Harvard Historical Studies series in 1896.[14] Africa and anti-colonialism, obviously, factored into Du Bois's thought early in his intellectual and political life, and it is here, during the most formative phase of his life and career, that we find the real roots of his Pan-Africanism – his belief in and commitment to the unification, decolonization, and liberation of continental and diasporan Africa. Indeed, it could be said that Du Bois's intellectual and political life both begins and ends with explorations of Africa, the African diaspora, slavery, Reconstruction, racism, sexism, colonialism, and capitalism.[15]

Bearing all of this in mind, throughout this book Du Bois's evolving thought is examined as an early form of intersectionality – a framework that emphasizes that race, gender, class, and sexuality, among other socio-political categories, are interconnected and frequently combine to create intersecting systems of oppression. Loosely situated within this framework, Du Bois's discourse can be explored as a kind of *embryonic intersectionality* – meaning an inchoate, not fully formed variant of intersectionality that, because of its prefigurative nature, is at times conceptually connected, and, at other times, intellectually awkward and discursively disjointed. Nevertheless, when taken together and ample attention is given to his contributions to the critique of racism *and* sexism *and* capitalism *and* colonialism, Du Bois's corpus registers as both an undeniable and unprecedented contribution to the origins and evolution of what scholars currently call intersectionality.[16]

Without question, an eclectic but consistently intersectional combination of ideas and interests unfolds across the landscape of Du Bois's life and work. In fact, each of the subsequent chapters of this book loosely corresponds with a major intersectional category (except for sexuality) and exposes readers to his incipient intersectionality. For example – and as will be discussed in chapter 1, "*The Philadelphia Negro*: Early Work and the Inauguration of American Sociology" – Du Bois was one of the very first empirical social scientists in the US, and *The Philadelphia Negro* provides both a history and sociology of the interconnections between race and class (i.e., the racialization of class) in black life and culture. Additionally, the chapter details the pitfalls of Du Bois's early efforts to use social science in the interest of social reform. Chapters 2 and 3 reveal Du Bois to be one of the most critical, contradictory, and controversial race theorists of the twentieth century. More specifically, the second chapter, "*The Souls of Black Folk*: Critique of Racism and Contributions to Critical Race Studies," analyzes Du Bois's 1903 classic, *The Souls of Black Folk*, for its contribution to the study and critique of race, anti-black racism, and critical race studies. Chapter 3, "'The Souls of White Folk': Critique of White Supremacy and Contributions to Critical White Studies," essentially inverts the framework from the previous chapter and provides a survey of Du Bois's work on whiteness, critique of white supremacy, and contributions to what is currently called critical white studies. Chapter 4, "'The Damnation of Women':

Critique of Patriarchy, Contributions to Black Feminism, and Early Intersectionality," treats Du Bois's critique of patriarchy (i.e., male supremacy) and contributions to black feminism and early intersectionality. Finally, chapter 5, "*Black Reconstruction*: Critique of Capitalism, Contributions to Black Marxism, and Discourse on Democratic Socialism," explores Du Bois's Marxist thought and developing democratic socialism via several of his key essays that synthesize elements of black economic nationalism with Marxism. The centerpiece of chapter 5 is Du Bois's black Marxist magnum opus *Black Reconstruction*, which was arguably the first application of Marxian concepts to African American enslavement and blacks' pivotal roles in the Civil War and Reconstruction.

Along with his contributions to the origins and evolution of intersectionality, this book explores Du Bois's contributions to *interdisciplinarity* – the practice of bringing the scholarship of two or more academic disciplines together to answer a research question or provide solutions to a problem. Du Bois's collective coursework at Fisk University, Harvard University, and the University of Berlin was incredibly interdisciplinary, and resulted in a BA in classics from Fisk in 1888; a BA in philosophy from Harvard in 1890; an MA in history from Harvard in 1891; doctoral studies in history, economics, politics, and political economy at the University of Berlin between 1892 and 1894; and, ultimately, a Ph.D. in history from Harvard in 1895.[17] After earning his doctorate, Du Bois began his teaching career as a professor of classics, teaching Latin, Greek, German, and English, from 1894 to 1896 at Wilberforce University, an African Methodist Episcopal institution in Ohio. He unsuccessfully attempted to add sociology to the curriculum at Wilberforce in 1894, and left the school in frustration for the University of Pennsylvania in 1896, where he was hired as an "Assistant Instructor" to research and write a study on the African Americans of Philadelphia, the previously mentioned *The Philadelphia Negro*.[18] At the University of Pennsylvania, however, Du Bois was still not free from frustration, writing in his autobiography, "I ignored my pitiful stipend" and "it goes without saying that I did no instructing, save once to pilot a pack of idiots through the Negro slums."[19] After his brief stay at the University of Pennsylvania, Du Bois accepted a position at Atlanta University, where he established one of the first sociology departments in the United States and edited 16 innovative interdisciplinary volumes known as the "Atlanta University Studies," which were published by Atlanta University Press consecutively between 1898 and 1914.[20]

From reformist to radical to revolutionary

Whether we turn to Du Bois's early reformist scholarship, his middle-period radicalism, or his late-life embrace of revolutionary politics, a certain dismissiveness pervades Du Bois studies. The general thought is that Du Bois was either a reformist *or* a radical *or* a revolutionary socialist. However, it is inconceivable that he could have occupied all three political positions throughout the course of his long life because it defies the adage of "radicalism in youth and conservatism in old age by reversing its order."[21] Du Bois's upending of the order of conventional political development is one of the main reasons studying his life and work remains important and instructive. Another reason why studying Du Bois's life and work continues to be crucial is because, in the long run, years of one-dimensional interpretations of his thought have led to his erasure both in the academy and in activist communities. For instance, Du Bois's *The Philadelphia Negro*, although often overlooked in the history of sociology, was, upon its publication in 1899, an utterly unprecedented and undeniably innovative work in urban sociology, industrial sociology, historical sociology, political sociology, sociology of race, and sociology of culture. Elijah Anderson asserted in his introduction to a reprint edition of *The Philadelphia Negro*: "W. E. B. Du Bois is a founding father of American sociology, but, unfortunately, neither this masterpiece nor much of Du Bois's other work has been given proper recognition." In fact, Anderson continued, "it is possible to advance through a graduate program in sociology in this country without ever hearing about Du Bois."[22]

Anderson's weighted words here help to highlight why an introduction to Du Bois's thought that surveys its full range and reach is desperately needed. Beyond his contributions to sociology or history or politics, among other academic disciplines, Du Bois's life and work continue to offer us much of practical value because we continue to search for solutions to many of the problems he spent a lifetime studying and critiquing. For example, Du Bois's writings on racism in the twentieth century remain relevant in the twenty-first century because we continue to be plagued by various forms of racism, whether we turn to the police brutality that triggered the Black Lives Matter Movement or the issues surrounding immigration in the US or Europe (e.g., Italy, Portugal, Slovakia, and the Czech Republic). His contributions to the critique of patriarchy prefigure the current discourse on "male feminism" and offer a powerful model to contemporary men seeking feminist-inspired forms of masculinity. His analysis of colonialism and its interconnectedness with racism (i.e., racial colonialism) continues to have great import for adequately understanding the ongoing struggles of formerly colonized continents such as Africa, Asia, and the Americas (i.e., North, Central, and South America). Lastly, Du Bois's often overlooked late-life work, especially *Black Reconstruction*, provides us with quintessential critiques of capitalism and global imperialism, and highlights the continuing overlap between racism, capitalism, and colonialism.

Du Bois: A Critical Introduction will probe the contradictions in Du Bois's thought that were integral to his evolution from reformist social scientist to radical intellectual-activist to revolutionary democratic socialist. As will be seen, Du Bois began his intellectual and political life committed to racial and economic reform, often displaying the influence of the bourgeois academics, social democrats, race liberals, and moderate Pan-Africanists he studied with and idolized at the time. During his reformist phase, he was committed to using egalitarian and legislative methods to achieve democratic social transformation. Throughout this period, Du Bois saw little or no revolutionary potential in the working class, especially the black working class. As a result, his early thought lacked a thorough understanding of, or commitment to, working-class folk as agents of their own emancipation. Dedicated to his "Talented Tenth" leadership strategy, Du Bois's early elitism led him to search for top-down solutions to social and political problems. His elitism gradually gave way to vanguardism – the belief that a small group of the most class-conscious, intellectually advanced, and politically sophisticated should lead the working class in their struggle against racism, colonialism, and capitalism. In the long run, this vanguardism caused him to misread many political situations, such as backing Joseph Stalin and Mao Tse-tung.

Over time, Du Bois shifted his political position from social reform to social revolution, and desperately searched for bottom-up solutions to social and political problems. In this regard, his intellectual and political evolution holds many lessons we could learn from and use today in our efforts to make sense of our epoch: from the contentious centrality of race, gender, and class in US politics, to popular revolutions across the Global South (i.e., formerly colonized or "Third World" countries), to recent worker uprisings in the US, Europe, Asia, Africa, and Latin America. Du Bois began his career a dedicated elitist but, after many missteps, evolved into a committed radical democratic socialist by his later years. He came to understand the carnage of world wars, race riots, lynchings, racial segregation, the disenfranchisement of women, colonialism, and imperialism as serious indictments of the triumphalist narratives of spreading democracy that Europe and the United States have propagated for centuries. It was Du Bois's search for solutions to the problems of racism, sexism, colonialism, and capitalism that forced him to gradually move beyond reformism and embrace radicalism, and eventually revolution. Ultimately, Du Bois's legacy is his incredible evolution from bourgeois social scientist to revolutionary internationalist. His legacy is also bound up in what his trajectory teaches us about oppressed peoples' awesome ability to transcend and try new things when deeply committed to transforming themselves and the world.

Perhaps more than anything else, Du Bois's indefatigable commitment to self-change and social change in the twentieth century provides us with a paradigm for transforming ourselves and the twenty-first century. As David Levering Lewis noted, "In the course of his long, turbulent career ... W. E. B. Du Bois attempted virtually every possible solution to the problem of twentieth-century racism – scholarship, propaganda, integration, cultural and economic separatism, politics, international communism, expatriation, Third World solidarity." Lewis importantly continued, "First had come culture and education for the elites; then the ballot for the masses; then economic democracy; and finally all these solutions in the service of global racial parity and economic justice."[23] Lewis helps to highlight both the aspirations and contradictions at the heart of this book.

Du Bois's dedication to racial justice, gender justice, decolonization, and an end to economic exploitation was an aspiration that brought numerous struggles, and at times caused contradictions and many mistakes, in determining the most appropriate course of action. Undoubtedly, his late-life enthusiastic commitment to the oppressed as agents of their own emancipation in many instances made him impetuous, and led him to misjudge calamitous political episodes such as the errors and horrors of Stalinism and Maoism. However, for those deeply interested in or committed to democratic social transformation, Du Bois's thought remains important precisely because he was right about some things and downright wrong about others, and frequently admitted it. In the end, it is Du Bois's trajectory from reformist to radical to revolutionary and his principled commitment to democratic social transformation, "rather than the solutions he proposed, that are instructive" – because Du Bois, Lewis shared, "was an intellectual in the purest sense of the word – a thinker whose obligation was to be dissatisfied continually with his own thoughts and those of others."[24] Du Bois's life and work, when objectively engaged and fully understood, provides us with a framework for not only identifying problems but developing viable solutions to them. Whether we turn to the resurgence of global racism and xenophobia, misogyny and gender injustice, the neocolonial conditions of the wretched of the earth and the Global South, the constantly changing character of capitalism and the misinterpretation of Marxism, or the seemingly never-ending imperialist wars, W. E. B. Du Bois's discourse offers us both extraordinary insights and cautionary tales.

To access the lessons Du Bois's legacy may teach us, we must ask a set of crucial questions: Why is it imperative for us to know *who* Du Bois was and *what* he contributed to contemporary thought? Even more – and methodologically speaking – why is it important to not only know *what* but *how*, in his own innovative intellectual history-making manner, Du Bois contributed when he contributed to contemporary thought? The real answers to these questions lie not so much in who Du Bois was, but more in the intellectual and political legacy he left behind. That is to say, the answers lie in the lasting contributions his discourse has historically made and is currently making to our critical comprehension of the ways the social inequalities and injustices of the nineteenth and twentieth centuries have informed and morphed into the social inequalities and injustices of the twenty-first century. Let us begin, then, with Du Bois's early social science in the interest of social reform in his seminal study *The Philadelphia Negro*.

1

The Philadelphia Negro:
Early Work and the Inauguration of American Sociology

Du Bois's urban sociology: *The Philadelphia Negro*

Building on, and decidedly going beyond, the methodological outline and orientation of his groundbreaking 1898 rural sociological work "The Negroes of Farmville," W. E. B. Du Bois's *The Philadelphia Negro* is widely considered his most comprehensive contribution to social science.[1] In many ways mirroring his discussion of the distinct history and heritage, racialization and criminalization, family life and conjugal conditions, education and illiteracy, and work and wages of the "country Negro" found in his Farmville study, *The Philadelphia Negro* added in-depth investigations of the disease and death rate, alcoholism and pauperism, electoral politics and religious practices of the "city Negro" to the incipient sociological enterprise. Much more methodical and meticulous than the rural study, almost 125 years after its publication, *The Philadelphia Negro* has garnered a unique place for itself in the annals of American social science. David Levering Lewis declared: "Some have made the debatable claim that *The Philadelphia Negro* is the first study of its kind in America, but its pride of place as the first scientific urban study of African Americans is as secure as the charge is misconceived that Du Bois's book is largely derivative."[2] Appearing to offer Lewis a rejoinder, sociologist Elijah Anderson exclaimed, "Du Bois's work takes on seminal status not only for the study of the urban poor but also for the study of race in urban America. Indeed, it is in this sense that *The Philadelphia Negro* was truly the first work of its kind." Then, concluding his contention with words that seem to dovetail with Lewis's views, Anderson asserted, "It was the first [study] to seriously address and profoundly illuminate what was then known as the 'Negro problem'" – the discourse on the civil rights and social roles of freedmen, freedwomen and their descendants in the US between the Reconstruction era (1865–77) and the World War II period (1939–45).[3]

Researched, written, and published under the auspices of the University of Pennsylvania and its affiliated welfare organization, the College Settlement Association (CSA), *The Philadelphia Negro* bears the marks of Du Bois's early elitism and emphasis on social reform. Partly on account of the white middle-class feminist paternalist reformism of the CSA – which, Lewis asserted, "was a feminist force to reckon with for civic leaders" – and partly owing to his own Eurocentrism, elitism, and assimilationism, Du Bois wrote "what amounted to two books in one – one that would not be immediately denounced or ridiculed by the arbiters of mainstream knowledge, influence, and order for its transparent heterodoxy; and a second one that would, over time, deeply penetrate the social sciences and gradually improve race relations policy through its not-immediately apparent interpretive radicalism."[4]

The Philadelphia Negro is both a book of social science and a plan of social reform. It is divided into four parts: part one provides a history of African Americans in the city of Philadelphia; part two engages "their present condition considered as individuals"; part three, "their condition as an organized social group"; and, lastly, part four, "their physical and social environment."[5] Squarely aligning himself with turn-of-the-twentieth-century progressivism – the idea that advancements in science, technology, social organization, and economic development are integral to improving the human condition – for Du Bois *The Philadelphia Negro* was a case study for "practical reform" of African American living conditions.[6] In other words, with *The Philadelphia Negro* he intended to offer solutions to the "Negro Problem." However, one major weakness of the book is that it vacillates between Du Bois's critique of the racial myths and social stereotypes swirling around recently emancipated African Americans and his obvious internalization of many of those same myths and stereotypes. To be specific, Du Bois sought to drive home the point of the "Negro group as a symptom" of their current conditions, and "not a cause." African Americans in Philadelphia were a "striving, palpitating group, and not an inert, sick body of crime."[7] But, Du Bois's own words in *The Philadelphia Negro* often reveal flashes of his embrace of Victorian moralism and elitism in his conception of social science in the interest of social reform.

Wedding history with sociology, Du Bois developed comprehensive questionnaires to capture the conditions of individuals, family relations, education, and employment. Working "morning, noon, and night," as he detailed in his autobiography, Du Bois personally interviewed 5,000 people.[8] His research was rigorous and the data he presented was exhaustive, touching on the ethos and central social institutions of the African American community. He was particularly adept at the presentation of statistics on African American health, marriage, family units, literacy, education, employment, religion, and crime. To fully comprehend the African American experience in Philadelphia at the dawn of the twentieth century, Du Bois believed his readers needed historical grounding. Hence, chapters III and IV of *The Philadelphia Negro* are devoted entirely to the history of African Americans in Philadelphia. Drawing on his graduate training at Harvard and the University of Berlin, for Du Bois sociology was more than mere analysis of the present social, political, and economic situation. The present is inextricable from the past in Du Bois's thought, and one of the most defining moments of African Americans' past was their enslavement. Consequently, he stressed "one cannot study the Negro in freedom and come to general conclusions about his destiny without knowing his history in slavery."[9] *The Philadelphia Negro* demonstrates that the most rewarding sociology for Du Bois is historical sociology, combined historical and sociological research that pays careful attention to the incessant evolution of the social organization, political practices, economics, and cultural traditions of a people. At this early point in his work, Du Bois strongly believed that systematic sociological inquiry, coupled with a detailed historical understanding and cultural comprehension of a social group, could provide the basis for a concrete plan and program of social reform.

Nevertheless, Du Bois's commitment to black progress was often undercut by his elitism. *The Philadelphia Negro* shows traces of his – however subtle – digestion and indelicate application of a homespun intra-racial Social Darwinistic elitism where the "better class" of blacks – the "talented few" in his words – were purportedly destined to rise above, and eventually rule over, the "low civilization" of the "great mass of Negroes." For instance, Du Bois ironically wrote, "there are many Negroes who are as bright, talented and reliable as any class of [white] workmen, and who in untrammeled competition would soon rise high in the economic scale, and thus by the law of the survival of the fittest we should soon have left at the bottom those inefficient and lazy drones who did not deserve a better fate."[10] Inexcusable elitism and assimilationism fill the pages of *The Philadelphia Negro* but, despite this, it has been repeatedly hailed – by black and white alike, bourgeois and proletarian – as a seminal text in the history and development of American sociology.[11]

Unquestionably contradictory and controversial, Du Bois's sociology was ultimately social policy-preoccupied and social praxis-promoting. Seemingly more concerned with "getting the facts straight" than with avoiding hurting black or white folks' feelings, *The Philadelphia Negro* spared nothing and no one in its quest to provide new, empirically based knowledge in the interests of social, political, and institutional transformation. Long before European American sociology sought to couple social theory with social praxis, Du Bois, literally, laid the foundations for liberation sociology in the United States.[12] In fact, part of what really and truly distinguishes Du Bois's sociological legacy from those of his European and European American sociological forebears and contemporaries is his still easily detected determination, and the unmistakable passion with which he deconstructed and reconstructed the then-inchoate empirical social scientific research methods in the interests of African Americans.

In essence, what Du Bois's early sociological work presents us with are the theoretical trials and tribulations, the conceptual growing pains, of his initial efforts to conceive, first, an African American and, later, a Pan-African critical theory specific to the special social, political, and economic needs of black folk. However, it should be underscored that it was not merely Du Bois's combination of social science and social reform that led him to "ambiguities, exaggerations, and biases."[13] More critically, what makes Du Bois's "ambiguities, exaggerations, and biases" even more ironic is that, even though he was diligently endeavoring to establish an empirical sociology in the interests of African Americans, his work – quite literally, his words – betray the fact that he was intellectually infected with Eurocentrism, elitism, assimilationism, certain elements of Social Darwinism, and a very subtle form of sexism which privileged the patriarchal conception of the African American family. In what follows, let us take a closer look at *The Philadelphia Negro*, accenting its prefiguring and pivotal place in Du Bois's discourse. By dividing our discussion along the lines of the *The Philadelphia Negro*'s primary themes, which coincide with its major chapters, we will be able to better grasp and grapple with its innovative and influential findings and more easily explore its "interpretive radicalism," as well as its interpretive elitism and conceptual conservatism.

Du Bois's sociology of "A City Within a City": *The Philadelphia Negro* and the racialization of the city

Undoubtedly, one of the major breakthroughs of *The Philadelphia Negro* is its detailed discussion of class formation among African Americans a mere three decades after the signing of the Emancipation Proclamation in 1863. Within the early world of sociology, the sociology of class was dominated by Max Weber's and Karl Marx's respective conceptions of class. In brief, Weber developed the three-class system, which is also known as the Weberian stratification. It is essentially a multidimensional approach to social stratification that captures the interplay between wealth, status, and power. He argued that a person's power is demonstrated in society through their status (i.e., social position), through their class in the economic sphere, and through their party (i.e., political organization) in the political sphere. Marx's class theory emphasizes that a person's position within a class hierarchy is determined by their particular role in the production process. Marxian class theory also contends that social, political, and ideological consciousness is determined by one's class position. From Marx's point of view, there was a class war and never-ending class struggle between those who control production (the bourgeoisie) and those who produce the goods or services in society (the proletariat). The Du Boisian theory of class differs from Weber's and Marx's conceptions of class in that Du Bois's theory takes into consideration the role race and racism play in class hierarchy and class struggles among racially colonized peoples, and especially black folk.

Even more meticulously than in his previous work such as "The Negroes of Farmville," Du Bois ventured into the uncharted regions of African American social classes and unprecedentedly determined that class formation and class conflict amongst African Americans were consequences of – of course – economics, employment, education, property ownership, and morals and manners, but also, and even more tellingly, racialization and assimilation – what he termed "color prejudice," the "color-line," "discrimination against

Negroes," the "tangible form of Negro prejudice," "a silent policy against Negroes," "veiled discrimination," and "social ostracism."[14] Seeming to simultaneously draw from, and commit a *conceptual coup d'état* in the midst of, Weber's and Marx's conceptions of class, Du Bois's concept of class, even in this early instance, is distinguished because of its critical attention to the ways in which the political economy of race and racism dictated and determined that social classes amongst African Americans could be more properly analyzed as *racial classes*.[15]

Even if all of the other sociological innovations of *The Philadelphia Negro* were to be overlooked, as they frequently have been, Du Bois's tenacious insistence on the ways in which African American social classes have been and remain degradingly racialized and, therefore, are always and everywhere more than mere socio-economic classes – *à la* the conventional sociological conception of class – should be calmly and cautiously considered for both its classical and contemporary sociological significance. Du Bois's sociology of racial classes reaches from the nineteenth century, across the twentieth century, and resonates with both the sociology of race and the sociology of class in the twenty-first century with its intense emphasis on African Americans' particular and peculiar class formations and class cultures. His sociology of racial classes registers as an early reminder that Weberian and Marxian conceptions of class, no matter how "universal" many sociologists believe them to be, were primarily tailored to fit the needs and greeds of Europeans, and not the needs of a non-European group such as African Americans who were, truth be told, enslaved, racialized, and colonized by Europeans from a wide range of class backgrounds: from bourgeoisie and petit-bourgeoisie to proletariat and lumpenproletariat.[16]

Part of what makes African American social classes "racial classes" is not simply their racialization at the hands of whites but, even more, the continued racial colonization of their lives and experiences under American apartheid.[17] Du Bois unrepentantly announced at the outset of *The Philadelphia Negro*:

> Here is a large group of people – perhaps forty-five thousand, a city within a city – who do not form an integral part of the larger social group. This in itself is not altogether unusual; there are other unassimilated groups: Jews, Italians, even [other white] Americans; and yet in the case of the Negroes the segregation is more conspicuous, more patent to the eye, and so intertwined with a long historic evolution, with peculiarly pressing social problems of poverty, ignorance, crime

and labor, that the Negro problem far surpasses in scientific interest and social gravity, most of the other race or class questions.[18]

Acknowledging that racial segregation was inextricable from African Americans' other "peculiarly pressing social problems," Du Bois ultimately declared that the "Negro problem far surpasses in scientific interest and social gravity, most of the other race or class questions."

For those who have wrongly claimed that Du Bois's class consciousness was a consequence of his later Marxist studies, here is clear proof to the contrary. However, we should acknowledge – as he did in his final autobiography, *The Autobiography of W. E. B. Du Bois* – that when Du Bois's early sociology of class is placed under scrutiny, it is found wanting, especially with regard to every class of African Americans other than the "better class of Negroes," or, rather, the "Negro aristocracy," as he put it.[19] For Du Bois, the Negro Problem, the *Negroization* or *process(es) of Negroizing* African Americans, went well above and well beyond "other race or class questions," because intentionally immigrating to America – without in any way diminishing the hardships and harsh conditions immigrants experienced – is extremely different from having endured the African holocaust, the Middle Passage, and African American enslavement, as well as subsequent racial segregation and outright racial terrorism. African American social classes, therefore, did not then, and certainly do not now, solely revolve around income, employment, and education, but also pivot on an axis involving the political economy of black lives lived in anti-black racist environments.

Du Bois made a major methodological contribution by emphasizing the importance of contextualizing the "Negro problem" within the various environments in which African American lives and struggles were persistently pathologized or problematized. "The student of these questions," Du Bois asserted, referring to his contention that the "Negro problem far surpasses ... most of the other race or class questions," "must first ask, What is the real condition of this group of human beings? Of whom is it composed, what sub-groups and classes exist, what sort of individuals are being considered?"[20] He went further to underscore his emphasis on contextualizing African Americans within the various environments in which they eke out their existences, sternly stating that the "student must clearly recognize that a complete study must not confine itself to the group, but must specially notice the environment; the physical environment of city, sections and houses, the far mightier social environment – the surrounding world of custom, wish, whim, and thought which envelops this group and powerfully influences its social development."[21] In any effort, then, with pretensions to present a "complete study" of African Americans, it is necessary to "specially notice [their] environment," as it is crucial to understanding their "social development." Above, Du Bois wrote of the "long historic evolution" of the Negro Problem and American apartheid. His remarks here point to the deeply historical dimension of his sociology, which has been collectively commented on by Manning Marable, David Levering Lewis, David Blight, Robert Gregg, Marcus Hunter, Gerald Horne, and Aldon Morris.[22]

Indeed, other ethnic and cultural groups had gone through their own unique trials and tribulations in their efforts to socio-economically adjust and "assimilate" to the new context of American industrial capitalist culture – *The Philadelphia Negro* offers brief discussions of the socio-economic histories of various "ethnic European" groups, such as the Jews and Italians mentioned above. However, according to Du Bois, what made their respective situations different from the situation of African Americans was the incessant and insidious interplay of the political economy of race and anti-black racism in the US. It is this comparative historical dimension of *The Philadelphia Negro* that further distinguishes Du Bois's sociological discourse from the "armchair cerebrations of sociology's nineteenth-century system-builders" and gave its innovative interpretations their critical theoretical thrust. For Du Bois, sociology was so much more than merely "history abstracted" and isolated to tease out and examine its social problematics – as if the social can somehow be fancifully suspended from not only the historical, but also the political and the economic.[23] In his 1898 classic, "The Study of the Negro Problems," with which he undeniably laid the foundation on which contemporary African American studies has been built, Du Bois observed that the "study of the Negro as a social group may be, for convenience, divided into four not exactly logical but seemingly most practicable divisions, viz.: 1. Historical study. 2. Statistical investigation. 3. Anthropological measurement. 4. Sociological interpretation."[24] Note that "Historical study" is first and foremost, and then "Statistical investigation" and "Anthropological measurement" are to be undertaken before "Sociological interpretation." This should be stressed, or else Du Bois's cutting-edge conception of racial classes, not to mention his homespun historical sociology, is bound to be overlooked.[25]

Throughout *The Philadelphia Negro*, Du Bois relentlessly reminded his readers that race and racism distorted and deformed African American social development. Sometimes assuming the passive voice of an objective and disinterested social scientist rattling off facts and figures, and at other times unequivocally and aggressively arguing in the interests of African Americans, Du Bois's African American history-, culture-, and political economy-informed social science repeatedly returned to comparative history to give its sociological interpretations in-depth acuity and unprecedented authority. For example, he thundered in a key passage:

> We grant full citizenship in the World-Commonwealth to the "Anglo-Saxon" (whatever that may mean), the Teuton and the Latin; then with just a shade of reluctance we extend it to the Celt and Slav. We half deny it to the yellow races of Asia, admit the brown Indians to an ante-room only on the strength of an undeniable past; but with the Negroes of Africa we come to a full stop, and in its heart the civilized world with one accord denies that these come within the pale of nineteenth century Humanity. This feeling, widespread and deep-seated, is, in America, the vastest of the Negro problems; we have, to be sure, a threatening problem of ignorance but the ancestors of most Americans were far more ignorant than the freedmen's sons; these ex-slaves are poor but not as poor as the Irish peasants used to be; crime is rampant but not more so, if as much, as in Italy; but the difference is that the ancestors of the English and the Irish and the Italians were felt to be worth educating, helping and guiding because they were men and brothers, while in America a census which gives a slight indication of the utter disappearance of the American Negro from the earth is greeted with ill-concealed delight.[26]

It is within this context of overt anti-black racism and American apartheid that African American social classes formed and fluttered here and there. Their classes could not and would not be "classes" in a Weberian or Marxian sense so long as the political economy of race and racism was – whether intentionally or unintentionally, consciously or unconsciously – embraced by whites (including "ethnic European" immigrants) from a wide range of class backgrounds: again, from bourgeoisie and petit-bourgeoisie to proletariat and lumpenproletariat. As the collective work of Allen Davis, Mark Haller, Theodore Hershberg, Philip Scranton, and Sam Warner demonstrates, there has long been a historical and sociological discourse surrounding the "late" urban "arrival time" of African Americans – that is, when compared with "ethnic European" immigrants – as the fundamental factor explaining their maladjustment within industrial cities and urban environments, consequently reducing or, in several cases, rendering invisible the salience of the politics of race and economics of racism.[27] *The Philadelphia Negro* unflinchingly challenges such misguided hypotheses by turning to the history of American apartheid and pointing out that, long before the Industrial Revolution and long after the Emancipation Proclamation and Reconstruction, African Americans were not allowed any form of individuation within the world of white supremacy, which – as the twentieth-century works of Richard Wright, Ralph Ellison, James Baldwin, Toni Morrison, Aimé Césaire, and Frantz Fanon eloquently illustrate – in time existentially translates into black invisibility and black anonymity. "No differences of social condition" or social class, Du Bois declared, "allowed any Negro to escape from the group, although such escape was continually the rule among Irish, Germans and other whites."[28]

In other words, elite African Americans' degraded racial status trumped their purportedly privileged class status – that is, their (theoretically) socially privileged position based on their education, employment, and income – and it is from this frame of reference that Du Bois delivered what was undeniably the first extended foray into African American class formation and class conflict.[29] "Before it was identified and described in *The Philadelphia Negro*, the class structure of Afro-America was mostly unknown, utterly myste-rious, and even widely assumed as nonexistent," David Levering Lewis quipped. He caustically continued, "Most white people supposed that the periodic appearance of exceptional or 'repre-sentative' black people was due to providence, 'mixed blood,' or some mysterious current passing through a dark, undifferentiated mass. Otherwise, there were only good Negroes and bad ones."[30] According to Marcus Anthony Hunter, "Du Bois's analysis points to an idea of *black heterogeneity* – the varied distinctions, perspectives, and peoples that constitute the black community." As a conse-quence, Hunter went further: "Du Boisian heterogeneity theorizes the concept as imbued with a consequential mix of racial tensions and intraracial distinctions. Such factors give rise to complex civil racialized societies that are compelled to live alongside one another within and across urban America."[31] Almost assuredly to the awe of his white readers, in *The Philadelphia Negro* Du Bois outlined four omnipresent classes or "grades," as he put it, of African Americans

– as easily identified in Philadelphia as they could be in New York, Chicago, Farmville, Atlanta, or Houston.[32]

The "talented few" and the "submerged tenth": Du Bois's concept of racially oppressed and economically exploited social classes

Seeming to prepare his readers for his intellectual history-making report, Du Bois softly intoned, "There is always a strong tendency on the part of the [white] community to consider the Negroes as composing one practically homogeneous mass. This view has of course a certain justification" – after all, he solemnly said, the "people of Negro descent in this land have had a common history, suffer today common disabilities, and contribute to one general set of social problems."[33] Then, like a lion calmly luring its prey into its lair, he sardonically said, "yet if the foregoing statistics have empha- sized any one fact it is that wide variations in antecedents, wealth, intelligence and general efficiency have already been differentiated within this group." Which is to say that, long before the births of Marx and Weber, African American social classes had "already been differentiated" and did not – and certainly not always and in every instance – quickly coincide with European or European American social classes or class struggles. Here we have returned to what was referred to above as Du Bois's *conceptual coup d'état* in the midst of Weber's and Marx's conceptions of class.

The first social class among African Americans was variously termed the "better class of Negroes," the "Negro aristocracy," and, most tellingly, the "talented few." They were, Du Bois delightfully disclosed, "Families of undoubted respectability earning sufficient income to live well; not engaged in menial service of any kind; the wife engaged in no occupation save that of house-wife, except in a few cases where she had special employment at home. The children not compelled to be bread-winners, but found in school; the family living in a well-kept home."[34] Of course, note should be made of Du Bois's – however demure – embrace of the patriarchal family model. Essentially, the husband and father was to be the bread-winner, and only, as Du Bois put it, "unworthy" or "unfor- tunate" women were left to protect and provide for themselves and, if applicable, their poor, fatherless children. One gets the distinct impression from reading *The Philadelphia Negro* that Du Bois beguilingly believed that "a woman's place is in the home." In holding that backward belief, he never offered viable options for the supposedly "unworthy" or "unfortunate" women who did not have homes, and courageously struck out on their own to build homes and, literally, create family. While Du Bois attributed a great deal of agency to African American men, his work was particularly weak when it came to identifying – and, even more, embracing – African American women's agency. We will return to Du Bois's ignorance of African American women's agency below, but it is important for readers to constantly bear this issue in mind in the meantime.

The second class of African Americans were the "respectable working-class." They lived "in comfortable circumstances, with a good home, and having steady remunerative work. The younger children in school."[35] The third class was candidly called the "poor." They were, Du Bois glibly shared, "persons not earning enough to keep them at all times above want; honest, although not always energetic or thrifty, and with no touch of gross immorality or crime. Including the very poor, and the poor."[36] The last and, as Du Bois disdainfully put it, the "lowest class" was one comprised of "criminals, prostitutes and loafers," the so-called "submerged tenth."[37] Therefore, in Du Bois's early articulation of African American social classes, there was a black bourgeoisie – a "Talented Few" or "Talented Tenth" – at the top, a "Submerged Tenth" at the bottom, and, sandwiched in-between, the black working class, on the one hand, and the black poor and "very poor," on the other hand.[38]

It could be easily averred that Du Bois's early articulation of African American social classes most readily resembles Marx's more famous conception of social classes – that is, bourgeoisie, petit-bourgeoisie, proletariat, and lumpenproletariat. However, to make too much of this – that is to say, the external or schematic similarities of their conceptions of class – would be to make a grave mistake. Du Bois's emphasis on the political economy of race and racism in dictating and determining African American class formation and African American class struggle obviously distinguishes his theory of class from Marx's and Weber's conceptions of class. By placing the role that race and racism play right alongside of politics and economics in class formation and class struggle, Du Bois developed a theory of class that spoke to the special needs of African Americans, and other racially colonized folk in capitalist countries.

Immediately following Du Bois's discussion of African American social classes in *The Philadelphia Negro* is a chapter on "The Contact of the Races," which begins with a section on "Color Prejudice."[39] The fact that Du Bois placed a chapter on racism directly after his unprecedented discussion of African American social classes speaks in no uncertain terms about the ways in which he was attempting to share with his readers not only the evolution and inner workings of African American social classes, but also the distinct ways that the politics of race and economics of racism dictated and determined African American class formation and African American class struggle in ways unfathomed by Weber, Marx, "late-nineteenth-century American social reformers," and, most certainly, European and European American social classes: from bourgeoisie and petit-bourgeoisie to proletariat and lumpenproletariat.[40] Du Bois acutely identified the ways in which anti-black racism was inextricable from the political economy of African American occupations in late-nineteenth-century Philadelphia. There was great difficulty, Du Bois reported, in "getting work," "keeping work," and "entering new lines of work," and this created a dire situation in which African Americans not only socio-economically suffered and resented whites but, eventually, resented and reviled each other and their (from their paradoxical perspective) "damn-blasted!" blackness.[41] "It is one of the paradoxes of this question," Du Bois divulged, "to see a people so discriminated against sometimes add to their misfortunes by discriminating against themselves."[42]

Unequivocally, then, Du Bois documented African Americans' own unique racialized class struggles, which were equally exacerbated and perpetuated not only by variations in education, employment, and income, but, perhaps even more intensely, by the aforementioned politics of race and economics of racism. For instance – and to expose Du Bois's problematic privileging of the "better class of Negroes" – let us turn to his discussion of the "aristocracy of the Negro." In his own unmistakably elitist words:

> Nothing more exasperates the better class of Negroes than this tendency to ignore utterly their existence.... In many respects it is right and proper to judge a people by its best classes rather than by its worst classes or middle ranks. The highest class of any group represents its possibilities rather than its exceptions, as is so often assumed in regard to the Negro. The colored people are seldom judged by their best classes, and often the very existence of classes among them is ignored. This is partly due in the North to the anomalous position of those who compose this class: they are not leaders or the ideal-makers of their own group in thought, work, or morals. They teach the masses to a very small extent, mingle with them but little, do not

largely hire their labor. Instead then of social classes held together
by strong ties of mutual interest we have in the case of the Negroes,
classes who have much to keep them apart, and only community of
blood and color prejudice to bind them together.[43]

We have established that Du Bois's early sociological work,
especially *The Philadelphia Negro*, was riddled with Eurocentrism,
elitism, and assimilationism. Therefore, we need not rehearse here
how incredibly elitist he was to imperiously assert, in essence, that
the frequently backward-thinking black bourgeoisie – who, as he
himself acknowledged, did not in any meaningful way fulfill the
central mission of the bourgeoisie, which is to invent, be "leaders,"
and be "ideal-makers" – best represented African Americans.[44] In
addition, we can forgo a full discussion of Du Bois's contention that
the African American aristocracy, which ironically does not "mingle
with" and – even more damning – does not "hire" members of
the black working class and the black masses, should "teach the
masses." Issues such as these will be engaged in greater detail
below. However, here it is important to highlight the last sentence
of the passage above: "Instead then of social classes held together
by strong ties of mutual interest we have in the case of the Negroes,
classes who have much to keep them apart, and only community
of blood and color prejudice to bind them together." Here, Du Bois
slightly overstated his case when he claimed, almost as if attempting
to directly counter Marx's conception of class, that "instead ... of
social classes held together by strong ties of mutual interest," in
the case of African Americans "*only* community of blood and color
prejudice ... bind them together."

It was not "only" black biology and anti-black racism that led to,
and held together, African American social classes, but also intra-
racial conflicts and contradictions, many stemming from African
Americans' historical and cultural evolution from enslaved "house
Negroes" and "field Negroes" to emancipated black moderates and
black militants. Ironically, Du Bois's deep sense of history in *The
Philadelphia Negro* penetratingly documented much of this historical
and cultural evolution but, once again, his inchoate mode of
analysis and interpretive framework displayed serious limitations,
which ultimately altered his analysis, tipping it toward conceptual
conservatism even in the midst of his interpretive radicalism and
sociological innovations.[45] Consciously seeking to go above and
beyond Du Bois's conception of class, racial classes can be said to
be classes in the conventional sense, as they are conscious of their

own class interests and harbor hostility toward other classes and their interests. However, racial classes are also classes in an unconventional sense, insofar as racialization and racial colonization collapse the respective non-white social classes into "one practically homogeneous mass," as Du Bois said above. In essence, this makes racial classes socially, politically, and economically impotent, and impedes the pursuit of their various class interests.

It is, indeed, the "community of blood and color prejudice" that "binds" racial classes "together," and certainly their respective socio-economic statuses seem to be secondary – if not, often, altogether trumped by the racialization of politics and economics in the US. On the one hand, racial classes simultaneously *are* and *are not* classes in the conventional sociological sense, because, although they evolved in the context of capitalism, just as many European and European American social classes did, the politics of race and economics of racism, literally, racially dehumanized and deformed their class formations and class struggles. On the other hand, Du Bois's interpretive elitism blinded him from seeing the ways in which it was not *"only* community of blood and color prejudice" that bound African American social classes "together," but also intra-racial class conflicts and contradictions, ranging from the "impulse of the best, the wisest and the richest ... to segregate themselves from the masses," to the clannishness of the "mass of the servant class, the porters and waiters, and the best of the laborers."[46]

It could possibly go without saying that members of the various African American social classes resented being confused with, or collapsed into, a social class other than their own – or, worse, confused with or collapsed into "one practically homogeneous mass" – by whites. However, what Du Bois, with his interpretive elitism in tow, overlooked was the fact that, above and beyond their "community of blood" and common experience of "color prejudice," intra-racially and intra-culturally African American social classes had incessantly seething and simmering relationships with one another, which, admittedly, were exacerbated and perpetuated by African American enslavement and its aftereffects, but also, truth be told, possibly built on pre-existing "traditional" or indigenous (i.e., pre-colonial and pre-capitalist) African conceptions of cultural, social, political, and economic classes. In fact, Du Bois himself hinted at as much when he revealingly wrote: "If the Negroes were by themselves either a strong aristocratic system or a dictatorship would for the present prevail. With, however, democracy thus prematurely thrust upon them, the first impulse of the best, the wisest and richest is to segregate themselves from the mass." He concluded, "This action, however, causes more of dislike and jealousy on the part of the masses than usual, because those masses look to whites for ideals and largely for leadership."[47]

The black working class and the black masses, then, do not look to the African American aristocracy, who insultingly "segregate themselves from the mass," but, rather, the black masses remonstratively, however unconsciously and covertly, frequently turn to whites for "ideals" and "leadership" – perhaps, in the twisted logic of "If you can't beat 'em, join 'em," as the saying goes. This is indicative of not *"only* community of blood and color prejudice" binding the black working class and the black masses together, but also a deep-seated sense of denial and betrayal at the hands of – yes, of course – whites, but the black bourgeoisie as well. Special note must be made of the intensity of the dialectic of white superiority and black inferiority that not only led W. E. B. Du Bois and the African American aristocracy to embrace and assimilate certain aspects of white middle-class culture and Victorian values, but also induced the black working class and the black masses to imbibe the values and culture of the white middle class.

Returning to the black working-class and the black masses' resentment, their "dislike and jealousy," the black bourgeoisie takes a page out of the white world's book and coarsely collapses the black working class and the "worthy poor" into the "Submerged Tenth," the black lumpenproletariat of criminals, pimps, and prostitutes.[48] Displaying his palpable elitist disdain, Du Bois wrote:

> it is just as natural for the well-educated and well-to-do Negroes to feel themselves far above the criminals and prostitutes of Seventh and Lombard Streets, and even above the servant girls and porters of the middle-class workers. So far they are justified; but they make their mistake in failing to recognize that however laudable an ambition to rise may be, the first duty of an upper-class is to serve the lowest class.[49]

Here, Du Bois seems to go simultaneously backward and forward: backward, of course, with his claim that the "well-educated and well-to-do Negroes" have a right to look down on not only the "criminals and prostitutes," but also the "servant girls and porters of the middle-class workers"; and forward, perhaps, in the sense that here we witness him wrestling with his conception of the responsibility or "duty" of the African American aristocracy, which, he unequivocally concluded, is "to serve the lowest class." Of course, Du Bois would go on wrestling with the question of the responsibility or "duty" of the African American aristocracy for the remainder of his life: first, putting forward his theory of the "Talented Tenth" in 1903, and then deconstructing and reconstructing the said theory into his often-overlooked 1948 doctrine of the "Guiding Hundredth."[50]

Although primarily known as a sociologist of race, and even more frequently as an innovator within the world of urban sociology, Du Bois's sociology of racial classes has been, and remains, ignored and excluded. Partly on account of his own interpretive elitism, and partly on account of his sociological negation, the relegation of Du Bois's sociology of racial classes to the periphery of the sociology of class has undeniably distorted, if not deformed, the discourse and development of this subdiscipline within sociology.[51] A similar assertion could be made about his sociology of the African American family, and, consequently, it is the main subject of the next section.

Du Bois's sociology of the urban African American family: black bourgeois patriarchy, white middle-class morality, and the burden of black women's sexuality

Critically building on our understanding of Du Bois's sociology of racial classes, now we turn to his equally innovative, as well as controversial and contradictory, sociology of the African American family.[52] Similar to his sociology of racial classes, Du Bois's interpretive elitism loudly leaps from the pages of *The Philadelphia Negro* in ways that enable us to take stock of not simply his elitism and assimilationism, but also his subtle sexism. For instance, Du Bois often linked poverty with immorality, frequently equating the alarming presence of unmarried African American women, especially unmarried mothers, and husbandless wives with promiscuity and degeneracy. As with his Farmville study, in *The Philadelphia Negro* unemployment was unerringly associated with "shrewd laziness, shameless lewdness," and "cunning crime."[53] The unemployed were essentially "good natured, but unreliable and shiftless persons who cannot keep work or spend their earnings thoughtfully."[54] From Du Bois's elitist frame of reference, and coming in a close second to the political economy of race and racism, many, if not most, of African Americans' social problems stemmed from the "large proportion of single men" and the even "larger number of widowed and separated" women, which indicated the "widespread and early breaking up of family life."[55]

The "early breaking up of family life" was the consequence of several socio-cultural factors, ranging from the history of the "lax moral habits of the slave regime" to "economic difficulties." As the "conditions of life for men are much harder than for women," Du Bois wrongly reported, "desertion and separation" are almost understandable for "a people comparatively low on the scale of civilization."[56] However, this was nothing other than a veiled, shockingly Eurocentric reference to the absence of the African American family, based on the bourgeois patriarchal paradigm. Du Bois's subtle sexism seeped into his analysis of the African American family and, ultimately, made his interpretive elitism all the more intense, especially with regard to African American women's conjugal conditions. He audaciously asserted that "a large number of these widows are simply unmarried mothers and thus represent the unchastity of a large number of women."[57]

In other words, Du Bois straightforwardly and haughtily labeled unmarried African American mothers as slightly better than "sluts" – actually he, indeed, did sociologically designate them as "sluts" – but, with equally unmitigated imperiousness, he quickly went on to add insult to injury by claiming that unmarried African American mothers and their often "unkept" and "undisciplined" children were likely to lapse into welfarism and crime: "The result of this large number of homes without husbands is to increase the burden of charity and benevolence, and also on account of their poor home-life to increase crime."[58] With words that seem to sadly prefigure the twentieth-century discourse on African American "welfare queens," Du Bois did not simply condemn poor black mothers to lives of promiscuity and unchaste charity – which was already condescendingly bourgeois, and otherwise bad enough – but also foretold the future of their children as one irrevocably bound up with the aforementioned "shrewd laziness, shameless lewdness," and "cunning crime."[59]

Although Du Bois ardently insisted on compassion in comprehending social scientific research as an instrument in the interest of social reform (especially African American uplift), his elitist, assimilationist, and, sometimes, sexist approach was not always empathetic to poor blacks in general, and unwed African American women's and mothers' lives and struggles in particular. Consequently, he frequently explained the life-struggles and low status of every social class of African Americans other than the "well-educated and well-to-do Negroes" in terms of their alleged "improper" sexual behavior, which eventually always ended with an elitist exegesis on what could be termed *the burden of black women's sexuality* – that is to say, the supposed heightened or hyperactive socio-sexual deviance of those condemned women who were "unmarried mothers" and, therefore, allegedly "represent the unchastity of a large number of women." It was not only a bourgeois patriarchal family paradigm that Du Bois used as his point of departure here, but also what he dubbed the "monogamic ideal."[60] African American men's complicity in African American women's and African American mothers' "unchastity" is given short shrift, if Du Bois can be said to have acknowledged it at all. Ironically, it is almost as if late-nineteenth-century African American women had miraculously developed a way to artificially inseminate themselves, and late-nineteenth-century African American men's promiscuity and "desertion" are rendered invisible, at best, or erased from the narrative of Du Bois's historical sociology altogether, at worst. In other words, where African American women's and African American mothers' "unchastity" appears in *The Philadelphia Negro*, African American men's "desertion" and their promiscuous and polygamous double-dealing disappear.

Because, as Du Bois audaciously said above, the "conditions of life for men are much harder than for women," black men's exclusion from industrial occupations and unions was taken as an unambiguous assault on the African American patriarchal family ideal. Unceasing stereotypical caricatures, emanating from white working-class minstrelsy to white middle-class highbrow journalism, proclaimed the patriarchal absence in African American families as clear proof of black men's emasculation, black women's licentiousness, and the arrant inferiority of black culture. Formed and deformed by white middle-class conceptions of the patriarchal family, black men and women twistedly sought to embrace, and bring their conjugal conditions and traditions in line with, white patriarchal sex roles and gender norms, and it was these warped "norms" which ultimately became the *sine qua non* of African American uplift, cultural development, and social survival.[61] Du Bois's early sociological discourse – especially as found in "The Negroes of Farmville" and *The Philadelphia Negro* – is, however uncomfortably, conceptually situated at the center of a discursive universe that was informed by white bourgeois patriarchal sex roles and gender norms, and also black nationalist intellectual-activists' agonizing acknowledgment of the horrid history of African American enslavement, racist sexual violence against black women, and the degradation of the African American family. Ironically, however, many, if not most, New Negro "race men" – Du Bois notwithstanding – attempted to counter minstrelesque mischaracterizations of the patriarchal absence in the African American family with their own homespun and hard-edged black bourgeois patriarchy and hyper-masculinity, which always seemed to register more as a knee-jerk reaction to minstrelesque mischaracterizations than as an authentic and autonomous articulation of African American manhood and the African American family.[62]

Caught within the double-bind of white *and* black bourgeois conceptions of the African American family, many New Negro "race men" desperately desired to prove whites' minstrelesque mischaracterizations wrong by demonstrating that they were, indeed, the masters of their houses and the heads of their families, which from their banal bourgeois-informed perspectives translated into irrefutable evidence of African American humanity, civilization, dignity, and piety. However, the New Negro "race men," patently pursuing an African American patriarchal family paradigm, did not realize that their obsessive preoccupations with achieving the patriarchal family, bourgeois morality, and Jeffersonian individuality in their incessant efforts to counter minstrelesque mischaracterizations was unwittingly leading them to embrace a white middle-class patriarchal family model in blackface – which, again unwittingly, distracted them from, and distorted their critical comprehension of, the political economy of race and racism within US culture and society. In other words, their reactionary black patriarchy was inadvertently playing right into the hostile hands of the white supremacist capitalist patriarchs who put forward the minstrelesque mischaracterizations in the first place, and who knew, furthermore, that, as long as African Americans, among other non-whites, viewed racism, sexism, and capitalism in isolation and disconnection – instead of as incessantly intersecting systems of exploitation, oppression, and violence – then, no true anti-racist, anti-sexist, and anti-capitalist social transformation would be quickly forthcoming.[63]

Du Bois doggedly attempted to situate his sociology of the African American family within the wider context of the urban environment. For example, his references to the instability and weaknesses of the black family were placed somewhere between the political economy of anti-black racism and black moral turpitude: "The causes of desertion are partly laxity in morals and partly the difficulty of supporting a family."[64] Du Bois, to be sure, did not downplay the incessantly interlocking nature of racial oppression and economic exploitation on African American families, illuminating the "economic stress" and the "grave physical, economic and moral disorder" they cause.[65] It sickened him that the "sorts of work open to Negroes [is] not only restricted by their own lack of training but also by discrimination against them on account of their race." He continued, "their economic rise is not only hindered by their present poverty, but also by widespread inclination to shut against them many doors open to the talented and efficient of other races." What is more, Du Bois unapologetically declared, "Everyone knows that in a city like Philadelphia a Negro does not have the same chance to exercise ability or secure work according to his talents as a white man."[66]

It was ultimately a combination of racial, sexual, moral, and economic factors, Du Bois concluded, that destabilized and degraded the African American family. Returning to his historical sociological lens, and also returning to his subtle sexism against black women and for black patriarchy, Du Bois sternly stated:

> it must be remembered that the Negro home and the stable marriage state is for the mass of the colored people of the country and for a large per cent of those of Philadelphia, a new institution. The strictly guarded savage home-life of Africa, which with all its shortcomings protected womanhood, was broken up completely by the slave ship, and the promiscuous herding of the West Indian plantation put in its stead. From this evolved the Virginia plantation where the double row of little slave cabins were but parts of a communistic paternalism centering in the Big House which was the real center of the family life. Even in Pennsylvania where the plantation system never was developed the slave family was dependent in morals as well as work upon the master. With emancipation the Negro family was first made independent and with the migration to cities we see for the first time the thoroughly independent Negro family. On the whole it is a more successful institution than we had right to expect, even though the Negro has had a couple of centuries of contact with some phases of the monogamic ideal. The greatest weakness of the Negro family is still lack of respect for the marriage bond, inconsiderate entrance into it, and bad household economy and family government. Sexual looseness then arises as a secondary consequence, bringing adultery and prostitution in its train. And these results come largely from the

postponement of marriage among the young. Such are the fruits of a sudden social revolution.[67]

Forgoing a full discussion of Du Bois's obviously Eurocentric and patriarchal statement concerning the "strictly guarded savage home-life of Africa, which with all its shortcomings protected womanhood," we will conclude our analysis of Du Bois's sociology of the African American family by focusing on his assertion that "Sexual looseness then arises as a secondary consequence" to African Americans' "lack of respect for the marriage bond, inconsiderate entrance into it, and bad household economy and family government." Irritatingly, Du Bois seems to deemphasize the enormous role slavery, Black Codes, Jim Crow laws, and other forms of racial segregation played in dehumanizing and degrading African Americans and the African American family.[68] Admittedly, and to his credit, he did invoke the "slave ship[s]," the "promiscuous herding of the West Indian plantation[s]," the "Virginia plantation[s]," the "little slave cabins," the "Big House," and the "plantation system" in general. However, to his discredit, Du Bois ultimately placed the responsibility for the crises of African American conjugal conditions almost squarely on African Americans, and especially black women. Again, the fault is not to be found with Du Bois's historical and sociological research methods, which were impeccable, and innovative for his intellectual milieu.[69] It was Du Bois's constantly recurring conceptual conservatism and interpretive elitism, reeking of both sexism and assimilationism, that repeatedly rendered his sociology of the African American family a sociology of black deviance, a sociology of black women's promiscuity, a sociology of black men's emasculation, and, even more despicably, a sociology of black children's criminalization.[70] Here, we have come back, once again, to the emphasis on the importance of methods of interpretation and modes of analysis grounded in, and growing out of, continental and diasporan African history, culture, and struggle.

Du Bois developed a merciless critique of "[un]protected womanhood" that spared neither "unmarried mothers," husbandless wives, widows, nor "well-to-do" married women who worked outside of their homes. Black bourgeois patriarchal familial and social etiquette dictated that "a woman's place is in the home." But, this ideal, like most ideals the black bourgeoisie borrowed from the white middle class, was not easily attainable for African American men and women, considering their dual burden of racial oppression and economic exploitation. It would be almost impossible to deny Du Bois's disdain for the moral failings of black men, repeatedly referring to them as "criminals," "gamblers," "idlers," "rogues," "rascals," "shrewd abettors," and "shiftless and lazy ne'er-do-wells."[71] However, black women who struggled to meet the white middle-class standards for womanhood, wifehood, and motherhood, which the black bourgeoisie superimposed on African American womanhood, wifehood, and motherhood, were summarily dismissed and scapegoated as the major contributors to, and essentially the continuing causes for, the instability of the African American family.

The social stratification and moral hierarchy of the black bourgeoisie rushes to the fore when we turn to Du Bois's rote ranking of African American women: humble and hard-working married women who worked outside of their homes had only a slightly higher moral and social standing than unmarried women. Indeed, they were respectable, but not as virtuous as those wives who were "engaged in no occupation save that of house-wife." It was these families "of undoubted respectability," and "earning suffi- cient income to live well," which Du Bois believed best represented African Americans.[72] Be that as it may, these families were few and far between (i.e., the "Talented Few"), and yet Du Bois, blinded by his interpretive elitism, continued to encourage African Americans, the large majority of whom were extremely economically exploited and poverty-stricken, to pursue this white middle-class patriarchal family model. Why did Du Bois incessantly advocate that African Americans assimilate white middle-class culture and values in *The Philadelphia Negro*? How could he not have seen how blatantly sexist many of his sociological assessments of black women's lives and struggles were? What role did internalized anti-black racism play in forming and deforming Du Bois's research methods, socio- logical observations, and sociological theorizations? This chapter concludes by briefly offering answers to each of these questions.

Du Bois's methodological innovations and interpretive limitations in *The Philadelphia Negro*

As discussed above, many have made mention of Du Bois's methodological innovations in *The Philadelphia Negro*. However, few have moved beyond merely mentioning Du Bois's methodological innovations to critically detailing the ways in which his classical research methods laid the foundation for many contemporary research methods. More attention has been given to what Du Bois borrowed – or, in many instances, how his methods were allegedly uncritically derived from European and European American early sociologists. Yet rarely have Du Bois's borrowings from African American intellectual and cultural history been discussed, and even more rarely do discussions of Du Bois as a mixed or multi-methodological innovator register. Along with the inadequate attention that Du Bois's methodological innovations have received has been the tendency on the part of the few who have accented and engaged his remarkable research methods to almost completely overlook his interpretive shortcomings due to his elitism and subtle sexism. On critical reflection, it is highly plausible that Du Bois may have been simultaneously methodologically progressive and interpretively regressive. In other words, and in many instances throughout *The Philadelphia Negro*, his thinking shows lucid signs of sociological breakthrough and, at the same time, Africological setback consequent to his seemingly unrepentant reliance on Eurocentric, elitist, and assimilationist frames of reference. This, to be sure, created a curious paradox in the ways Du Bois's sociological legacy has been interpreted, and continues to be reinterpreted.[73]

In terms of Du Bois's methodological innovations, the influence of Charles Booth and Jane Addams seems to be easily detected in *The Philadelphia Negro*, but the myriad influential texts emanating from African American intellectual and cultural history have been conspicuously and consistently left in the lurch.[74] Sociological research methods that sensitively engaged African American lives and struggles in the late nineteenth century were virtually nonexistent, and white sociology's "natural laws" and negative assessments of black culture were almost always based on Eurocentric evolutionary grand theorizing rather than empirical evidence.[75] There was no other recourse for Du Bois if, indeed, he wanted to critically study African Americans. He would have to, literally, invent research methods tailored to the particular – and, often, peculiar – lives and struggles of African Americans, which he knew, from his graduate studies at the University of Berlin and Harvard, went well beyond rote racial oppression and included economic exploitation, miseducation, continued racial colonization, and the innumerable absurdities and agonies of American apartheid. As if directly refuting those who have repeatedly argued that his research methods were derivative of late-nineteenth-century white sociological research methods, in his posthumously published autobiography, Du Bois declared:

I started [*The Philadelphia Negro*] with no "research methods" and I asked little advice as to procedure. The problem lay before me. Study it. I studied it personally and not by proxy. I sent out no canvassers. I went myself. Personally I visited and talked with 5,000 persons. What I could, I set down in orderly sequence on schedules which I made out and submitted to the University [of Pennsylvania] for criticism. Other information I stored in my memory or wrote out as memoranda. I went through the Philadelphia libraries for data, gained access in many instances to private libraries of colored folk and got individual information. I mapped the district, classifying it by condition; I compiled two centuries of history of the Negro in Philadelphia and in the Seventh Ward.[76]

Even when placed alongside Jane Addams's *Hull House Maps and Papers* and Charles Booth's *Life and Labor of the People in London*, methodologically *The Philadelphia Negro* is distinguished because – if for no other reason – it applied social scientific research methods to, and conducted empirical sociology in the interests of, African Americans.[77] What is more, if we were to situate *The Philadelphia Negro* within the context of early sociological inquiry in the United States, then we come back to Phil Zuckerman's contention that "Years before the famous studies of the Chicago School, Du Bois's sociological output was characterized by a hands-on, empirical research methodology to a much greater and more respectable degree than that of his more famous contemporaries."[78] Alluding to those who have compared *The Philadelphia Negro* with Florence Kelley's watershed Hull House work, Martin Bulmer wrote, "More important, his [i.e., Du Bois's] conception of science was a more rigorous one than that of Florence Kelley, and it precluded too close identification with philanthropy and social intervention."[79]

Synthesizing disparate parts of early white sociological discourse with strands of incipient Pan-Africanist, black nationalist, black Christian, black bourgeois and black ethnological uplift thought, Du Bois's sociological perspective and experiences were unlike those of his "more famous contemporaries": partly because many of them worked within intellectual and social reform communities which fostered constant sociological dialogue, and partly because Du Bois had neither the luxury nor largess of long-term research funding or a research team. The fact that with *The Philadelphia Negro* Du Bois can be said to have single-handedly inaugurated empirical sociology in the United States has not been completely lost.[80] For example, Bulmer offered a series of important corroborative points:

For fifteen months, Du Bois immersed himself in the detailed empirical study of the Seventh Ward, the largest concentration of black people in a city which at that time had a black population of 45,000, the largest anywhere in the North. His experience of carrying out the study was different from that of Charles Booth or Florence Kelley, for he worked on his own with little support from others. Although nominally attached to the University [of Pennsylvania] with the position of "Assistant Instructor," he had a one-year appointment which was not renewed, no office there, his name did not appear in the university catalogue, he taught no students, and he had only peripheral contact with members of the sociology department. His time was spent entirely in the black district, his principal social contacts, perforce, were with black rather than white Philadelphians. Color distanced him too from the white philanthropists who had initiated the study, and [this] meant that his contact with them was not on a regular basis.... The contrast between the Seventh Ward study and Hull House was marked. Florence Kelley was a resident of Hull House and full participant, W. E. B. Du Bois resided above a cafeteria belonging to the Philadelphia Settlement and was not a participant in the work of the Settlement.[81]

Taking all of this into serious consideration, those seeking to render methodological comparisons or interpretations of *The Philadelphia Negro* should do so cautiously because, as Bulmer observed, Du Bois labored "morning, noon, and night" under comparably different conditions than those of his "more famous contemporaries." The "comparably different conditions" have been either unintentionally overlooked or intentionally erased by those sociologists who, for whatever reason, refuse to sincerely consider the horrors of the African holocaust and African American enslavement, as well as their aftereffects on the discourse and development of sociology in the United States. Basic logic tells us that it is extremely possible that the Native American holocaust may have altered, or had some sort of significant impact on, the ways sociologists approach the lives and struggles of Native Americans; basic logic, also, tells us that it is extremely possible that the Jewish holocaust may have altered, or had some sort of significant impact on, the ways sociologists approach the lives and struggles of Jews; and, finally, basic logic tells us that it is extremely possible that the Armenian holocaust may have altered, or had some sort of significant impact on, the ways sociologists approach the lives and struggles of Armenians. Why, then, are the horrors of the African holocaust and African American enslavement, as well as the lingering legacy of Black Codes, Jim Crow laws, and other forms of racial segregation, not considered with the same spirit of sociological seriousness that "basic logic" reveals that we should hold with regard to the aforementioned?

Part of Du Bois's methodological innovation revolved around his intense emphasis on a comprehensive history of African Americans' heterogeneity and the gathering of empirical evidence prior to sociological theorizing concerning their lives and struggles.[82] Hence, it will be recalled, Du Bois emphatically exclaimed: "One cannot study the Negro in freedom and come to general conclusions about his destiny without knowing his history in slavery."[83] When viewed from the sociological world of the twenty-first century, *The Philadelphia Negro*, with its dull facts and figures, seems like a fairly typical empirical sociological investigation of African Americans in Philadelphia at the turn of the twentieth century. However, when situated within the sociological world it evolved out of and, in several senses, eventually epistemically exploded, *The Philadelphia Negro*'s interdisciplinarity not only took the "master's tools" and initiated the work of dismantling the "master's house" – to poorly paraphrase Audre Lorde – but also deftly demonstrated the disciplinary decadence and epistemic apartheid of sociology, especially American sociology, at its inception.[84]

In "The World Was Thinking Wrong About Race," Mia Bay unapologetically announced:

> Du Bois's study of the Philadelphia Negro has emerged as a classic across the disciplines precisely because it was written before the modern disciplines of sociology, anthropology, history, and economics were fully formed. Although justly celebrated for its contributions to all these fields, *The Philadelphia Negro*'s relationship to the more amorphous social science of its own day has been overshadowed by the retrospective appreciations it has received from scholars intent on establishing it as a pioneering work within their various nascent disciplines.[85]

Bay's last point should be emphasized, as it helps to directly highlight the disciplinary decadence and epistemic apartheid of sociology, among other traditional disciplines. Her assertion also highlights the importance of the emphasis on reinterpreting Du Bois employing interdisciplinary modes of analysis that have been grounded in, and continue to grow out of, classical and contemporary, continental and diasporan African lives and struggles. After all, to speak candidly, continental and diasporan Africans were, in most instances, at the heart of Du Bois's various discourses. Is it, then, too much to contend that continental and diasporan African histories, cultures, and struggles should be central to Du Bois scholars' and students' methods of interpretation, if, indeed, their Du Bois studies are to be free from the Eurocentrism and assimilationism that Du Bois unwittingly bequeathed to seemingly every generation of African American intellectuals since *The Philadelphia Negro*'s publication?

The Philadelphia Negro boldly blurred the boundaries between history, sociology, anthropology, and political economy in their intellectual infancy, and it put forward a pioneering empiricism that continues to inspire awe. "Its intellectual achievement has been assessed, above all," Bay argued, "in terms of its innovative use of social science practices that became commonplace long after it was published, such as participant observation, census-taking, the interview, and the historical and economic analysis of government data." Nevertheless, "such appreciations tend to measure mostly the symbolic significance – as a 'black first' – of a book so neglected in its own day that most of its innovations were not so much picked up as rediscovered by later social scientists."[86] More than merely "a 'black first,'" *The Philadelphia Negro* challenges those who have either completely ignored it within the world of white sociology or attempted to ghettoize it within the world of "black sociology." With implications for history, sociology, anthropology, and political economy in general, and historical sociology, urban sociology, industrial sociology, sociology of work, sociology of economics, sociology of race, sociology of culture, sociology of deviance, sociology of religion, sociology of education, and sociology of crime in particular, *The Philadelphia Negro*'s sociological empiricism seems to hold it together in the same way that its aforementioned Eurocentrism, elitism, and assimilationism incessantly threaten to tear it apart.[87]

Du Bois's methodological innovations and sociological empiricism were, in many instances, muted by his misinterpretations as a result of Eurocentrism and elitism. It would be virtually impossible to deny Du Bois's uneasy intellectual adherence to white middle-class culture and Victorian values, as well as his internalization of anti-black racist myths and subtle sexist stereotypes. As mentioned above, Du Bois sometimes employed the crude characterizations of African Americans – especially African American women, wives, and mothers – rampantly running throughout the white sociological discourse of his era. With the very dispassionate and disinterested social scientific detachment he would later mercilessly criticize, Du Bois Eurocentrically referred to African Americans as a "half-developed race" and "a people comparatively low in the scale of civilization."[88] He essentially accepted white middle-class culture, and in particular the white middle-class Victorian values and gender norms of family life, as universal "civilized" and "high culture" criteria to "judge" black behavior, regardless of social class. Therefore, ironically, even as he pointed out that "There is always a strong tendency on the part of the [white] community to consider the Negroes as composing one practically homogeneous mass," Du Bois himself seemed susceptible to white bourgeois and anti-black racist thinking concerning African American social classes.[89]

Du Bois was explicitly Eurocentric, elitist, and assimilationist throughout *The Philadelphia Negro* and, in effect, advocated that African Americans should openly embrace and assimilate European and European American "civilization" and culture as quickly as possible, if they were to survive the endless onslaught of American apartheid and European global imperialism. Here, then, we have returned to Du Bois's lame "If you can't beat 'em, join 'em" logic, which both pervades and perplexes *The Philadelphia Negro*. At this early point in his intellectual and political development, he did not dare demand a radical democratic socialist transformation of the white supremacist colonial capitalist patriarchal system that Europeans and European Americans had erected. Explicit evidence of Du Bois's Eurocentrism, elitism, and assimilationism recurringly surfaces when and where we come to his condescending comments concerning African American social classes, especially the differences in their conjugal conditions and family life. Du Bois's various interpretive limitations caused him to neglect the nuances of African American culture, at best, or completely disregard the distinctiveness of African American culture, at worst – and the real rub is that his various interpretive limitations led him to these myopic misinterpretations of African American culture even as he methodically and meticulously chronicled it in innovative and unprecedented ways. Here, then, we have come full circle and returned to the crux of the contention that, in *The Philadelphia Negro*, Du Bois was simultaneously methodologically progressive and interpretively regressive.

We turn now to an exploration of Du Bois's *The Souls of Black Folk*, which is widely regarded as his greatest contribution to the discourse on race and critique of racism. Although interpretively much more consistent than his urban and rural sociology, Du Bois's discourse on race and critique of racism, nonetheless, is not free from controversy and contradictions. Race and racism, as he emphasizes throughout *The Souls of Black Folk*, have historically presented, and continue currently to present, contemporary society in general, and contemporary social science in particular, with one of its greatest "problems." Let us, then, consciously cross the color-line and enter the racially colonized world within the Veil.

2

The Souls of Black Folk: *Critique of Racism and Contributions to Critical Race Studies*

Introduction to black folk's souls

Between 1897 and 1910, W. E. B. Du Bois served as Professor of History and Economics at Atlanta University, an African American institution established during the Reconstruction era in 1865. At Atlanta he laid the groundwork for, and ultimately created, a sociology program squarely focused on post-emancipation African American life and culture, specifically in the South.[1] During his first five years at Atlanta University, he published a series of essays in academic journals, progressive magazines, and liberal periodicals, including the *Annals of the American Academy of Political and Social Science*, the *Atlantic Monthly*, the *Nation*, the *World's Work*, the *Outlook*, the *Southern Workman*, the *Independent*, *Harper's Weekly*, the *Missionary Review*, the *Literary Digest*, the *Dial*, and the *Brooklyn Eagle*. Du Bois drew from these essays to form the basis of his next and most famous book, *The Souls of Black Folk*, which was published in 1903.[2] A unique mix of history, sociology, political criticism, ethnography, autobiography, biography, eulogy, and fiction, *The Souls of Black Folk* is held together by Du Bois's remarkable vision of a truly democratic America free from racial hierarchy. The book contains 14 chapters. Of these, 9 had been previously published, but subsequently substantially revised, and the remaining 5 chapters were composed specifically for *The Souls of Black Folk*.[3]

Each chapter opens with two epigraphs: one from a "white" poet, and the other a couple of bars from a "black" spiritual. "It is crucial to recognize that Du Bois," Brent Hayes Edwards observed:

chooses *not* to include the lyrics to the spirituals, which often serve
to underline the arguments of the chapters: Booker T. Washington's
idealism is echoed in the otherworldly salvation hoped for in "A
Great Camp-Meeting in the Promised Land," for example; likewise
the determined call for education in "Of the Training of Black Men"
is matched by the strident words of "March On."

Du Bois, Edwards emphasized, withheld the lyrics to "mark another
barrier for the reader, in another form – to suggest, again, the inner
life 'within the Veil,' a mode of knowledge and 'striving' that
remains difficult to reach, if not inaccessible, using the imperfect
and limited means of white culture."[4] At the outset of each of the
book's chapters, then, Du Bois addresses his readers on both sides
of the "Veil" and the "color-line": the "Veil" is Du Bois's trope for
the microaggressions that impact black folk on an individual or
personal level, and the "color-line" is his metaphor for the Black
Codes, Jim Crow laws, and other forms of racial segregation that
socially and spatially divide black and white folk.

The diverse, multi-genre chapters of *The Souls of Black Folk* are
part of a cohesive story about the triumphs and tragedies of black
life in the post-emancipation white-dominated world. As Du Bois
stated in "The Forethought": "Herein lie buried many things which
if read with patience may show the strange meaning of being
black here at the dawning of the Twentieth Century. This meaning
is not without interest to you, Gentle Reader; for the problem of
the Twentieth Century is the problem of the color-line."[5] The first
chapter, "Of Our Spiritual Strivings," details the "unreconciled"
strife at the heart of African American life after the Civil War, when
blacks were repeatedly rebuffed and denied entry into American
democracy. Chapter II, "Of the Dawn of Freedom," continues
the story begun in the first chapter by focusing on the failures of
the Freedmen's Bureau, which symbolizes the government's half-
hearted efforts and lack of commitment in addressing the challenges
of the formerly enslaved during the Reconstruction period (*circa*
1865–77). The third chapter, "Of Mr. Booker T. Washington and
Others," offers a merciless critique of the accommodationist policies
of the most prominent African American leader of the era, and
especially calls into question Washington's emphasis on industrial
education for blacks in the South. Chapter IV, "Of the Meaning of
Progress," is a reflection on Du Bois's first experiences teaching in
rural Tennessee and his return visit there ten years later, only to
find the "awful shadow of the Veil" still firmly in place, and much

regress instead of progress.[6] The fifth chapter, "Of the Wings of Atalanta," focuses on the peril that lay ahead of Atlanta and the wider Southern world if higher education is not widely available to African Americans. Du Bois specifically warned against the "greed of gold" and those who "interpret … the world in dollars."[7] "The need of the South is knowledge and culture," he asserted, and "to make men, we must have ideals, broad, pure, and inspiring ends of living, – not sordid money-getting, not apples of gold."[8] In chapter VI, "Of the Training of Black Men," Du Bois continues his emphasis on higher education for African Americans by arguing that black colleges and universities should not be railroaded into privileging trade training over liberal arts education.

The next three chapters are all centered around African American life in Dougherty County, Georgia, and offer readers a window into a world where debt, racism, and the color-line demarcate a "Black Belt" throughout the South, from the Carolinas to Texas, where black freedom is often indistinguishable from black bondage. Chapters X, XI, and XII dive even deeper into the world "within the Veil": "Of the Faith of the Fathers" focuses on the rise and important role of the black church not simply for black religious culture, but for African American history and culture more generally; "Of the Passing of the First-Born" is Du Bois's poignant eulogy for his 2-year-old son, Burghardt Gomer Du Bois, who died of diphtheria in 1899; "Of Alexander Crummell" is a brief biography of the iconic African American minister and proto-Pan-Africanist who lived and worked in Liberia for 20 years and implored African Americans to join him in the uplift of Africa. *The Souls of Black Folk* comes to a close with a short story and a paean to the spirituals. More specifically, chapter XIII, "Of the Coming of John," revisits several of the tragic themes surrounding the underside of the post-emancipation period taken up in previous chapters, such as "Of the Training of Black Men," "Of the Black Belt," and, most especially, "Of the Sons of Master and Man," but does so in fictional form. The fourteenth and final chapter, "The Sorrow Songs," uses black music as a metaphor for black people in America and powerfully picks up Du Bois's gift theory trope with the assertion that black music "has been neglected, it has been, and is, half despised, and above all it has been persistently mistaken and misunderstood; but notwithstanding, it still remains as the singular spiritual heritage of the nation and the greatest gift of the Negro people."[9]

At the core of *The Souls of Black Folk* is Du Bois's contention that African Americans perceive their history and culture, and quite literally their lives, from the point of view of the white world. This, in turn, leads African Americans to "double-consciousness" – African Americans' recognition of their African or black consciousness and their imposed American or white consciousness, and the arduous struggle to reconcile the two. For Du Bois, the entire history of blacks in the United States is the history of this struggle and the ways each African American at some point in their lives ends up questioning whether they are African, or American, or able to be both. At the dawn of the twentieth century, Du Bois believed that African Americans had no other recourse but to merge their African consciousness with their American consciousness to create a hybrid that preserved the best of both their African and American heritages. To achieve this synthesis, African Americans would need to continue what they began during the Reconstruction years and carry on the struggle to expand freedom and democracy to include blacks as well as whites. As the chapters "Of Mr. Booker T. Washington and Others," "Of the Meaning of Progress," "Of the Wings of Atalanta," and "Of the Training of Black Men" clearly indicate, Du Bois also placed a special emphasis on education as a key element in overcoming double-consciousness. However, African Americans' acquisition of knowledge invariably made them aware of their history of enslavement and post-emancipation segregation in a nation that proudly professed to be free and democratic. Hence, *The Souls of Black Folk*, above all else, is a book about contradictions: black folk's contradictions and conflictual relationships with their Africanness and Americanness, and white folk's contradictions with their conceptions of freedom, democracy, and the very meaning of America.

As alluded to above, *The Souls of Black Folk* is an incredibly interdisciplinary text, drawing directly on history, sociology, politics, economics, education, and religion. For example, chapters I through III ("Of Our Spiritual Strivings," "Of the Dawn of Freedom," and "Of Mr. Booker T. Washington and Others") hinge on the historical "strivings" of the "souls of black folk"; chapters IV through IX ("Of the Meaning of Progress," "Of the Wings of Atalanta," "Of the Training of Black Men," "Of the Black Belt," "Of the Quest of the Golden Fleece," and "Of the Sons of Master and Man") symbolize the educational and sociological "strivings" of the "souls of black folk"; and chapters X through XIV ("Of the Sons of Master and Man," "Of the Faith of the Fathers," "Of the Passing of the First-Born," "Of Alexander Crummell," and "The Sorrow Songs") represent the political and religious "strivings" of the "souls of black folk."[10] Du Bois's contributions to the discourse on race and critique of racism in *The Souls of Black Folk* revolve around his efforts to capture the complexities of what it means to be black in a white world. That is to say, subtly revealing the racialization of virtually every aspect of not only black life, but white life as well, is central to the book. History, politics, economics, education, and religion have all been racialized in the US, and *The Souls of Black Folk* provides a metaphorical map that enables its readers to navigate, and perhaps ultimately synthesize, the "two worlds" – one black and one white – that remained unreconciled at the opening of the twentieth century.[11]

In *The Souls of Black Folk* Du Bois created several seminal concepts of race and critiques of racism to complement his earlier efforts to establish the social scientific study of race and racism begun in *The Philadelphia Negro*. Many of the concepts of racial lived-experience that Du Bois articulated in *The Souls of Black Folk* are intellectually interconnected and endlessly intersect. Ultimately, these concepts offer several of his most enduring contributions to the discourse on race and critique of racism. Undoubtedly, his concepts of "double-consciousness" and the "color-line" are significant. However, his theory of blacks' "Veiled" visibility and invisibility, as well as his emphasis on blacks' unique "second-sight" in the white world, are equally relevant with regard to the discourse on race and racism. Lastly, Du Bois's gift theory, which stresses the importance of both black and white America recognizing African Americans' distinct gifts to US history and culture, both in slavery and in freedom, is a part of the aforementioned cluster of concepts that connect *The Souls of Black Folk*'s 14 chapters. In what follows, we explore *The Souls of Black Folk* through five of its major metaphors and core concepts: the Veil, the color-line, double-consciousness, second-sight, and the gift theory.

"The strange meaning of being black"

Du Bois begins *The Souls of Black Folk* by exploring the "strange meaning of being black." The meaning of blackness is not only important for African Americans, but for whites as well, because the central premise of the book is that the "problem of the Twentieth Century is the problem of the color-line."[12] In the wake of the Civil War and Reconstruction, Du Bois understood race and racism to be central to America's past, present, and future. Consequently, the

14 chapters of *The Souls of Black Folk* are all, in one way or another, examinations of America's racial hierarchy and how that hierarchy has undermined the development of American democracy. Du Bois writes from different perspectives and speaks in different voices throughout *The Souls of Black Folk* because race and racism are multidimensional, polyvocal, and ever changing, and consequently require varied kinds of criticism and conceptual counter-attacks. Throughout the book, Du Bois writes in a series of pronouns that change from chapter to chapter. This range of pronouns alternates from personal observations ("Between me and the other world there is ever an unasked question"[13]) to second-person appeal ("I pray you, then, receive my little book in all charity"[14]), third-person statements ("he simply wishes to make it possible for a man to be both a Negro and an American"[15]), and collective struggle ("by every civilized and peaceful method we must strive for the rights which the world accords to men"[16]). These changes in tone and points of view render the book's central subject – the "spiritual world in which ten thousand thousand Americans live and strive" – as complex, cultured, and full of human ingenuity as any other group of people, especially white people.[17]

Instead of some inert, fixed phenomenon frozen in space and time, the world within the Veil, the world on the other side of the color-line, has been and remains in a state of constant transformation, as a consequence of it being impacted by history but also as a result of it making history. But racial microaggressions (the Veil) and racial segregation (the color-line) have shrouded the "spiritual world in which ten thousand thousand Americans live and strive," and this has caused African Americans and much of their history and culture to be ignored or erased or otherwise rendered invisible. As Du Bois shared:

> The shadow of a mighty Negro past flits through the tale of Ethiopia the Shadowy and of Egypt the Sphinx. Through history, the powers of single black men flash here and there like falling stars, and die sometimes before the world has rightly gauged their brightness. Here in America, in the few days since Emancipation, the black man's turning hither and thither in hesitant and doubtful striving has often made his very strength to lose effectiveness, to seem like absence of power, like weakness. And yet it is not weakness.[18]

Beyond the subtle reference to his growing Pan-Africanism, which links African Americans' "mighty Negro past" with the "tale of Ethiopia the Shadowy" and "Egypt the Sphinx," in *The Souls of Black Folk* Du Bois reveals to his readers that the Veil obscures the perception of those who created, perpetuate, or otherwise benefit from the maintenance of the color-line. African Americans' past in many ways determines their present and future. Hence, throughout *The Souls of Black Folk*, Du Bois provides his readers with much-needed mini-history lessons, chronicling the lives and struggles of the black folk who seem to "flash here and there like falling stars," and sadly "die sometimes before the world has rightly gauged their brightness." It is the Veil that dampens and ultimately darkens African Americans' "brightness," that obfuscates and minstrelizes their lives and struggles. Du Bois wanted his readers to see African Americans on their own terms and from their own points of view, which is one of the reasons he created so many racial metaphors and concepts to capture African Americans' anguished experience of racial domination and racial discrimination. Whether we turn to the metaphor of the Veil, which denotes blacks' experience of racial microaggressions, or the color-line concept, which symbolizes blacks' experience of systemic racial segregation, Du Bois translated his social scientific findings from *The Suppression of the African Slave Trade*, *The Philadelphia Negro*, and several of his Atlanta University Studies into accessible concepts that could reach across the borders and boundaries of race, religion, education, politics, and social class. As Robert Stepto observed, part of the brilliance of *The Souls of Black Folk* is that Du Bois, literally, turns "data into metaphor."[19]

"The two worlds within and without the Veil"

One of the most significant racial metaphors Du Bois developed based on his social scientific data was the Veil. The "Veil" is the trope Du Bois created to represent the barrier between black and white folk as a consequence of anti-black racist microaggressions. Microaggressions are essentially indirect or subtle forms of discrimination against members of a marginalized group. At the outset of *The Souls of Black Folk*, readers are made aware of the centrality and significance of the Veil when Du Bois states in "The Forethought": "Leaving, then, the white world, I have stepped within the Veil, raising it that you may view faintly its deeper recesses, – the meaning of its religion, the passion of its human sorrow, and the struggle of its greater souls."[20] Du Bois's use of the Veil metonym, along with its corollary concept of the color-line, was prescient in the sense that it continues to capture the racialization of African Americans' lives and struggles: from late-nineteenth-century Black Codes and Jim Crow laws to the twentieth-century racial segregation that led to the Civil Rights Movement, to the twenty-first-century "new Jim Crow" system and anti-black racist police brutality that led to the Black Lives Matter Movement.[21]

Where the color-line calls to mind the racially segregated white and black social worlds, Du Bois's discourse on the Veil points to the ways racial discrimination impacts African Americans on an interpersonal or individual level. In many ways, *The Souls of Black Folk* suggests that the Veil at best blurs, and at worst blinds, whites to blacks' distinct individual identities and personal qualities. Thus, the Veil's significance is dual, as it affects both blacks and whites, but does so very differently. Although both blacks' and whites' lives and experiences revolve around the very same color-line, it is their divergent relationships to the Veil, to the interpersonal barrier created by anti-black racist microaggressions, that is one of the major themes of the book. However, the Veil is not only the obstacle created by whites' microaggressions. It works both ways and also doubles as a kind of cultural armor or cloak African Americans can use to disguise or shield their "inner thoughts," their "inner feelings," and indeed their "inner life."[22] Hence, Du Bois writes of "raising it [the Veil] that you [i.e., whites] may view faintly its deeper recesses." It is not merely whites who wield the Veil for purposes of domination and discrimination. Blacks can upend it and creatively use it in the interest of protection, affirmation, and liberation.

Du Bois's discourse on the Veil accentuates not only African Americans' agency, but also their ability to create an anti-racist culture of resistance and human redemption in the midst of the mayhem of the post-emancipation white-dominated world. The Veil has been and can continue to be used by the racially oppressed to *conceal*. However, it can also be used by the racially oppressed to *reveal*, if – and this is an extremely important "if" – an earnest opportunity presents itself, as Du Bois deemed it did in *The Souls of Black Folk*. He stated: "Herein lie buried many things which if read with patience may show the strange meaning of being black here in the dawning of the Twentieth Century.... I have sketched in swift outline the two worlds within and without the Veil."[23] Du Bois uses the Veil to make both black and white folk aware of the fact that, even after the Emancipation Proclamation and the Reconstruction era, there remain "two worlds": one world for whites and another world for blacks, and between these "two worlds" is a "Veil of Color," a yawning chasm of racism – racism at the individual level (the Veil) and racism at the social level (the color-line).[24]

The "strange meaning of being black," Du Bois declared, "is not without interest to you, Gentle Reader" – which refers to both black and white "Gentle Reader[s]," because the "problem of the Twentieth Century," he prophesied, with words that continue to resonate and ring true, "is the problem of the color-line."[25] *The Souls of Black Folk*, therefore, was written with "Gentle Reader[s]" from both the world "within" and the world "without" the Veil in mind – that is to say, for those blacks who unceasingly searched for the "strange meaning of being black" in a white world; and for those whites who had consciously or unconsciously upheld the color-line after the collapse of Reconstruction and the rising tidal wave of anti-black racial violence that rolled across the United States as the twentieth century dawned. If there were any doubts as to Du Bois's sincerity on the part of whites, he solemnly wrote: "I pray you, then, receive my little book in all charity, studying my words with me, forgiving mistake and foible for sake of the faith and passion that is in me, and seeking the grain of truth hidden there."[26] He equally assuaged the potential suspicions of his black readers by bluntly asserting: "And, finally, need I add that I who speak here am bone of the bone and flesh of the flesh of them that live within the Veil?"[27]

Du Bois's discourses on the Veil and the color-line are significant because they represent one of the first efforts by a social scientist to articulate a *critical social theory of racial oppression, racial exploitation, and racial violence*. That is to say, in *The Souls of Black Folk*, Du Bois advances a theory that is critical of the ways in which racial oppression, racial exploitation, and racial violence breed misunderstandings and microaggressions between, first, the black folk they racially segregate (the Veil); second, the black folk they systemically racially divide and socially separate (the color-line); and, third, as a result of each of the aforementioned, the black folk they cause to suffer from a severe inferiority complex that induces them to constantly view themselves from whites' supposedly "superior" points of view (double-consciousness). The Veil's processes and practices of containment and concealment racially (re)organize, literally, everything that crosses the color-line, every interaction between the "two worlds within and without the Veil." As a result, the Veil blurs the vision of – or, more frequently, blinds – those who are white and who wish not to view non-whites (i.e., non-whites' humanity, history, and culture). Although whites may render blacks anonymous and invisible in the white world, blacks are never invisible to each other. As Du Bois pointed out in *The Philadelphia Negro*, blacks are not a "homogeneous mass," and especially not within the world of the Veil.[28] However, one of the consequences of whites' socio-political dominance and their ability to amplify their ideology of black sub-humanity is that blacks begin to internalize the diabolical dialectic of white superiority and black inferiority, which in turn leads to what Du Bois cryptically called "double-consciousness" (see below).

In their efforts to combat the internalization of the dialectic of white superiority and black inferiority, blacks need to become acutely aware of their "double-consciousness" and how their utilization of white values and white culture as criteria to judge black lives and struggles is detrimental to black liberation, Du Bois emphasized. As Arnold Rampersad observed, the "term 'soul'" throughout *The Souls of Black Folk* "was used synonymously with consciousness."[29] That is to say, Du Bois advocated for African Americans to dialectically deconstruct and radically reconstruct their "double-consciousness" into a *critical black consciousness* – meaning: a critical and compassionate consciousness grounded in and growing out of continental and diasporan African history, culture, and struggle. This is a consciousness or awareness that consistently harbors a radical humanism that refuses to denigrate or demonize whites or other non-whites but, instead, is open to aligning with all who sincerely seek to reclaim and rehabilitate their long-denied humanity as a consequence of white domination and racial colonization.[30]

As for whites living within racially divided worlds, Du Bois audaciously argued that they are affected just as much as blacks. The striking difference, however, is that whites seemed willing to accept a blithe blindness to black social suffering, black political disenfranchisement, and black economic exploitation, and the myriad ways each of the aforementioned is inextricable from white privilege, white social wealth, and white political power as a consequence of whites' quarantining black life to the world within the Veil and whites' creation of the color-line. As will be witnessed in the next chapter, Du Bois was one of the first social scientists to seriously consider the recurring effect that whites' complicity – whether active or passive – in the construction and maintenance of the color-line had on the "souls of white folk." From Du Bois's perspective, race and racism have never been simply black or non-white people's problem, but a human problem that should concern all humanity. Anywhere societies are racially divided, even though they may not be "legally" or "officially" racially divided anymore, the quality of both white and non-white life suffers.

"The problem of the twentieth century is the problem of the color-line"

In *The Souls of Black Folk*, Du Bois deployed the vivid and often lyrical language of the Veil, as well as its conceptual complement the "color-line," to make his discourse on race and racism accessible to as wide an audience as possible.[31] Du Bois came to the conclusion that there are some sentiments, some "finer feelings," especially certain lived-experiences and lived-endurances prevalent in the non-white world, which simply cannot be captured in the highbrow language of – to use Du Bois's words – "calm, cool, and detached" white social science.[32] In 1904, Du Bois asserted that, in writing *The Souls of Black Folk*, he found that it was "difficult, strangely difficult, to translate the finer feelings of men into words."[33] Early twentieth-century America did not view the Veiled race (i.e., his beloved "black folk") as "men" – by which Du Bois meant *human beings*. Hence, his task was doubly difficult when compared and contrasted with the work of his white social-scientific peers at the turn of the twentieth century. Du Bois's biographer David Levering Lewis hit the nail on its head when he revealingly wrote: "Three years into yet another century of seeming unassailable European supremacy, *Souls* countered with the voices of the dark submerged and unheard."[34] The meaning of *The Souls of Black Folk* is crystal clear, according to Lewis: until Du Bois's "Gentle Reader[s]" "appreciated the message of the songs sung in bondage by black people," which was one of the only ways enslaved Africans could truly express themselves, then, "Du Bois was saying, the words written in freedom by white people would remain hollow and counterfeit."[35]

Lewis went on to point to the personal pain and soul-searching Du Bois endured to compose a work of such simultaneous gruesomeness and grandeur. Observing Du Bois's extraordinary "courage in abundance," especially considering the lynching-laden historical moment in which he composed *The Souls of Black Folk*, a usually cool-penned Lewis, palpably bristling with intellectual enthusiasm and excitement, exclaimed:

He also possessed in equal measure – passion mediated by the written word. The shaping empire of intellect reigned over both. From the first page of *The Souls of Black Folk*, Du Bois's mind, courage, and passion interact to create a splendid diapason. It is as though the small hurts and large insults of his own life ... have fused with those of the Sam Hoses and Ida B. Welles and ten millions more to merge Du Bois, for a noetic moment in history, uniquely with the souls of all black people.[36]

Some scholars may have overlooked the social-scientific significance of *The Souls of Black Folk* because of its remarkable lyricism.[37] However, their visceral reactions to the volume unequivocally reinforce precisely why Du Bois's discourse on the Veil has resonated with so many, both within and without academe. The theory of the Veil is interconnected with the concept of the color-line, but they should not be, as they frequently have been, collapsed into one and the same thing, or made synonymous. Du Bois used the metaphor of the Veil to expatiate the "personal disrespect and mockery" blacks experience in their interpersonal interactions with whites.[38] As the Veil fans out and blankets the social world, it becomes the "ridicule and systematic humiliation" of the color-line – the Black Codes, Jim Crow laws, racial segregation, and other forms of American apartheid.[39] *The Souls of Black Folk* reveals that, even though the color-line is either inconsequential or invisible to most whites, it is of great consequence and, in fact, highly visible when viewed from the perspective of blacks.[40]

Du Bois was infuriated by the ways African Americans were being ill-treated at the turn of the twentieth century. In specific, he was deeply bothered by the harsh black living conditions he witnessed in the South during his Fisk University years (*circa* 1885–8), which only worsened as the 1880s morphed into the 1890s. From Du Bois's point of view, the 1896 Supreme Court decision of *Plessy* v. *Ferguson*, which made Jim Crow segregation based on "race" the official law of the land, effectively sanctioned the rise of the Ku Klux Klan, the increase in lynchings, and anti-black racist rioting and mob violence. The period was so bleak for black folk that historian Rayford Logan referred to it as the "nadir" of the African American experience.[41] The concept of the color-line is one of the many ways Du Bois sought to make post-enslavement forms of anti-black racism at the turn of the twentieth century visible to those who lived "without the Veil." The *Plessy* v. *Ferguson* decision was merely a legal manifestation of the post-enslavement, deeply racially divided country that America was quickly becoming during its post-Reconstruction years (*circa* 1877–1917). It is in this sense that it could be argued that the *Plessy* v. *Ferguson* decision registers as a subtextual source hovering in the background, underwriting and informing every word written in *The Souls of Black Folk*.[42]

The color-line is clearly observed in the chapter "Of the Coming of John," the only fiction in *The Souls of Black Folk*, where a white John's and a black John's destinies are intertwined and determined by their race, proximity to each other, and the observance of the color-line. As Du Bois shared:

> Thus in the far-away Southern village the world lay waiting, half consciously, the coming of two young men, and dreamed in an inarticulate way of new things that would be done and new thoughts that all would think. And yet it was singular that few thought of two Johns, – for the black folk thought of one John, and he was black; and the white folk thought of another John, and he was white. And neither world thought the other world's thought, save with a vague unrest.[43]

Both Johns, John Jones (black John) and John Henderson (white John) lived their lives along the color-line. Both received education. Both spent time in the North. However, upon returning "home" to the South – Altamaha, Georgia – there was a stark contrast in their lives, experiences, and opportunities. White John was, to put it plainly, young, white, and free to do as he pleased. Black John, on the other hand, was young, black, and completely constrained by the color-line, that yawning racial chasm between the black and white social worlds. Before he went North to study, black John had a reputation as "a good boy, – fine plough-hand, good in the rice-fields." Indeed, he was "handy everywhere, and always good-natured and respectful." But, his mother, Peggy Jones, wanted more for her son and stressed education. Consequently, black John took his studies seriously and excelled at history, ethics, and astronomy.[44]

Less than a decade after the *Plessy* v. *Ferguson* decision, Du Bois created historical fiction to conceptually capture and convey the cruelty of the color-line. To that end, black John went to ask the white Judge of his hometown "for the privilege of teaching the Negro school."[45] The exchange between black John and the white Judge is revealing, as black John "found it so hard and strange to fit [into] his old surroundings again."[46] The white Judge, perhaps sensing that black John had been transformed by his Northern educational experience, sternly stated:

"You've come for the school, I suppose. Well John, I want to speak to you plainly. You know I'm a friend to your people. I've helped you and your family, and would have done more if you hadn't got the notion of going off. Now I like the colored people, and sympathize with all their reasonable aspirations; but you and I both know, John, that in this country the Negro must remain subordinate, and can never expect to be the equal of white men. In their place, your people can be honest and respectful; and God knows, I'll do what I can to help them. But when they want to reverse nature, and rule white men, and marry white women, and sit in my parlor, then, by God! we'll hold them under if we have to lynch every Nigger in the land. Now, John, the question is, are you, with your education and Northern notions, going to accept the situation and teach the darkies to be faithful servants and laborers as your fathers were, – I knew your father, John, he belonged to my brother, and he was a good Nigger. Well – well, are you going to be like him, or are you going to try to put fool ideas of rising and equality into these folks' heads, and make them discontented and unhappy?"[47]

While black John is met with much discouragement, white John, free from the constrictions of the color-line, could do as he damn-well pleased, and, indeed, he did. One day, white John, seeking to enjoy his inherited Southern white *and* male supremacist privileges, attempted to sexually assault Jennie, the "little brown kitchen-maid," and black John's younger sister. Hurt and headstrong, and emotionally overwhelmed by the many millions of ways white supremacy dehumanizes black folk, black John killed white John for the offense, and the story ends with black John waiting on the white lynch mob to perform the commonplace anti-black racist ritual so characteristic of the era, the "nadir." Du Bois seems to be saying that both black lives and white lives lived along the color-line are cursed and imprisoned. Neither are free from the ravages of racism and, based on the story's end, neither blacks nor whites will survive so long as there is a color-line.[48]

Because blacks are veiled in invisibility in the white world, Du Bois brought whites' tendency to approach blacks more as problems than as humans to his readers' attention at the outset of *The Souls of Black Folk*, thereby innovatively inverting whites' pathological approach to black humanity, black history, and black culture. In other words, Du Bois problematized whites' problematic conceptions – or, rather, misconceptions – of blacks by audaciously asserting blacks' humanity and agency. Cautiously lifting the Veil so that whites might have a window into the black world, he wryly wrote:

Between me and the other world there is ever an unasked question: unasked by some through feelings of delicacy; by others through the difficulty of rightly framing it. All, nevertheless, flutter round it. They approach me in a half-hesitant sort of way, eye me curiously or compassionately, and then, instead of saying directly, How does it feel to be a problem? they say, I know an excellent colored man in my town; or, I fought at Mechanicsville; or, Do not these Southern outrages make your blood boil? At these I smile, or am interested, or reduce the boiling to a simmer, as the occasion may require. To the real question, How does it feel to be a problem? I answer seldom a word.[49]

Although Du Bois deceptively claims that he seldom answers a word in response to the often unasked and insulting question, "How does it feel to be a problem?," *The Souls of Black Folk* should be seen as part of his ever-evolving and often intricate answer, or, rather, his synoptic *solution*, to what could be called the "White Problem" or, put another way, the "Problem of white folk" – which is to say, whites' problematic, (hyper)racial colonial approach to black lives and struggles. Both the Veil and the color-line are invisibly (to most whites) and visibly (to most blacks) present in each and every one of their interactions; in all of the cracks and crevices of the crucial questions that could have and should have been earnestly asked of one another; in the many millions of racial myths and cultural stereotypes that the media produce for mass consumption and, as far as one can see, for mass confusion. Du Bois's vision of the Veil, then, is also a *critical theory of willful white blindness to black humanity, black history, and black culture*. This phrase emphasizes whites' ability, theoretically and technically speaking, to see blacks and their humanity, history, and culture if – and, again, this is an extremely important "if" – they choose to do so, but also, and here's the real rub, whites' tendency to intentionally turn a blind-eye to black humanity, black history, and black culture – or, further, whites' custom to selectively see certain "exceptional" blacks (usually Booker T. Washington-styled blacks, black entertainers, and black athletes), despite whites' apparent inability to authentically see the ongoing suffering and social misery of the black masses, who continue to live within the world of the Veil and whose lives are cruelly quarantined to the color-line.[50]

From Du Bois's perspective, if whites wanted to, or even needed to, really and truly *see* and appreciate blacks' (not just "exceptional" blacks') humanity, they could (through protracted processes of learning to love and appreciate blacks on blacks' own terms) transgress and transcend their white blindness to blacks and blackness – that is to say, whites' blindness to real (as opposed to their unreal or fictitious fantasies of) blacks and blackness. However, in order to do this, whites would have to open themselves, not just to blacks', but to all non-whites', humanity, history, culture, and, most importantly, their respective struggles for racial, social, and economic justice. Here it is important to stress that the "color-line," as conceived of by Du Bois, was never merely a matter of racial discrimination and racial segregation in the United States. In point of fact, the color-line is both national and international, which is why the opening sentence of "Of the Dawn of Freedom" reads: "The problem of the twentieth century is the problem of the color-line, – the relation of the darker to the lighter races of men in Asia and Africa, in America and the islands of the sea."[51]

Even in the chapter "Of Mr. Booker T. Washington and Others," Du Bois's early internationalism is on display when he asserted that the "recent course of the United States toward weaker and darker peoples in the West Indies, Hawaii, and the Philippines" essentially replicates many of its racial colonial policies and practices used against African Americans. He makes the connections between the national color-line and the global color-line clear. Considering the globality of the color-line, Du Bois poignantly asked, "where in the world may we go and be safe from lying and brute force?"[52] Du Bois's latent anti-imperialism, which is in the background rather than the foreground of *The Souls of Black Folk*, would blossom and become more pronounced in his work after World War I, especially in his books *Darkwater*, *Dark Princess*, *Color and Democracy*, and *The World and Africa*.[53]

"It is a peculiar sensation, this double-consciousness, this sense of always looking at one's self through the eyes of others"

Du Bois, as his work undoubtedly demonstrated, was willing to raise the Veil and cross the color-line. But, the question begs, how many whites at the turn of the twentieth century were willing to cross with him? It could almost go without saying that there was, for the most part, a stubborn refusal to cross the color-line on the part of most whites. Perceptively anticipating that this would be the case, Du Bois developed the concept of double-consciousness to capture the excruciating anguish that the diabolical dialectic of white superiority and black inferiority inflicted on blacks.[54] The related theory of second-sight explained the unique insight blacks gained as a result of their experience of the whites-on-the-top and blacks-on-the-bottom racial hierarchy. Du Bois's discourse on the Veil dovetails with his concept of double-consciousness because it also seeks to explain that blacks' efforts to gain self-consciousness in a white-dominated world will be, by default, always and everywhere damaged and distorted, because the most prevalent and pervasive ideas and images of blacks and blackness in white-dominated societies are those predicated on, and prefabricated by, the dialectic of white superiority and black inferiority.

In other words, where the Veil metaphorically represents the ways the color-line is constantly cloaked in a dark cloud of misconceptions, miscommunications, and misgivings between the "two worlds within and without the Veil," double-consciousness conceptually captures not only the often-overlooked fact that blacks internalize the racial hierarchy of the white world, but also the fact that part and parcel of the white world's ideology is the constant blanketing of the white-dominated black world with anti-black racist and white supremacist (mis)conceptions of blacks and blackness. The concept of double-consciousness, therefore, boldly broaches the taboo topic (among both blacks and whites) of blacks' intense internalization of white supremacist creations and disseminations of blackness. Undoubtedly, Du Bois had double-consciousness in mind above when he stated that *The Souls of Black Folk* would explore the "strange meaning of being black here in the dawning of the Twentieth Century."[55]

Du Bois's vision of the Veil provides his "Gentle Reader[s]" with an opportunity to transgress willful white blindness to blackness, and to actually see blacks and their history, culture, and struggle with new eyes. However, his vision of the Veil is also about revealing the truth long buried in the blood-soaked soil of a racially colonized and racially divided nation and world. In *The Souls of Black Folk*, the trope of the Veil is certainly about mourning and memorializing those African Americans who agonizingly endured the "holocaust of war, the terrors of the Ku-Klux Klan, the lies of carpet-baggers, the disorganization of industry, and the contradictory advice of friends and foes," only to be "left … bewildered serf[s] with no new watchword beyond the old cry for freedom."[56] But the Veil also represents all of those veiled figures, especially women in African, African American, and Caribbean cultures and societies, who for so long have passed unnoticed, attentively observing without being respectfully observed or acknowledged, always seemingly concealing more than they are revealing.[57]

Even though Du Bois was willing to work with whites in their earnest efforts to transgress their blindness to black humanity, black history, and black culture, he was not willing to do so at the expense of downplaying or diminishing the physical and psychological damage that life within the Veil and life along the color-line had on the "souls of black folk." The conceptual culmination of Du Bois's efforts to make both blacks and whites aware of this damage was, of course, his discourse on double-consciousness. He revealingly wrote, in perhaps the most widely commented-upon passage in *The Souls of Black Folk*:

> After the Egyptian and Indian, the Greek and Roman, the Teuton and Mongolian, the Negro is a sort of seventh son, born with a veil, and gifted with second-sight in this American world, – a world which yields him no true self-consciousness, but only lets him see himself through the revelation of the other world. It is a peculiar sensation, this double-consciousness, this sense of always looking at one's self through the eyes of others, of measuring one's soul by the tape of a world that looks on in amused contempt and pity. One ever feels his two-ness, – an American, a Negro; two souls, two thoughts, two unreconciled strivings; two warring ideals in one dark body, whose dogged strength alone keeps it from being torn asunder.
>
> The history of the American Negro is the history of this strife, – this longing to attain self-conscious manhood, to merge his double self into a better and truer self. In this merging he wishes neither of the older selves to be lost. He would not Africanize America, for America has too much to teach the world and Africa. He would not bleach his Negro soul in a flood of white Americanism, for he knows that Negro blood has a message for the world. He simply wishes to make it possible for a man to be both a Negro and an American, without being cursed and spit upon by his fellows, without having the doors of Opportunity closed roughly in his face.[58]

Here, with these hallowed words, Du Bois indelibly etched his name into the annals of American literary and cultural history. Although the Veil and the color-line are central tropes in *The Souls of Black Folk*, Du Bois's concept of double-consciousness and its corollary concept of second-sight are also essential to understanding *The Souls of Black Folk*. These concepts are also vital to comprehending the contradictions of racial discrimination and racial segregation in a nation that pretentiously prides itself on its cultural liberalism and commitment to democracy.[59] Observe that Du Bois's "doubling" discourse connected the Veil with second-sight (the "Negro is a sort of seventh son, born with a veil, and gifted with second-sight in this American world"). Moreover, for Du Bois, America was, to those "born with a veil," "a world which yield[ed] [them] no true self-consciousness, but only lets [them] see [themselves] through the revelation of the other world."[60]

Then, as if faithfully harking back to his stated intention at the book's opening – that is, to candidly explore the "strange meaning of being black here in the dawning of the Twentieth Century" – Du Bois revealed the dual nature of double-consciousness: it is simultaneously a curse (i.e., the inability to see oneself except "through the eyes of others") and a blessing (i.e., it gives blacks "second-sight," which enables them to perceive and offer solutions to the key problems of "this American world"). Black lives, Du Bois correctly assumed, would be "strange" and "peculiar" to whites because of the Veil and the color-line. The concept of double-consciousness asserts that the Veil that obscures whites' view of blacks, and the color-line that racially divides the white world from the black world, simultaneously create a "double self," a "double life," a tortured "two-ness" in blacks' souls.[61] In fact, the "racial fault-lines" of the color-line ultimately drive blacks to constantly question whether they are Africans or Americans (and even whether they are human or sub-human) to such an excruciating degree that their souls become doubled and divided, much like the "American world" they live in.[62] Du Bois's concept of double-consciousness encapsulates the psychological consequences of blacks' racial colonization. It illustrates the ways that the color-line that racially divides society is replicated within black souls and ultimately translates into "two-ness": "two souls, two thoughts, two unreconciled strivings" – indeed, "two warring ideals in one dark body."[63]

"[T]he Negro is a sort of seventh son, born with a veil, and gifted with second-sight in this American world"

Being both a curse and a blessing, double-consciousness does not simply convey black folk's inability to see themselves except "through the eyes of others." It also makes it clear that, even though they are "born with a veil," they have been "gifted with second-sight in this American world." Du Bois distressingly wrote of "two souls, two thoughts, two unreconciled strivings; two warring ideals in one dark body, whose dogged strength alone keeps it from being torn asunder." But a question begs: Where do blacks get the "dogged strength" that keeps their souls and bodies "from being torn asunder"? After painting such a bleak picture of the "souls of black folk," and their trials and tribulations in the white world, this seems like a fair question, and, indeed, it is a query which Du Bois ingeniously answered with his notion of blacks' "second-sight."[64] Second-sight symbolizes blacks' ability, even in the face of unfathomable adversity (i.e., holocaust, enslavement, colonization, segregation, etc.), to see the strengths and weaknesses of both Africa (the black world) and America (the white world), and the ways these "two worlds" could and should learn from – and, even more, aid – each other.

Du Bois described African Americans in the passage above as being "gifted with second-sight," and it is their experiences in, and visions of, the "two worlds within and without the Veil" that ultimately distinguish their special contributions to American and world culture and civilization. In essence, where the majority of whites suffer from a social blindness to blackness, blacks have been blessed (or "gifted," in Du Bois's words) with second-sight as an ironic consequence of their having endured racial colonization and other forms of racial oppression at the hands of whites. But blacks, Du Bois admonishes, should never take their giftedness for granted, as it is neither automatic nor axiomatic: because double-consciousness, truth be told, constantly makes second-sight dangerously double-edged and always and ever enervating, because of both the intensity and depth of blacks' internalization of white supremacist (mis)conceptions of blacks and blackness and the paradoxes of the trajectory and transmutations of the American and global color-line. With this in mind, we see that, at its conceptual core, double-consciousness is about double or divided selves in the process of spiritually, psychologically, and socially evolving out of tortured "two-ness" into "self-conscious manhood" – which is to say, self-conscious humanhood. However, it should be emphasized, the only way to achieve self-conscious humanhood is through ongoing anti-racist struggle or, as Du Bois put it, continuous "striving."[65]

Second-sight provides blacks with a window into the "two worlds within and without the Veil." It also enables them to begin the dialectical process(es) of decolonization and human liberation by critically calling into question double-consciousness. Once this process is initiated, it, literally, gives African Americans *second-sight* – that is, first, the ability to view the "two worlds within and without the Veil"; second, the capacity to see the special contributions that both the "souls of black folk" and the "souls of white folk" have made to America and the wider world; and, ultimately and most importantly, the means to sift through and synthesize the best of the "souls of black folk" with the best of the "souls of white folk" in the interest of creating, as Du Bois declared, "a better and truer self," a "better and truer" nation, and a "better and truer" world. This was Du Bois's sensational solution to the problem of double-consciousness. The "Negro," armed with second-sight, would have to "merge his double self into a better and truer self." However, in this "merging he wishes neither of the older selves to be lost. He would not Africanize America, for America has too much to teach the world and Africa. He would not bleach his Negro soul in a flood of white Americanism, for he knows that Negro blood has a message for the world."[66] In the end, then, second-sight will enable African Americans to not simply see, but also synthesize, black and white "gifts" and "messages" and, in the fullness of time, articulate America's special truths to the wider world.[67]

"We have brought our three gifts and mingled them with yours"

To fulfill the mission that Du Bois charged black folk with, they, first and foremost, needed to familiarize themselves with their history, culture, and struggle without the intrusions of Eurocentric interpretations of their lives and dire conditions. It is in this sense that *The Souls of Black Folk* is brimming with impressively abridged swaths of African American history, which, according to Lewis, represent the "kind of feat that was to become [Du Bois's] signature."[68] As it relates to African Americans' discovering their "gifts" to the United States, Du Bois's forays in social, political, and cultural history were meant to expose his "Gentle Reader[s]" to the "truth hidden there" at the heart of American history since the nation's inception. In the last chapter of *The Souls of Black Folk*, "The Sorrow Songs," Du Bois unapologetically argued that African Americans had given America three preeminent "gifts," and that America would not be America "without her Negro people":

Your country? How came it yours? Before the Pilgrims landed we were here. Here we have brought our three gifts and mingled them with yours: a gift of story and song – soft, stirring melody in an ill-harmonized and unmelodious land; the gift of sweat and brawn to beat back the wilderness, conquer the soil, and lay the foundations of this vast economic empire two hundred years earlier than your weak hands could have done it; the third, a gift of the Spirit. Around us the history of the land has centered for thrice a hundred years; out of the nation's heart we have called all that was best to throttle and subdue all that was worst; fire and blood, prayer and sacrifice, have billowed over this people, and they have found peace only in the altars of the God of Right. Nor has our gift of the Spirit been merely passive. Actively we have woven ourselves with the very warp and woof of this nation, – we fought their battles, shared their sorrow, mingled our blood with theirs, and generation after generation have pleaded with a headstrong, careless people to despise not Justice, Mercy, and Truth, lest the nation be smitten with a curse. Our song, our toil, our cheer, and warning have been given to this nation in blood-brotherhood. Are not these gifts worth the giving? Is not this work and striving? Would America have been America without her Negro people?[69]

Here, it is important to highlight how Du Bois's "gift theory" hinges on his conception of second-sight, so much so that second-sight, it could be argued, is a subtle subtextual theme that informs each and every sentence of *The Souls of Black Folk*.[70] Take note above of Du Bois's discourse on the dialectic of black gifts and white indebtedness, which, in a white-dominated world, means that whites acknowledge neither blacks' gifts nor their white indebtedness to the black givers of the gifts. Second-sight is not simply about blacks' ability to identify and appreciate their gifts to America and the wider world. It is also about blacks sharing the lessons of their lives and struggles with others, especially other non-whites struggling against the various forms of European imperialism and racial colonialism. Even more, second-sight is about seeing, educating, and supporting authentic white anti-racist allies involved in the struggle for racial, social, political, and economic justice.

This, of course, means that, someway and somehow, blacks will have to counter double-consciousness and the diabolical dialectic of white superiority and black inferiority. Because, without breaking free from double-consciousness, blacks will not be able to fully appreciate or put into practice their second-sight, or self-consciously see that their lived-experiences and lived-endurances of the horrors of the African holocaust and African American enslavement, as well as their experiences of post-emancipation American apartheid, could make an incalculable contribution to human culture and civilization. In other words, the cure (second-sight and self-consciousness) is partially contained in the poison (the Veil and double-consciousness). Indeed, African Americans' experience of the African holocaust, enslavement, and racial segregation not only represents a deconstruction and reconstruction of what it means to be black in a white supremacist world, but also critically calls into question whites' racial hierarchy, which denotes which human beings count as "human," "sub-human," and/or "non-human."[71]

Du Bois, *The Souls of Black Folk*, and the prelude to "The Souls of White Folk"

With whites undeniably wielding enormous (if not unparalleled) power within the black world, Du Bois turned his attention to developing a critical social theory of the "souls of white folk." In fact, soon after the publication of *The Souls of Black Folk*, Du Bois came to the realization that, in order to really and truly grasp and seriously grapple with the "souls of black folk," he would also have to critically engage the "souls of white folk." He deepened and developed his discourse on race and critique of racism by unswervingly critiquing the specific race and type of racism that continued to plague the racially colonized and racially divided (especially blacks) along the color-line: whites and white supremacy. Undeniably the first critical social theorist of race to systematically explore the international, national, regional, and local dimensions of white supremacy, Du Bois's work in this area can be said to contribute to what many contemporary race scholars call: critical white studies. Consequently, we now turn our attention from Du Bois's discourse on the "souls of black folk" to his critical social theory of the "souls of white folk."

3

"The Souls of White Folk": *Critique of White Supremacy and Contributions to Critical White Studies*

Introduction: "The Souls of White Folk," *The Souls of Black Folk*, and critical social theory of white supremacy

Long acknowledged as one of the foundational figures in the field of critical white studies, it could be argued that W. E. B. Du Bois was a major intellectual architect of not only "black studies," but also "white studies," particularly *critical* white studies. Over the last several decades, some critical white studies scholars have turned to Du Bois's heretofore overlooked 1910 essay "The Souls of White Folk" as a key point of departure for their work.[1] Other critical white studies scholars have looked to Du Bois's 1935 classic *Black Reconstruction*, and specifically the chapters "The White Worker" and "The White Proletariat in Alabama, Georgia, and Florida," as sources for inspiration and indispensable aids in their critical analysis.[2] However, an inchoate *critical social theory of white supremacy* can be observed in an attentive reading of Du Bois's 1903 classic *The Souls of Black Folk*. For instance, in "W. E. B. Du Bois and the Construction of Whiteness," Keith Byerman shared that, although "W. E. B. Du Bois's construction of blackness through the trope of double-consciousness has been much commented on," we would be remiss to overlook the fact that the "'twoness' he described resulted from white attitudes and behavior." Indeed, the concept of double-consciousness marked whiteness just as much as it did blackness, and "while Du Bois's critics during his life certainly felt they knew his views on the subject of whiteness – he was either white-hating or white-loving – his texts of the early twentieth century in fact reveal considerable subtlety in his representations."[3]

When we engage the "considerable subtlety" in Du Bois's depictions of whiteness, we not only detect how "white attitudes and behavior" are integral to understanding double-consciousness, but also discover how he "reverses the gaze of racial domination in order to make whites the object rather than the subject of attention." Throughout *The Souls of Black Folk*, he used "irony, parody, and sarcasm to reconfigure racial power, especially the power of self-definition stolen from blacks in the reality of double-consciousness."[4] Consequently, *The Souls of Black Folk* is centered around both blackness *and* whiteness. It stands to reason that an analysis of one is inextricable from an analysis of the other, and Du Bois was one of the first social scientists to emphasize and critically explore this key point. Building on Byerman's analysis, David Owen, in "Whiteness in Du Bois's *The Souls of Black Folk*," importantly observed that "Du Bois understood the relational nature of blackness and whiteness" and that, indeed, "interrogating one necessarily involves reflecting on the other."[5] Because black identity is "fundamentally shaped by the racial order of white supremacy in which it is formed," according to Owen, Du Bois's concept of double-consciousness demonstrates that, on the one hand, "black identity is mediated through whiteness" and, on the other hand, "white identity is also formed by means of a mediation through blackness."[6]

In other words, because of the "relational nature" of blackness and whiteness, Du Bois "couldn't consider one without at the same time considering the other." Nevertheless, Owen offered this critical caveat, "Du Bois's radical re-framing of the understanding of race in America in terms of whiteness and its relationship to blackness thus does not re-center whites and whiteness." On the contrary, developing a critical theory of whiteness is "essential to adequately understanding and critiquing white supremacy." By critically "destabilizing the hegemony of whiteness through exposing it as the unquestioned norm," Owen continued, "Du Bois generates a new framework for the critique of white supremacy."[7]

Hence, here at the outset, it is important to understand why Du Bois's contributions to critical white studies need to be explored in any serious introduction to his intellectual life and legacy. The intent here is not to "re-center whites and whiteness," but to objectively examine Du Bois's critical social theory of white supremacy and the ways it discursively dovetails with his critical social theory of the "souls of black folk." Bearing this in mind, several vital points should be emphasized in our exploration of Du Bois's contributions to critical white studies contained in *The Souls of Black Folk*: (1) Du Bois's privileging of the black worldview (i.e., second-sight) over the dominant white worldview; (2) Du Bois's problematization of whiteness, i.e., his identification of the "white problem" – meaning, the problem of white supremacy; (3) Du Bois's emphasis on the ways in which white supremacy is integral to understanding, and inextricable from, blacks' anguished experience of double-consciousness; (4) Du Bois's utilization of the Veil as a discursive device to conceptually capture and convey the ways white supremacy impacts both blacks and whites; and (5) Du Bois's aiming of several key passages of *The Souls of Black Folk* directly at white readers in an effort to disrupt their, whether conscious or unconscious, relationships with white supremacy.

The Souls of Black Folk's contributions to critical white studies: Du Bois's critical social theory of the souls of white folk in *The Souls of Black Folk*

Du Bois began *The Souls of Black Folk* by characterizing the "white world" as the "other world."[8] In doing so, he challenged the normativity of whiteness and, in essence, inverted the longstanding tendency within the white world to "other" blacks and blackness. Consequently, *The Souls of Black Folk* stands in stark contrast to earlier articulations of the black experience marketed to white readers – such as Frederick Douglass's *Narrative of the Life of Frederick Douglass*, published in 1845, William Wells Brown's *Narrative of William W. Brown, A Fugitive Slave*, published in 1847, and Booker T. Washington's *Up from Slavery*, published in 1901 – because *The Souls of Black Folk* decidedly eschewed the assimilationist and accommodationist impulses of most African American literature that made its way to white readers at the turn of the twentieth century.[9] Unlike Douglass, Brown, and Washington, Du Bois was not preoccupied with proving to white readers that blacks possessed the spiritual, ethical, intellectual, and psychological faculties to qualify as full-fledged, bona fide human beings, based on the norms of the white world. As a consequence of white supremacy, he understood many of the white world's views and values to be *anti-human* in general, and *anti-African* (read: *anti-black*) in particular, which he documented and discussed in detail in his first book, *The*

Suppression of the African Slave Trade to the United States of America, 1638–1870, published in 1896.[10] Put another way, *The Souls of Black Folk* can be read as an assault on the ideology of white supremacy. It is an unambiguous challenge to the entire value system undergirding the artifice of white supremacy.[11]

Instead of the Other representing blacks, as per usual within the white world, in *The Souls of Black Folk* whites are the Other, and their world is the "other world." Tellingly, Owen asserted, "By othering the *white* world, Du Bois reverses the typical perspective on matters of race by shifting the point of view from the white to the black perspective, from dominant to marginalized worldview."[12] It is Du Bois's inversion of the "typical perspective on matters of race" that creates in his readers, and "most especially in his white readers," a "kind of cognitive dissonance." By othering whiteness and the white world, Du Bois opens up the "necessary discursive space for the credible expression of the black experience" and the sharing of "racial truth[s]."[13] A couple of things should be noted here. First, regarding "racial truth[s]," Byerman stressed that *The Souls of Black Folk* "provides a massive dose of the racial truth that whites have refused to acknowledge." He elaborated further that whites "have to be coddled initially," which is why Du Bois strikes a "deferential tone" in "The Forethought" of *The Souls of Black Folk*, because "contrary to their self-image," whites "lack the moral and intellectual strength to face reality" – meaning, the "racial truth[s]" they have "refused to acknowledge."[14] It should also be observed that Du Bois's technique of inverting the "typical perspective on matters of race," his innovative "shifting the point of view from the white to the black perspective," from "dominant to marginalized worldview" would come to be called "subaltern theory" within the field of postcolonial studies by the end of the twentieth century. Hence, once again, Du Bois's work proves prescient.[15]

Conceptually connected to Du Bois's othering of white normativity and privileging of the black perspective over the white perspective is his calling into question and problematizing of whiteness and white supremacy. In the discussion of *The Souls of Black Folk* in the previous chapter, emphasis was placed on the "ever ... unasked question" between Du Bois and the "other world": "How does it feel to be a problem?" Du Bois shared that the question typically prompted "flutter[ing]," "feelings of delicacy," "half-hesitan[cy]," "curious[ity]," and sometimes even "compassion."[16] Obviously, to reiterate, the "other world" Du Bois is referring to here is the white world, the world "without the Veil," as he put it. Because whites live "without the Veil" and the experience and epistemology that come along with it, Du Bois emphasizes their "awkwardness and ineptitude" surrounding discussions of race and racism. When Du Bois notes the numerous ways he is asked, "How does it feel to be a problem?," he is touching on a taboo topic and revealing the unspoken axiom that most whites conceive of themselves as being free from the "race problem," and their belief that blacks are, in fact, the epitome of the race problem. Incapable of conceiving of him as a whole human being, let alone a social scientist with advanced degrees from Harvard University and the University of Berlin, Du Bois's white interlocutor overdetermines him based on his race and makes the false assumption that the only thing Du Bois is likely to be conversant in is race.

However, by documenting the "dangerous innocence and incompetence" inherent in the question, and whites' lack of understanding of race and racism in general, Du Bois "reverses the gaze of racial domination in order to make whites the object rather than the subject of attention," as Byerman asserted above. "If Du Bois is to achieve his purpose of making blacks a part of American culture," Byerman continued, "he must deconstruct and defamiliarize the assumptions of those who exercise cultural hegemony." One of the myriad ways Du Bois "deconstruct[ed] and defamiliarize[d]" throughout *The Souls of Black Folk* was "by offering his own version of white voices," and "by pointing out what whites *really* mean when they speak to him."[17] It is in this way that Du Bois, ultimately, "reverses the act of racial definition," and put into play what might be termed *racial redefinition*, whereby the racially colonized have the power to racially reimagine their racial colonizers.[18]

With the question, "How does it feel to be a problem?," in one way Du Bois is clearly observing that it is a *white question* about the "strange meaning of being black."[19] In another way, the question could be interpreted as marking the questioner as white and an adherent of the white worldview and white value system. The racial reality of the matter is that blacks simply do not need to ask each other such absurd and asinine questions because: (1) they have an intimate understanding of the interiority of the black experience; and (2) they do not conceive of themselves as problems in the world "within the Veil" and on their side of the "color-line." Blacks and blackness are only perceived of as being problematic within the racial hierarchy of white supremacy, and by bringing this "racial truth" to whites' attention Du Bois not only "deconstruct[s] and defamiliarize[s] the assumptions of those who exercise cultural hegemony," but he also deftly practices *racial redefinition*. Byerman offers insight:

> Only by making whites aware of their position as a racial group rather than as the norm against which blacks (and others) are negatively judged is it possible to reconfigure the social order. His reframing of racial identity in this way, so that the anxiety of whites about their privilege is placed in the foreground, allows him to structure the notion of "problem" in a fundamentally different way. The effort to make him (and others like him) the problem exposes underlying white uncertainty about their own identity and status. If speaking to Du Bois causes anxiety and discomfort among people who otherwise move effectively through the world, then he may not be the problem at all. If they have to prove themselves to him, if they are limited in their understanding of him, if they can be so easily made the target of his humor, and, finally, if *the* problem of the coming century is a color-line they created and maintain (as they do in the scenario he depicts), then *they* are the problem.[20]

Recall, Du Bois stated that he seldom answers a word when the question, "How does it feel to be a problem?," is put to him. Instead of answering the question directly, Du Bois spends the bulk of *The Souls of Black Folk* describing the agonizing experience of having this question hovering over and haunting every inter-action blacks have with whites. Moreover, by not answering the question directly, and by subtly redirecting the question to whites and white supremacy, Du Bois spurns the tacit presumptions of the question, which are that not only are blacks the reason for the race problem, but they are responsible for it as well. In fact, the question ultimately merges blacks with their problems: within the white world, blacks are not people with problems, they are, to put it bluntly, *black problems*, a problem people. However, a careful reading of *The Souls of Black Folk* from the black point of view reveals that the race problem is, in fact, a *white problem* because whites created the social construction of race, invented institutions to perpetuate the racial hierarchy at the heart of white supremacy, and historically and currently benefit the most from the continu-ation of racial colonialism, racial capitalism, and white supremacy. Again, Owen offers insight, "it is not blacks that are the problem but the norming of whiteness itself that is." Without a doubt, it is the "presumption of the white perspective that is problematic, not the mere presence of blacks in a society structured by white supremacy."[21]

In *The Souls of Black Folk*, when Du Bois rhetorically asks, "Why did God make me an outcast and a stranger in mine own house?," he is giving voice to the ways in which white supremacy *others* blacks and makes them constantly question whether they are, in fact, a problem.[22] It also makes them question why they are "outcast[s]" and "stranger[s]" in their own country. Hence, Du Bois gives the distinct impression that within the white world blacks are perceived as "problems," "outcast[s]," and "stranger[s]." He, tongue-in-cheek, admitted that "being a problem is a strange experience."[23] Du Bois's irony reveals that he does not believe that he and his beloved black folk are a problem, and that, whether they like it or not, black folk must contend with the "typical perspective on matters of race" which sees them as "problems," "outcast[s]," and "stranger[s]." In essence, the norming of whiteness translates into the privileging of white views and values over all other views and values, and most especially black views and values. In the white world, whites are considered normal. In the white-dominated black world, whites and whiteness are normal and blacks and blackness are considered abnormal in light of the hegemony of white supremacy. Because of the ubiquity of white supremacy, the impact of the norming of whiteness on blacks and the black world is most often unrecognized by whites except when they are presented with the most egregious acts of anti-black racist violence.[24]

It is contending with, and always having to account for, the normativity of white supremacy that creates double-consciousness: blacks' consciousness of their own views, values, and interests, but also their consciousness of the superimposition of the dominant white world's views, values, and interests over black views, values and interests. Consequently, on the one hand, double-consciousness symbolizes the angst surrounding blacks being racially oppressed by, and racially excluded from, the dominant white world. On the other hand, double-consciousness represents Du Bois's effort to raise whites' awareness of the normative assumptions of white supremacy and how the said assumptions racially traumatize and dehumanize blacks. More simply said, with the concept of double-consciousness Du Bois seeks to raise both black and white *critical* consciousness. He seeks to raise black consciousness of the pitfalls of the white perspective and the problems surrounding blacks accepting and internalizing *the dialectic of the normality of whiteness and the abnormality of blackness*. Similarly, he seeks to raise white consciousness of the fallacy of the racial neutrality of whiteness, the racial trauma and racial terrorism inherent in white supremacy, and the myriad microaggressions that whites mete out against blacks in almost every interaction between blacks and whites.

It is when Du Bois touches on blacks' interactions with whites that we are introduced to his theory of the Veil in *The Souls of Black Folk*. He opens the book by "stepp[ing] within the Veil, raising it that you may view faintly its deeper recesses," and emphasizing the "two worlds within and without the Veil."[25] He assures his readers that he has an intimate understanding and lived-experience of the Veil when he concludes "The Forethought" with the following sentence: "And, finally, need I add that I who speak here am bone of the bone and flesh of the flesh of them that live within the Veil?"[26] Elsewhere in the book, he writes of the Veil as both *the marker and mask of difference*, famously personalizing the impact of the Veil and the ways it contributed to the racial colonization of his childhood:

And yet, being a problem is a strange experience, – peculiar even for one who has never been anything else, save perhaps in babyhood and in Europe. It is in the early days of rollicking boyhood that the revelation first bursts upon one, all in a day, as it were. I remember well when the shadow swept across me. I was a little thing, away up in the hills of New England, where the dark Housatonic winds between Hoosac and Taghkanic to the sea. In a wee wooden school-house, something put it into the boys' and girls' heads to buy gorgeous visiting-cards – ten cents a package – and exchange. The exchange was merry, till one girl, a tall newcomer, refused my card, – refused it peremptorily, with a glance. Then it dawned upon me with a certain suddenness that I was different from the others; or like, mayhap, in heart and life and longing, but shut out from their world by a vast veil. I had thereafter no desire to tear down that veil, to creep through; I held all beyond it in common contempt, and lived above it in a region of blue sky and great wandering shadows. That sky was bluest when I could beat my mates at examination-time, or beat them at a foot-race, or even beat their stringy heads.[27]

The fact that this is a childhood story should be underscored, because it not only indicts Du Bois's white classmates, but the white adults who created and condoned the "tall newcomer['s]" *anti-black racist etiquette*. The "tall newcomer" was symptomatic of the anti-black racist attitudes and social practices of the larger society. Consequently, with this story, Du Bois is basically sharing his *racial initiation* with his white readers, who more than likely have no real understanding or experience of racial initiation. It does not matter that all the other white children seem to previously accept little "Willie" Du Bois, the only black student at his school (and in his town). Within the twisted logic of white supremacy, the "tall newcomer" is entitled to white privilege and, therefore, need not accept Du Bois's greeting card or acknowledge his humanity, simply because he is black.[28] It should also be noted that all the other white children, in essence, conceded the "tall newcomer['s]" right to claim her *white privilege* – her *white right* to reject non-whites "peremptorily," as Du Bois painfully put it.

Whether the "tall newcomer" was polite or impolite is beside the point. In this instance, any white person, including white children, have the white right to racially remind any black person (child, adult, or even an elder) that they are considered less than human (sub-human at best, and non-human at worst) within the racial hierarchy of white supremacy. No apology is needed. It is both the de jure and de facto law of the land. Not one of Du Bois's white classmates took a principled stand against the "tall newcomer['s]" anti-black racism; obviously, if one of them had rebuffed racism the characteristically scrupulous Du Bois would have made mention of it. Not one of Du Bois's teachers (who were all white) did anything to assist him and he very likely did not feel comfortable going to them for redress. It would appear that this was his first fateful experience of double-consciousness.[29]

With his racial initiation all but complete, after this humiliating incident Du Bois was painfully aware of the Veil and had "no desire to tear down that veil, to creep through," because he began to hold white folk in "common contempt." However, he did have a desire to make whites aware of their role in the construction and perpetuation of the Veil (and its corollary the color-line). Du Bois also held the belief that it is important for whites to understand how the "awful shadow of the Veil" is connected to blacks' experience of double-consciousness, as when he continued the questioning broached above:

> Why did God make me an outcast and a stranger in mine own house? The shades of the prison-house closed round about us all: walls strait and stubborn to the whitest, but relentlessly narrow, tall, and unscalable to sons of night who must plod darkly on in resignation, or beat unavailing palms against the stone, or steadily, half hopelessly, watch the streak of blue above.[30]

It is obvious that Du Bois did not live within the world of the Veil by choice, but instead by force (i.e., the enforcement of the color-line

– American apartheid). Describing it as a "prison-house," the trope of the Veil allowed Du Bois to bring the violence of the normalization of whiteness to his white readers' attention metaphorically. Moreover, by metaphorically discussing the racial hierarchy of white supremacy, Du Bois was able not only to identify the "color-line" – or, rather, the racial divide between black and white America – but also to critique the oppression, subordination, and marginalization of blacks consequent to the "color-line." Part of the reason Du Bois emphasized privileging the black perspective over the white perspective when it comes to matters of race is because most whites do not think of themselves as having a racial identity, have no intimate understanding of race or racism, and have never really experienced racial trauma or racial terrorism. As a result, the Veil and the color-line are most often hyper-visible to blacks and largely invisible to the majority of whites, except when whites are presented with the most monstrous expressions and operations of anti-black racist violence. The metaphor of the Veil is Du Bois's way of conceptually conveying the racial barrier between blacks and whites on a personal or individual level, and the metonym of the color-line is Du Bois's way of conceptually conveying the racial barrier between blacks and whites on a larger social, political, and economic level.[31]

The Veil covering blacks and their blackness is meant to quarantine and hide them from the white public's view. As with other utilizations of veils in different contexts, they are typically used to mask or, at the least, obscure the person covered by them. Du Bois's metaphor of the Veil symbolizes the historic and current repercussions of the obscured and protracted history of anti-black racism and white supremacy in the United States. Even more, Du Bois's metaphor of the Veil is intended to raise whites' consciousness of blacks' enslavement, racial segregation, and economic exploitation for whites' historic and current material profit and psychological benefit.[32] From Du Bois's point of view, white supremacy did not come into being accidentally, and, just as no one randomly dons a veil, his metaphor of the Veil accents the intentionality of white supremacy to render blacks and blackness invisible. Here, then, we may conclude that *the Veil is whiteness* in so far as whiteness dictates and determines who can be seen and heard in the white-dominated private sphere. It also stands to reason that *the color-line is whiteness* because only whiteness can dictate and determine when and where one can be seen, heard, and travel in the white-dominated public sphere.[33]

It is readily accepted that one of the major aims of *The Souls of Black Folk* is to raise blacks' consciousness of the Veil, the color-line, double-consciousness, second-sight, and their special gifts to the United States.[34] In light of the above analysis, a claim could be made that a related aim of *The Souls of Black Folk* is to raise whites' consciousness of: (1) blacks' life behind the Veil and quarantined along the color-line; (2) blacks' dilemma of double-consciousness and the special second-sight that grows out of grappling with double-consciousness; and, finally, (3) blacks' seminal gifts to the United States. Even more, and squarely based on the above discussion, *The Souls of Black Folk* can be said to be aimed at raising whites' consciousness of whiteness and white supremacy, and especially the ways in which whiteness and white supremacy are integral to, and ubiquitous throughout, US history, culture, society, politics, economics, education, religion, etc.[35] Throughout *The Souls of Black Folk*, Du Bois demonstrates that he is a master of indirection and expert of innuendo by raising whites' consciousness of whiteness and white supremacy by means of metaphor and metonym. He also cleverly *critiques by questioning* throughout *The Souls of Black Folk*, adroitly asking:

How does it feel to be a problem?[36]

Do not these Southern outrages make your blood boil?[37]

Why did God make me an outcast and a stranger in mine own house?[38]

Will America be poorer if she replace her brutal dyspeptic blundering with light-hearted but determined Negro humility? or her coarse and cruel wit with loving jovial good-humor? or her vulgar music with the soul of the Sorrow Songs?[39]

If worse come to worst, can the moral fibre of this country survive the slow throttling and murder of nine millions of men?[40]

... shall we teach them trades, or train them in liberal arts?[41]

To be sure, behind the thought lurks the afterthought, – suppose, after all, the World is right and we are less than men?[42]

These are merely samples of some of the questions Du Bois asks throughout *The Souls of Black Folk* and, bearing our discussion above in mind, it could be suggested that each question doubles as a critique of the absurdity of whiteness and white supremacy. By questioning the virtually unquestioned norms of whiteness and white supremacy, Du Bois created an innovative, innuendo-filled way to simultaneously raise whites' consciousness of, and to critique, whiteness and white supremacy. In other words, by making the unfamiliar familiar, by centering blackness and decentering whiteness, Du Bois intellectually opened up a new world to his white readers and exposed them to the depth and complexity of the "souls of black folk." Whether using the metaphor of the Veil or the metonym of the color-line, in detailing the enslavement, racial segregation, and economic exploitation of blacks Du Bois makes visible one of the long-invisible major mechanisms of the maintenance of whiteness and white supremacy to his white readers. Literally *unveiling* whiteness and white supremacy, by describing the racial oppression and economic exploitation of blacks that is typically veiled or cloaked or hidden from the white public's view, Du Bois ingeniously repurposed the Veil and robbed it of much of its power, because he exposed whites not only to the horror and harsh living conditions lurking behind the Veil, but also to the undeniably creative and complex black lives, thoughts, and cultural practices burgeoning behind it.[43]

In essence, *The Souls of Black Folk* brings to light precisely what the Veil is supposed to keep shrouded in darkness. When Du Bois explains the black experience in multidimensional terms, when he compares and contrasts the despondency of blackness with the hegemony of whiteness, he makes public precisely what the Veil was constructed to keep private. This is also to say, he makes the invisible visible by illustrating the relationality between the agony of the black experience and the euphoria of the white experience. When whites objectively engage Du Bois's poignant and provocative revelations in *The Souls of Black Folk*, it becomes virtually impossible to avoid the audacious assertions of black humanity hidden in the shadows of US history, culture, and politics. Because whiteness operates in an imperialist manner, racially colonizing everything from social institutions and politics to education and religion, by default it racially colonizes and marginalizes blacks and blackness. Du Bois's eloquent articulation of the black experience *unveils* the invisibility of the tyrannical anti-black racist nature of whiteness and white supremacy for his white readers. Moreover, his stark descriptions of the black experience for his white readers calls into question the neutrality and normalcy of whiteness, and particularly the anti-black racism embedded in the white perspective. In this way, even if only in the pages of *The Souls of Black Folk*, whiteness is problematized and ultimately deconstructed to the point where its dominance over all things historical, cultural, intellectual, social, political, economic, and religious in the US can be called into question by both blacks and whites. And, by collectively calling whiteness into question, Du Bois exposes and undermines the maintenance of white supremacy.[44]

If for no other reasons, *The Souls of Black Folk* is significant because, on the one hand, with it Du Bois provided an unprecedented labyrinthine examination of blacks, blackness, and the black experience. On the other hand, *The Souls of Black Folk* is seminal because it *unveiled* for his white readers the false neutrality and normalcy of whiteness, and the myriad ways whiteness serves as a central cog in the wheel of white supremacy. Indeed, Du Bois's revelations to his white readers are just as important as his prophetic pronouncements to his black readers. For whiteness to work at an optimal level in the interest of white supremacy, it must itself don a veil and hide its operations and machinations from the majority of white folk. Part of what makes *The Souls of Black Folk* an undeniable classic is the fact that Du Bois not only lifted the Veil so that the world "within the Veil" (i.e., the black world) could be seen, but also lifted the Veil so that the world "without the Veil" (i.e., the white world) could be seen by his white readers. By *unveiling* – literally – by calling into question and making many taken-for-granted white norms visible, by emphasizing the anti-black racist elements inherent in the normativity of whiteness, Du Bois exposes the insidious nature of the neutrality and normalcy of whiteness. In other words, it makes perfect sense for whiteness and white supremacy to be invisible to whites within the racial logic of the white dominated world.

The invisibility of whiteness and white supremacy are necessary for their maintenance and perpetuation because, without *veiling* them, the delusions and contradictions of whiteness and white supremacy are rendered apparent – as opposed to transparent – to whites. Consequently, throughout *The Souls of Black Folk*, there are a series of subtextual signifiers, allusions, effigies, double entendres, critical questions, metaphors, metonyms, etc., which reframe, and refocus Du Bois's white readers' attention on, the reality and false neutrality of whiteness and the ways whiteness is an integral part of the inner workings and extension of white supremacy. The fact that Du Bois developed a way to chronicle and critique whiteness and white supremacy without directly identifying them, not only ingeniously *unveiled* them and made them visible, but essentially rendered them vulnerable to the questions and critiques of anyone who dared to impartially engage *The Souls of Black Folk*. He was not simply trying to save the "souls of black folk," but also desperately trying to save the "souls of white folk" as well.

"The Souls of White Folk['s]" contributions to critical white studies: Du Bois's critical social theory of the souls of white folk in "The Souls of White Folk"

Traditionally, "white supremacy" has been treated in race and racism discourse as *white domination of, and white discrimination against, non-whites*, and especially blacks.[45] It is a term that often carries a primarily legal and political connotation, which has been claimed time and time again to be best exemplified by the historic events and contemporary effects of: first, the African holocaust, African colonization, and African diasporan enslavement; second, the "failure" of Reconstruction, the racist ritual of late-nineteenth- and early-twentieth-century lynching, and the rise of Black Codes and Jim Crow segregation in the United States; and, third, post-Civil Rights Movement liberal racism in America and continued white neo-colonial and racial rule throughout Africa, and especially apartheid in South Africa.[46] Considering the fact that state-sanctioned racial segregation and black political disenfranchisement have seemed to come to an end, "white supremacy" is now seen as classical nomenclature which no longer refers to contemporary racial and social conditions. However, instead of being a relic of the past that refers to an odd or embarrassing moment in the march toward multiracial democracy by the United States and South Africa (among many other anti-black racist nations and empires), it remains one of the most appropriate ways to characterize current racial colonial national and international conditions. That is to say, white supremacy has been and remains central to modernity (and "postmodernity") because "modernity" (especially in the sense in which this term is being used in European and European American academic and aesthetic discourse) reeks of racial domination and discrimination. It is an epoch (or aggregate of eras) which symbolizes not simply the invention of race, but the perfection of a particular species of *international* racism: global white supremacy.[47] Hence, European modernity is not merely the moment of the creation of race, but, even more – as Theodore Allen argued in *The Invention of the White Race* – it served as an incubator for the invention of the white race and a peculiar Pan-European imperialism predicated on the racial colonization, economic exploitation, cultural degradation, and, at times, physical decimation of non-white peoples' cultures and civilizations.[48]

In "The Souls of White Folk," which was initially published in the *Independent* in 1910, then substantially revised and republished in *Darkwater* in 1920, Du Bois stated, "Everything considered, the title to the universe claimed by White Folk is faulty."[49] Where his engagement of whiteness in *The Souls of Black Folk* revolved around indirection, in "The Souls of White Folk" he directly dissected whiteness and connected it to the evils of global imperialism. In fact, when the essay is carefully read, even the title "The Souls of White Folk," coming in the intellectual aftermath of *The Souls of Black Folk*, ironically reveals that white supremacy not only dehumanizes blacks, but robs whites of their souls and renders them heartless in their interactions with blacks (and other non-whites). In their centuries of enslavement by and service to whites, blacks developed the ability to see whites both as they wanted to be seen (i.e., as Christian and democratic) and as they really are from the black perspective (i.e., racial oppressors and racial terrorists). Consequently, Du Bois opened "The Souls of White Folk" emphasizing his unique "second-sight" and that he is "clairvoyant" when it comes to white folk:

> I see in and through them. I view them from unusual points of vantage. Not as a foreigner do I come, for I am native, not foreign, bone of their thought and flesh of their language. Mine is not the knowledge of the traveler or the colonial composite of dear memories, words and wonder. Nor yet is my knowledge that which servants have of masters, or mass of class, or capitalist of artisan. Rather I see these souls undressed and from the back and side. I see the working of their entrails. I know their thoughts and they know that I know. This knowledge makes them now embarrassed, now furious. They deny my right to live and be and call me misbirth! My word is to them mere bitterness and my soul, pessimism. And yet as they preach and strut and shout and threaten, crouching as they clutch at rags of facts and fancies to hide their nakedness, they go twisting, flying by my tired eyes and I see them ever stripped, – ugly, human.[50]

With the second-sight of his "tired eyes," Du Bois sees whites not as they wish to be seen – as Christian, angelic, and democratic

– but "ever stripped," "ugly," and all too "human." The accentuation of white nakedness, of "see[ing] in and through" whites, of viewing whites "from unusual points of vantage" immediately conveys to the reader that "The Souls of White Folk" was written from the subaltern point of view of the "black gaze."[51] Whites may present themselves as powerful, but Du Bois's underscoring of their nakedness indicates a kind of vulnerability that is typically associated with the powerless (i.e., non-white folk in white supremacist societies). The ability to see the vulnerability and frailty of white folk is an aspect of black folk's gift of second-sight. For Du Bois, whiteness is a façade, which is why he stated, "I know their thoughts and they know that I know. This knowledge makes them now embarrassed, now furious." Hence, the mere fact that white folk believe they are superior to black folk does not change the reality that blacks and other non-whites are, in fact, not in any way inferior to whites. This is one of the central points of "The Souls of White Folk." Although whites "preach and strut and shout and threaten," the reality is:

> Europe has never produced and never will in our day bring forth a single human soul who cannot be matched and over-matched in every line of human endeavor by Asia and Africa. Run the gamut, if you will, and let us have the Europeans who in sober truth over-match Nefertari, Mohammed, Rameses and Askia, Confucius, Buddha, and Jesus Christ. If we could scan the calendar of thousands of lesser men, in like comparison, the result would be the same; but we cannot do this because of the deliberately educated ignorance of white schools by which they remember Napoleon and forget Sonni Ali.[52]

Here, Du Bois is critiquing the racial colonization of education, the "deliberately educated ignorance of white schools," just as much as he is critiquing white religion by invoking Jesus, Muhammad, Buddha, and Confucius. In doing so, he demonstrates that white supremacy is pervasive and woven through every fiber of the fabric of US history, culture, education, religion, politics, economics, and society. This means that it is not just Ku Klux Klansmen who embrace white supremacy, but also unwitting white schoolteachers who teach "Napoleon and forget Sonni Ali," among other iconic non-white historical figures.[53] Indeed, it is a paradox: in order for whites to be noble, blacks must be ignoble. If whites are superior, by default, within the racial hierarchy of white supremacy, blacks must be inferior. But what happens when blacks refuse their assigned role as sub-human, inferior beings within the world of whiteness? What happens when black folk resist white supremacy and the racial terrorism overtly and covertly used to maintain it? Even more, what happens when blacks bubble over and ask, as Du Bois did in *Darkwater*: "Who made these devils? Who nursed them in crime and fed them on injustice? Who ravished and debauched their mothers and their grandmothers? Who bought and sold their crime and waxed fat and rich on public iniquity?"[54] As he did throughout *The Souls of Black Folk*, Du Bois carried over his characteristic "critique by questioning" technique in "The Souls of White Folk." White supremacy simply could not go unquestioned and unchecked.

Any form of black resistance to whiteness – whether intellectual or physical, moderate or militant – makes mechanisms for the maintenance of white supremacy necessary. As a result, whites have a range of devious devices at their disposal to, often literally, whip or beat blacks into submission and make them conform to white supremacy. Anything can be justified in the name of whiteness because white supremacy is its own morality.[55] Racial hatred, racial sexual assault, and racial terrorism are acceptable, even if they fly in the face of each and every professed principle of Western civilization, because white supremacy is circuitous and provides its own judge, jury, jailer, and executioner. As a consequence, in Du Bois's discourse, Byerman opined, whiteness is "associated with all possible evil and sinful qualities: demonic Christianity, greed, war, violent colonialism, theft, delusion, cruelty, exploitation, dishonesty," etc.[56] Where America represents freedom and democracy for whites, it symbolizes slavery and tyranny for blacks.[57] Du Bois stated:

> I see again and again, often and still more often, a writing of human hatred, a deep and passionate hatred, vast by the very vagueness of its expressions. Down through the green waters, on the bottom of the world, where men move to and fro, I have seen a man – an educated gentleman – grow livid with anger because a little, silent, black woman was sitting by herself in a Pullman car. He was a white man. I have seen a great, grown man curse a little child, who had wandered into the wrong waiting-room, searching for its mother: "Here, you damned black—." He was white. In Central Park I have seen the upper lip of a quiet, peaceful man curl back in a tigerish snarl of rage because black folk rode by in a motor car. He was a white man. We have seen, you and I, city after city drunk and furious with

ungovernable lust of blood; mad with murder, destroying, killing, and cursing; torturing human victims because somebody accused of crime happened to be of the same color as the mob's innocent victims and because that color was not white! We have seen, – Merciful God! in these wild days and in the name of Civilization, Justice, and Motherhood, – what have we not seen, right here in America, of orgy, cruelty, barbarism, and murder done to men and women of Negro descent.[58]

Note the power and poignancy of Du Bois's solemn refrain: "He was a white man." Instead of viewing white men as conventional patriarchal protectors and providers, blacks most often see them as enslavers, violators, and the cruelest of racial colonizers. With the repeated phrase "He was a white man," Du Bois is able to accentuate the racial trauma and racial terrorism at the heart of white supremacy, and the millions of microaggressions that whites inflict on blacks. When Du Bois writes of whites' "ungovernable lust of blood," being "mad with murder, destroying, killing, and cursing," and "torturing human victims," he is referencing the lynchings and race riots that culminated in, and marked, the "Red Summer of 1919."[59] However, he is also revealing to his readers that white supremacy is unadulterated racial violence – both physical and psychological racial violence – and that blacks live in a violent world created by whites who have long held a bloodlust and deathwish for blacks. Du Bois sadly said:

Up through the foam of green and weltering waters wells this great mass of hatred, in wilder, fiercer violence, until I look down and know that today to the millions of my people no misfortune could happen, – of death and pestilence, failure and defeat – that would not make the hearts of millions of their fellows beat with fierce, vindictive joy! Do you doubt it? Ask your own soul what it would say if the next census were to report that half of black America was dead and the other half dying.[60]

American democracy is a fallacy, according to Du Bois. White superiority is undercut by its irrational insistence on black inferiority, and its "ungovernable lust of blood" and "torturing human victims." What kind of democracy is predicated on slavery? This is a damning question, indeed. Within the twisted logic of white supremacy, if blacks were to die off or be killed off, then whites would no longer be reminded of the fact that American democracy is a fallacy.[61] From racial segregation to mass incarceration, even after all of the trials and tribulations African Americans have endured since the Emancipation Proclamation, there is no immediate threat of them being extinct for the foreseeable future. As a result, the black reminders of the failures of white democracy will continue to haunt America. As long as whites refuse to repair their relationship with blacks, whiteness – as Byerman put it above – will be "associated with all possible evil and sinful qualities: demonic Christianity, greed, war, violent colonialism, theft, delusion, cruelty, exploitation, dishonesty," etc. That is to say, utilizing their second-sight, blacks see the demonism at the heart of white conceptions and expressions of Christianity, instead of perceiving them as democratic and Christian.

The New Oxford American Dictionary defines demonism as "action or behavior that seems too cruel or wicked to be human." Consequently, connected to the above question, "What kind of democracy is predicated on slavery?," is a corollary question: What kind of Christianity condones slavery, colonization, racial segregation, and economic exploitation? As Byerman flatly put it, "demonic Christianity," a kind of Christianity that exculpates morally monstrous acts. In "The Souls of White Folk," Du Bois systematically exposes the underbelly of the major elements and institutions of white civilization and illustrates that each – whether we turn to politics, economics, education, religion, or the arts – is, in fact, not neutral and has been used to perpetuate and maintain white supremacy. Demonstrating the double-speak of demonic Christianity, Du Bois declared:

> A true and worthy ideal frees and uplifts a people; a false ideal imprisons and lowers. Say to men, earnestly and repeatedly: "Honesty is best, knowledge is power; do unto others as you would be done by." Say this and act it and the nation must move toward it, if not to it. But say to a people: "The one virtue is to be white," and the people rush to the inevitable conclusion, "Kill the 'nigger'!"[62]

In America, white Christianity is essentially *white religious superiority* and, much like white supremacy in general, white religious superiority has its own sick and twisted *anti-black racist ethics.* Because white religious superiority is white supremacy under the guise of religion, it can justify the most abominable anti-human atrocities in human history in light of the fact that, within the world of white supremacy, God is white and has ordained and endowed white people with a divine mission to deliver the "pagan, heathen, and infidel" non-white world – especially blacks – from their idolatry and "ancestor worship," their false gods and superstition.[63] With his second-sight, Du Bois can see that white folks' lily-white God is nothing more than the specter of whiteness and white supremacy. However, again using second-sight, as Du Bois pointed out above irony abounds here, as white folks' religion is most often nothing more than a repurposed, whitened and lightened religion based on the religions of black and brown folks, and especially the revelations and prophecies of Jesus, Muhammad, Buddha, and Confucius. If, in fact, Jesus, Muhammad, Buddha, and Confucius all belong to races and cultures that whites deemed "inferior," doesn't it raise the question of whites' inability to create a "major" religion of their own? They, literally, racially colonized the religions of the various non-white people whose lives and lands they racialized and colonized. It is whites' racial colonization of non-white religions that underscores the "demonic" nature of their conception of Christianity.

Much like the stories that have been handed down to us regarding demons evilly devouring everything they possibly can, whiteness symbolizes a particular kind of demonism that redirects all energy, instruments, and institutions toward the racial colonization of all views and values that do not advance the continuance and maintenance of white supremacy. White supremacy, in point of fact, invented race and racism. White supremacy has undoubtedly utilized science and technology to develop the most advanced weapons of war and mass destruction in human history. White supremacy has created a political system that promotes domination rather than liberation, tyranny rather than democracy. White supremacy coincides with capitalism and, as a result, it engineered an economic system that privileges human greed over human need, profits over people.[64] Is it any wonder, then, that there are subtle forms of demonism free-floating throughout historic and current white Christianity?[65] For Du Bois, there are no two ways about it, white religion historically has been and currently is a "miserable failure":

These super-men and world-mastering demi-gods listened, however, to no low tongues of ours, even when we pointed silently to their feet of clay. Perhaps we, as folk of simpler soul and more primitive type, have been most struck in the welter of recent years by the utter failure of white religion. We have curled our lips in something like contempt as we have witnessed glib apology and weary explanation.

Nothing of the sort deceived us. A nation's religion is its life, and as such white Christianity is a miserable failure.

Nor would we be unfair in this criticism: We know that we, too, have failed, as you have, and have rejected many a Buddha, even as you have denied Christ; but we acknowledge our human frailty, while you, claiming super-humanity, scoff endlessly at our shortcomings.[66]

Whether we turn to white politics and white economics, or white religion and white education, whiteness is caught in a catch-22. On the one hand, whiteness claims it is superior to, and therefore the opposite of, non-whiteness, especially blackness. On the other hand, whiteness – especially by virtue of Christianity and capitalism – is based, and has historically built, on non-white cultures and civilizations, especially black cultures and civilizations.[67] It is in this way that whiteness breaks its own rules. Instead of whiteness being "pure" and made up of exclusively white cultural, technological, and scientific components, in reality it is a highly hybridized ideology that owes as much to the non-white world as it does to the white world. White identity is an ideological identity based on domination and delusions of superiority, and the combination of domination and delusion frequently leads to psychopathic and self-destructive behavior. For example, in his 1915 essay "The African Roots of the War," Du Bois contended that no one should be shocked by the cruelty and carnage of World War I, because white supremacy is a *do-it-yourself ideology* that allows each ideologue to make it up as they go along.[68] In other words, white supremacy is, literally, an *anything-goes ideology* that ultimately leads to whites' inhumanity to other whites.

Taking into consideration the fact that white supremacy is historically specific and plays itself out differently in different local settings, it seems logical that the varying versions of white supremacy will eventually come into conflict with each other. There is no honor among thieves, as it were, and the greed at the heart of white supremacy ultimately turns in on itself, robbing and looting, cannibalizing and colonizing other whites. Delusions of grandeur coupled with greed lead to wars amongst whites and, as Du Bois declared:

War is horrible! This the dark world knows to its awful cost. But has it just become horrible, in these last days, when under essentially equal conditions, equal armament, and equal waste of wealth white men are fighting white men, with surgeons and nurses hovering near? ... This is not Europe gone mad; this is not aberration nor insanity; this is Europe; this seeming Terrible is the real soul of white culture – back of all culture, – stripped and visible today. This is where the world has arrived, – these dark and awful depths and not the shining and ineffable heights of which it boasted. Here is whither the might and energy of modern humanity has really gone.[69]

Note Du Bois's emphasis that this "seeming Terrible is the real soul of white culture ... stripped and visible." Here he returns to his earlier theme of white nakedness with which he began "The Souls of White Folk." Recall, he opened the essay revealing that his "tired eyes" can see (with his second-sight) white folk "ever stripped," "ugly," and "human," and not as the super-human whites wish to be seen. Although he writes that "This is not Europe gone mad; this is not aberration nor insanity; this is Europe," he is, however, indirectly, connecting white nakedness to white madness. White supremacy is irrationality. It is insanity. Indeed, white supremacy only makes sense within the framework of what was dubbed above a "do-it-yourself" or "anything-goes" ideology. Hence, if one were to critically and systematically study the history of Europe and America (essentially "New Europe"), utilizing black folk's second-sight, it would reveal the origins and evolution of these two interconnected psychopathic cultures and "civilizations" predicated on white supremacy. Europe and America represent the unadulterated irrational ideals of white supremacy, but they are not merely emblematical and ideological, they are also actual and actional. Because white supremacy undergirds and informs white identity and white behavior, it operates on multiple levels: ideological, individual, and institutional, among many others. The ubiquity of white supremacy makes it an out-of-control and over-the-top form of imperialism, and its greed and quest to colonize everything and anything makes even the most mediocre white person adopt beliefs and participate in behaviors that are not only imperious, grandiose, and grotesque, but contrary to both white and non-white humanity. In other words, when all the smoke clears and all the dust settles, *white supremacy is the racial colonization of humanity. White supremacy is the devolution and dehumanization of humanity*. It is, ultimately, the destruction of humanity.[70]

Du Bois asked: "How many of us today fully realize the current theory of colonial expansion, of the relation of Europe which is white, to the world which is black and brown and yellow?" Undoubtedly, this question still stands and continues to haunt us in the twenty-first century, as does Du Bois's answer to the question. "Bluntly put," he shared "that theory is this: It is the duty of white Europe to divide up the darker world and administer it for Europe's good."[71] As a consequence, "The Souls of White Folk" is not simply about saving white souls, but more concerned with the damage that the sickness infecting white souls (i.e., white supremacy) has done and is doing to black (and other non-white) souls. Long before the recent discourse on critical race theory and critical white studies, Du Bois called into question white superiority and white privilege, as well as the possibility of white racelessness and/or white racial neutrality and white universality. He was one of the first critical race theorists to chart the changes in race relations from de jure to de facto forms of white supremacy, referring to it, as early as 1910, as the "new religion of whiteness."[72]

White supremacy will not end until the views and values endemic to it and associated with it are rejected and replaced by radical anti-racist, critical multicultural, and uncompromising ethical views and values. The rejection of white supremacy and the replacement of white supremacist views and values involves not only blacks and other non-whites but, truth be told, whites as well. As the examples of the Emancipation Proclamation, Reconstruction, and the Civil Rights Movement indicate, changes in the law and its interpretation and application do not always translate into racial justice and radical democratic social transformation. White supremacist social views and values linger long after amendments have been made and laws changed. Therefore, law-focused critical race theory and critical white studies provide, at best, only a partial solution to the seemingly unceasing and more surreptitious problem of white supremacy in the twenty-first century.[73]

The conception and critique of white supremacy developed here does not seek to sidestep socio-legal race discourse as much as it intends to supplement it with the work of Du Bois and others in radical politics and critical social theory. One of the main reasons this supplemental approach to critical race theory and critical white studies is important is because, typically, legal studies of race confine theorists to particular national social and political arenas, which is problematic considering the fact that white supremacy is a global imperialist system. In fact, Du Bois declared, "whiteness is the ownership of the earth forever and ever, Amen!"[74] Here, he is sardonically hinting at the cardinal difference between white supremacy and most other forms of racism: its worldwide or global historical, cultural, social, political, legal, and economic influence and impact. White supremacy serves as the glue that connects and combines racism with colonialism, and racism with capitalism, and, logically then, each of the aforementioned with the others. It has also been argued that white supremacy exacerbates sexism by *sexing racism* and *racing sexism*.[75] Thus, white supremacy as a global racism intersects and interconnects with sexism, and particularly patriarchy, as a global system that oppresses and denies women's human dignity and right to be humanly different from men, the ruling gender.

With regard to Du Bois's critique of white supremacy, it is not simply a global and social phenomenon, but a personal and political one as well. That is to say, for Du Bois white supremacy is simultaneously systemic and systematic, and also a matter of racist cultural mores and manners, which teeter-totter between idealist, materialist, and constructionist accounts of race. For example, an idealist account of race says simply (or not so simply) that white racism against non-whites, and especially blacks, is not so much a matter of race as it is of culture. Racial idealists argue that European culture and its pre-colonial history of color symbolism and religious views (such as Europeans' conceptions of themselves as "civilized" whites, and non-whites as "wild," "savage," "heathen," or "ethnic" Others; the positive and negative associations regarding the colors white and black; and the ways their racist cultural interpretations of Christianity support not only white/black color valuations and devaluations but also the "civilize and Christianize" missions of European racial colonialism and imperialism) set the stage for what would later become whiteness and white supremacy.[76]

Materialist accounts of race, which are primarily inspired by Marxist theory, maintain that racism does not have to do with culture as much as it does with political economy. Europeans needed a cheap labor force to exploit and work their imperially acquired continents, countries, colonial settlements, and tropical plantations. For the racial materialists, it was not about "religion" or "civilization" or "science," but an obscene economics and politics predicated on super-exploitation, which was always and everywhere reduced to its lowest and most racist level.[77] Finally, racial constructionists contend that *race* is an outgrowth of human beings' inherent ethnocentrism, but that *racism* is a result of Europe's push for global dominance and worldwide white supremacy. In this view, no matter who invented race, the reasons for its origination, and whether it is scientifically sound, it is a historical artifact that most modern (and "postmodern") human beings use, either consciously or unconsciously, to make interpersonal, socio-cultural, and politico-economic decisions. "Whites" and "non-whites" do not exist prior to the imperial expansion that helped to birth, raise and rear European modernity. But this is all beside the point to the constructionists. What is relevant is *the invention of whiteness* and its classical and contemporary uses and abuses, and the ways it has evolved over several centuries, transitioning from de jure to de facto form, and transforming the racial rules and ethnic ethics of who counts as "white" and "non-white" – or, more properly, "human" and "non-human."[78]

Du Bois's writings on race do not fit nicely or neatly into any of the aforementioned theories of race. As even a cursory review of his concepts of race and critiques of racism reveals, at different intervals throughout his long life and career he harbored what would be considered aspects of each of the three accounts of race discussed above. For Du Bois, as intimated earlier, white supremacy is not simply a global and social phenomenon, but a personal and political one as well. Hence his assertion in "The Souls of White Folk": "The discovery of personal whiteness among the world's peoples is a very modern thing."[79] Take special note of the connection Du Bois makes between "personal whiteness" and "modernity," to use the latter term loosely. His dialectical approach to white supremacy accentuates its interconnections and intersections with other systems of exploitation, oppression, and violence because, in his critical discourse, racism is one of several "very modern" interconnecting and intersecting hegemonic variables. However, it is white supremacy's *globality*, the fact that it is a worldwide racist system or "racial polity," as Charles Mills maintains, that marks it for much-needed special consideration and critique.[80]

In his critique of the global aspects of white supremacy, Du Bois critically engaged its origins and evolution, locating its genesis, uniqueness, and ubiquitousness in European imperial global expansion, domination, and colonization. What distinguished white supremacy from local, national, and regional racisms, such as those that historically existed and currently continue to exist between certain non-white groups, is its international imperial nature and modern world-historic influence and effects. At the heart of the history of white supremacy, as quiet as it is kept, is a prolonged practice and promotion of an extremely acute form of *cultural racism* and *cultural theft*. For Du Bois, whites were "super-men" and "world-mastering demi-gods" with "feet of clay."[81] By this, he means whites, with all their claims of superiority and "super-humanity," are or appear to be super-strong because they built their empires on the "gifts" – which is to say, on the inventions and innovations, on the sciences and civilizations, and on the cultures and contributions – of the racially colonized others, the folk now known as "non-whites," whom whites, generation after jostling generation, whether actively or passively, have racially colonized and quarantined to the world within the Veil and life along the color-line.[82]

But, as the "super-men" with "feet of clay" comment reveals, and as Du Bois's theory of second-sight above suggests, the "colored" and racially colonized are well aware of whites' weakness, of their Achilles' heel: their imperial push for global domination – that is to say, their centuries-spanning project of setting up systems of exploitation, oppression, and violence – unwittingly and ironically created intra-imperial cultural tensions, racist sibling rivalries amongst whites themselves.[83] Indeed, it also created the context and laid the foundation for the very anti-imperial "colored"/colonized hammer that Du Bois boldly believed would smash the imperial white "super-men['s]" "feet of clay." In "The Souls of White Folk," Du Bois audaciously asserted:

> The greatness of Europe has lain in the width of the stage on which she has played her part, the strength of the foundations on which she has builded, and a natural, human ability no whit greater (if as great) than that of other days and races. In other words, the deeper reasons for the triumph of European civilization lie quite outside and beyond Europe, – back in the universal struggles of all mankind.
>
> Why, then, is Europe great? Because of the foundations which the mighty past have furnished her to build upon: the iron trade of ancient, black Africa, the religion and empire-building of yellow Asia, the art and sciences of the "dago" Mediterranean shore, east, south, and west, as well as north. And, where she had builded securely upon this great past and learned from it she has gone forward to greater and more splendid human triumph; but where she has ignored this past and forgotten and sneered at it, she has shown the cloven hoof of poor, crucified humanity, – she has played, like other empires gone, the world fool!
>
> If, then, European triumphs in culture have been greater, so, too, may her failures have been greater.[84]

Here Du Bois notes major "gifts" or contributions to culture and civilization that various non-whites have made throughout human history, many of them in their pre-colonial (or, rather pre-*European* colonial) periods.[85] He does not diminish or attempt to downplay the "greatness of Europe," but observed that the "triumph of European civilization lie[s] quite outside and beyond Europe." From Du Bois's perspective, each racially colonized group – or, rather, each "race" – has a "great message ... for humanity."[86] He was extremely confident in the greatness of black folk's past and present "gifts" *and* spirit of giving, even in the face of – and often, it seemed, in spite of – their lived-experiences and lived-endurances of holocaust, enslavement, colonization, segregation, and so forth.[87]

Conclusion: Du Bois, critical white studies, and critical social theory of white supremacy

Generic racism, if there is such a thing, essentially entails racial domination and discrimination. White supremacy does not simply racially oppress, as Du Bois asserted above. Being the fraternal twin (or, at the least, a sibling of some sort) of capitalism, it racially oppresses in the interest of nonpareil racial colonial economic exploitation. It symbolizes the intensification of economic exploitation by adding a racist dimension to capitalist greed and colonial gain. Hinging on a diabolical dialectic that sees whites as superior and non-whites as inferior, white supremacy consumes the non-white world and claims non-whites' contributions to human culture and civilization as European or white contributions to culture and civilization. This is so because, as discussed earlier, from the white supremacist point of view, non-whites have never possessed, and do not now possess culture or civilization and, therefore, could not possibly contribute to the upbuilding of something they have never possessed and do not now possess. Further, white supremacy enables and utterly encourages whites to loot the knowledge banks and cultural treasure troves of the non-white world, similar to the way they did when they established racial colonialism and racial capitalism, because it is a global system that recognizes and rewards based on the embrace of white hegemonic views and values, white conquest, and racial colonization.

Moving beyond a strictly materialist (politico-economic or class-centered) account of race and racism, and hitting at the heart of white supremacy, above Du Bois asked the "colored world" and those whites who would open themselves to moral and materialist questions: "How many of us today fully realize the current theory of colonial expansion, of the relation of Europe which is white, to the world which is black and brown and yellow? Bluntly put, that theory is this: It is the duty of white Europe to divide up the darker world and administer it for Europe's good."[88] Part of Du Bois's critique of white supremacy reveals his reliance on racial materialist arguments, while the other portion of his critique revolves around his own homegrown cultural nationalism, which later in his life evolved into a combination of Pan-Africanism, Marxist internationalism, democratic socialism, and radical humanism that sought to highlight commonalities and kinships amongst non-whites, based on their struggles against European imperial expansion and all-out white (cultural, social, political, economic, legal, educational, religious, and aesthetic) domination and discrimination.[89] Du Bois's critical comments in "The Souls of White Folk" deserve quotation at length here, as his argument is elaborated throughout several carefully constructed paragraphs that poignantly capture the crux of his critique of white supremacy:

> The European world is using black and brown men for all the uses which men know. Slowly but surely white culture is evolving the theory that "darkies" are born beasts of burden for white folk. It were silly to think otherwise, cries the cultured world, with stronger and shriller accord. The supporting arguments grow and twist themselves in the mouths of merchant, scientist, soldier, traveler, writer, and missionary: Darker peoples are dark in mind as well as in body; of dark, uncertain, and imperfect descent; of frailer, cheaper stuff; they are cowards in the face of mausers and maxims; they have no feelings, aspirations, and loves; they are fools, illogical idiots – "half-devil and half-child."[90]

Emphasis should be placed on Du Bois's slight discursive shifts here. He undeniably touches on racial colonialism's intersections and interconnections with capitalism by pointing to "all the uses" whites have put non-whites to: field work, house work, construction work, military work, sex work, etc. He, then, highlights the ways the white world has a tendency to view non-whites as either "devils" or "children," bringing issues of non-whites' perceived non-humanity ("devils") or their "minority" status ("children") to the fore, simultaneously exposing both whites' inhumanity, at worst, or paternalism, at best, toward their racial colonial subjects, or their racial "property." Continuing his discourse on white folk's dehumanization and racial colonization of non-whites, Du Bois sternly stated:

Such as they are civilization must, naturally, raise them [i.e., non-whites], but soberly and in limited ways. They are not simply dark white men. They are not "men" in the sense that Europeans are men. To the very limited extent of their shallow capacities lift them to be useful to whites, to raise cotton, gather rubber, fetch ivory, dig diamonds, – and let them be paid what men think they are worth – white men who know them to be well-nigh worthless.

Such degrading of men by men is as old as mankind and the invention of no one race or people. Ever have men striven to conceive of their victims as different from the victors, endlessly different, in soul and blood, strength and cunning, race and lineage. It has been left, however, to Europe and to modern days to discover the eternal world-wide mark of meanness, – color!

Such is the silent revolution that has gripped modern European culture in the later nineteenth and twentieth centuries. Its zenith came in Boxer times: White supremacy was all but world-wide, Africa was dead, India conquered, Japan isolated, and China prostrate, while white America whetted her sword for mongrel Mexico and mulatto South America, lynching her own Negroes the while.[91]

The "civilized" (read: whites) are simultaneously a race in a socio-cultural and politico-economic sense, although they do not think of themselves in racial terms, and they throw temper tantrums when they are thought of in racial terms, or as being racialized or raced. They can steal and kill the "uncivilized" (read: non-whites) without regard to rank or reason, and they can at any moment change the rules of the racial hierarchy and racial history because they alone are decidedly and definitively the authors of human culture and civilization, and most certainly the architects of science and technology. As Du Bois demonstrated above, white supremacy is not simply about racial domination and discrimination. That is to say, white supremacy cannot quickly be reduced to racism, and especially as it is understood in contemporary racial discourse. Much more, white supremacy robs the raced or non-whites of their right to be human, of their right to self-definition and self-determination. It reduces human beings to the status of things.

Du Bois's critique of white supremacy also hits head-on the issue of white personhood and black (or non-white) subpersonhood. Recall above he asserted: "They [the 'colored' and colonized] are not simply dark white men. They are not 'men' in the sense that Europeans are men." Whiteness and maleness are prerequisites for personhood in the world that European modernity made. A person, in this world, is one who is rational, self-directing, and morally and legally equal with a white male. Since white males created the laws of this world, only white males are equal and given moral, legal, and extralegal consideration. Therefore, as the 1857 *Dred Scott* v. *Sandford* Supreme Court decision demonstrates, "a black man has no rights which a white man is legally bound to respect."[92] White rights are intimately intertwined with the denial of black rights.[93] Or, to put it another way, white personhood is inextricable from black subpersonhood.

In *The Racial Contract*, Charles Mills contends: "Whiteness is defined in part in respect to an oppositional darkness, so that white self-conceptions of identity, personhood, and self-respect are then intimately tied up with repudiation of the black Other. No matter how poor one was, one was still able to affirm the whiteness that distinguished one from the subpersons on the other side of the color-line."[94] And, who or what are these "human things," to borrow a phrase from Du Bois's discourse, on the "other side of the color-line"?[95] Mills went further to explain: "Subpersons are humanoid entities who, because of racial phenotype/genealogy/culture, are not fully human and therefore have a different and inferior schedule of rights and liberties applying to them. In other words, it is possible to get away with doing things to subpersons that one could not do to persons, because they do not have the same rights as persons."[96]

Even in its mildest and most unconscious forms, white supremacy is one of the extremest and most vicious human rights violations in history because it plants false seeds of white superiority and black inferiority in the fertile ground of the future. It takes human beings and turns them into the sub-human or non-human "things," making them non-white means to a white imperial end. Du Bois's critical social theory of the "souls of white folk" and critique of white supremacy registers, then, as not only a radical critique of an increasingly illusive and nebulous racism, but an affirmation of black humanity and an epoch-spanning assertion of Pan-African and other oppressed peoples' inherent right to human rights, civil rights, and social justice.

Du Bois's critical race theory is distinguished, perhaps above all else, by its commitment to non-whites' rehumanization and whites' human redemption. It was not simply the Veil, the color-line, and double-consciousness that impeded a truly democratic society, but equally white blindness, white forgetfulness, and whites' treatment of blacks and black gifts as property.[97] Where he began his adventures in critical race theory toying with partially essentialist, reformist, and gradualist strains, historical happenings on the world scene and the increasing economic exploitation of blacks in white supremacist societies led him to couple his critical race theory with a more concerted Marxist critique of capitalism's connections with racism. As a consequence, Du Bois developed many of the first major concepts in critical race studies. However, racism and capitalism were not the only issues Du Bois believed were deterring an authentically multiracial and multicultural democratic society. There was also the problem of gender domination and discrimination, something he consistently engaged, but an issue that most Du Bois scholars have buried beneath a barrage of criticism regarding his black radicalness, critical coquetry with Marxism, and sociological deviations when compared and contrasted with the work of his white male peers. The next chapter, therefore, will be devoted to Du Bois's often-overlooked critique of patriarchy, contributions to black feminism, and early intersectionality.

4

"The Damnation of Women": Critique of Patriarchy, Contributions to Black Feminism, and Early Intersectionality

Introduction: Du Bois's inchoate intersectionalism

For many scholars and critics, W. E. B. Du Bois represents the archetypal "race man," caught within the confines of the "Victorian attitude of heteronormative masculinity" that dominated his epoch. Nagueyalti Warren went so far as to contend that Du Bois "cannot seem to escape the masculinist framework that presents the male as normative." But, even with his "masculinist worldview," Warren observed: "Although his theory was better than his practice regarding his relationship with women, his philosophical position was more correct than most men of his age and class."[1] A decade and a half prior to Warren, Joy James convincingly argued that Du Bois actually practiced "a politics remarkably progressive for his time and ours." James further noted, "Du Bois confronted race, class, and gender oppression while maintaining conceptual and political linkages between the struggles to end racism, sexism, and war."[2] Building on James's contention that, even if Du Bois is not a "feminist" by modern standards, he was, at the very least, undeniably "pro-feminist," Warren asserted that Du Bois "was perceptive about the constraints of motherhood, the ways in which societal restrictions turned [women] into housewives, and limitations placed upon their intellectual growth and work opportunities. He called this limitation the damnation of women."[3] Consequently, Du Bois's contributions to black feminism are filled with foibles. However, it is only when we critically engage these incredibly contradictory contributions that we are able to observe his inchoate intersectionality or, as James put it above, his confrontation of "race, class, and gender oppression." Many of the social and political problems of the twentieth century have been carried over into the twenty-first century, especially the problems of racism, sexism, capitalism, and colonialism. Amazingly, particularly when compared with the work of others of his era, Du Bois's discourse eventually evolved into an inchoate intersectional framework that – according to Susan Gillman and Alys Eve Weinbaum in *Next to the Color-Line: Gender, Sexuality, and W. E. B. Du Bois* – "juxtaposed" race-*with*-gender-*with*-class to such an innovative extent that they audaciously announced, "there could hardly be a more opportune time than the present to reengage his writings from the widest possible conceptual and historical vantage point."[4]

In Du Bois studies, there has been a long history of disrupting and disconnecting (as opposed to, *à la* Du Bois himself, intersecting, interconnecting, and juxtaposing) the various social variables he critiqued and sought solutions to. The inclination to disrupt and disconnect the major foci of Du Bois's discourse in many ways erases – or, at the least, renders invisible – the implicit or "veiled" racially gendered critical logic and language at play in, and that is integral to, his renowned discourse on race and racism. In other words, Gillman and Weinbaum weigh in again:

> as readers of Du Bois, we have finally arrived at a historical juncture when the daunting expansiveness of Du Bois's grammar – not to mention his life and work, spanning two centuries and straddling the globe – requires reinvigoration and renewal by scholarly and political concerns that have, over the past three decades, become inextricable from "the problem of the color-line" that Du Bois formulated and against which he fought on multiple fronts.[5]

Indeed, Du Bois did fight "on multiple fronts," and one of the pitfalls of attempting to force his work to fit into Eurocentric, patriarchal, and/or bourgeois conceptions of who counts as a social scientist, or what counts as social science, is that much of Du Bois's social scientific distinctiveness is lost.[6]

This chapter takes its cue from Gillman and Weinbaum, among several of the other contributors to their anthology, not simply by reframing Du Bois's comparative and conjunctive analysis within the context of women, gender, and sexuality studies, but also in light of the fact that their anthology seems to give short shrift to

Du Bois's contributions to social scientific approaches to the study of gender in general, and black feminist social science in particular. In terms of identifying and analyzing Du Bois's contributions to both humanities and social scientific approaches to the study of gender in general, and African American women in particular, the focus here is on how Du Bois maintained, as James asserted above, "conceptual and political linkages" between various anti-racist, anti-sexist, anti-colonialist, and anti-capitalist intellectual traditions and socio-political movements.[7] Unlike most of his white male social science contemporaries, Du Bois did not downplay or attempt to erase gender domination and discrimination. On the contrary, over time his work placed the critique of sexism and racism right alongside – or, rather, in juxtaposition to – the critique of capitalism, class analysis, and class conflict theory.[8]

In tune with the thinking of many Marxist feminists and socialist feminists, Du Bois grew to be critical of both capitalism and patriarchy. He came to understand women, in general, to have great potential as agents of democratic social transformation because of their simultaneous experience of capitalist exploitation and sexist oppression. However, similar to contemporary black feminists, Du Bois ultimately understood African American women in particular to have even greater potential as agents of radical democratic social change on account of their simultaneous experience of racism, sexism, and economic exploitation, whether under capitalism or colonialism. Du Bois's discourse on African American women, therefore, has immense import for the discussion at hand because it provides us with a paradigm and point of departure for developing an intersectional critical social theory that is simultaneously critical of racism, sexism, capitalism, and colonialism.

Although there is much in Du Bois's African American women-focused work that warrants our attention, this chapter will prioritize those aspects of his social and political thought that register as significant contributions to the discourse and development of black feminism and *intersectionality* – which is to say, the critique of the overlapping and interlocking systems of exploitation, oppression, and violence arising as a result of racism, sexism, capitalism, and colonialism. Most Du Bois scholars agree that his major contribution to African American women's studies is his 1920 essay "The Damnation of Women," which was published in *Darkwater*.[9] Therefore, the bulk of the discussion here will utilize "The Damnation of Women" as the primary point of departure.

Du Bois, damnation, and women: "The Damnation of Women" and the advent of intersectional thought

In his enduring essay "The Damnation of Women," Du Bois stated that there are three "great causes" in the modern world to which every human being should devote special concern and careful consideration: the "problem of the color-line," the "uplift of women," and the "peace movement."[10] Women in general, and African American women in particular, Du Bois sardonically remarked, "existed not for themselves, but for men." He went on to assert, "They were not beings, they were relations and these relations were enfilmed [*sic*] with mystery and secrecy."[11] Where the majority of his African American male contemporaries argued "a woman's place is in the home," Du Bois did not associate femininity with fragility or domesticity. He was an increasingly consistent defender of black womanhood, criticizing both white supremacist *and* black masculinist myths and stereotypes aimed at African American women. According to Barbara McCaskill, "in his capacity as editor of the *Crisis*, Du Bois enjoined African American men to resist emulating the gender oppression of those white men who dismissed women as their inferiors." She continued, "If African American womanhood were threatened, then at stake was the survival of the darker race itself."[12]

An example of Du Bois's pro-feminist politics from the *Crisis* can be found in his 1912 essay "The Black Mother," in which he defended black women, and black motherhood in particular, against the white supremacist assaults and assumptions of both white men and white women.[13] Three years later, a galled Du Bois called African American men's open and uncritical acceptance of male supremacy into question.[14] His black brothers were thinking and doing the unpardonable: disenfranchising their black sisters in much the same manner that whites historically have done to blacks, and the rich have done to the poor. Even if it meant becoming the laughing-stock of the land, Du Bois would – in the venerable spirit of Frederick Douglass and Charles Lenox Remond long before him – be disloyal to the putrid patriarchal privileges and practices of "this man-ruled world," he ardently exclaimed.[15]

In his classic 1915 *Crisis* essay "Woman Suffrage," which was a defense of women's right to vote and pursue political offices, Du Bois took Howard University dean Kelly Miller to task for comments he made against women's suffrage and feminist political practice.[16] Du Bois, a fierce advocate of women's rights and women's suffrage, stated that dean Miller and men of his ilk who contended that the "bearing and rearing of the young is a function which makes it practically impossible for women to take any large part in general, industrial and public affairs; that women are weaker than men; that women are adequately protected under man's suffrage; that no adequate results have appeared from woman suffrage and that office-holding by women is 'risky,'" are not only aping the assertions of white supremacists and white masculinists, but also putting forward "ancient" arguments. From Du Bois's black male-feminist perspective, "The actual work of the world today depends more largely upon women than upon men."[17]

Just as Du Bois argued in *The Philadelphia Negro* that "The world was thinking wrong about race," in "Woman Suffrage" he intended to show Kelly Miller and his black male-chauvinist colleagues that "this man-ruled world" was thinking wrong about gender (the "problem of gender"), and the "woman question" in particular.[18] Du Bois chided, with his unique women-centered wisdom: "The statement that woman is weaker than man is sheer rot: It is the same sort of thing that we hear about 'darker races' and 'lower classes.' Difference, either physical or spiritual, does not argue weakness or inferiority."[19] Here, by comparing masculinist sentiment ("woman is weaker than man") with white supremacist ideology (aimed at the "darker races") and bourgeois thought (derisive toward the "lower classes"), Du Bois innovatively accentuates the intersections and interconnections between sexism, racism, and classism. Consequently, Du Bois's discourse helped to lay the groundwork for the race, gender, and class paradigm currently utilized within contemporary intersectional social and political theory, decades before the major intersectionalists of the late twentieth and early twenty-first century were born.[20] From Du Bois's inchoate intersectionalist optic, African American men who argue women's inferiority wish to dominate and discriminate against women based on their differences from men. This, however, is no different than the white racist theorist who theorizes black inferiority and sub-humanity; and no different than the bourgeois thinker who theorizes the vices and vulgarities of the urban underclass, and especially non-white inner-city youth.

The connection that Du Bois makes between sexism, racism, and classism also indicates that he is, to a certain extent, not only conscious but also *critical* of the supposed gender neutrality and universality of men's patriarchal thought and practice. What is more, Du Bois's male-feminist thought in this instance demonstrates that he is aware that the black men who argue women's inferiority wish to dominate and discriminate against women based on women's differences *not* simply from "men" – in some supposed "general," "neutral," or "universal" sense – but from the vantage point and socio-political position of *white* and *wealthy* men. "Men," as with "women," only exist in archetypal form, as pure raceless and classless entities, in the heads of established-order academicians.

Du Bois's male-feminist critical social thought points to a set of subtle pre-reflective parenthetical signifiers (adjectives), which are subtextual markers included along with the purportedly neutral and universal terms (i.e., "man," "woman," "boy," and "girl"). So, in all actuality, when Kelly Miller and other patently pro-patriarchal men argue against women's equality based on their (i.e., women's) perceived differences – read: deficiencies and deviations – from the supposed male norm, they are arguing against women's equality based on the *white* male as the archetype, as the norm. Moreover, Miller and men of his ilk do not simply take the *white* male as the mean to measure women's humanity (or lack thereof), but also, whether unwittingly or otherwise, use the *bourgeois* or *wealthy* white male as the model male or, even more, as the universal embodiment of authentic humanity.

The foregoing analysis reveals, at the least, two things. First, most men's worldview in white and male supremacist capitalist societies is simultaneously race-, gender-, and class- specific *and* hegemonic. And, second, the aforementioned helps to highlight the fact that, although many African American men may be deeply devoted to the struggle against white supremacy and for black liberation, without serious, sustained, and simultaneous intersectional analysis and struggle against racism *and* sexism *and* capitalism, black liberation will be nothing more than, as Frantz Fanon put it in *The Wretched of the Earth*, "a fancy-dress parade and the blare of the trumpets."[21] Domination and discrimination would still be with us, part and parcel of our daily lives and struggles, and nothing would have changed except for the color (and class or caste in some respects) of the oppressors. In Fanon's words: "There's nothing save a minimum of readaptation, a few reforms at the top, a flag waving: and down there at the bottom an undivided mass [of women, especially non-white women], still living in the middle ages, endlessly marking time."[22]

"The Damnation of Women" is a major breakthrough in Du Bois's discourse because it clearly demonstrates his growth as a serious critical social theorist *and* early intersectionalist. For example, in his most famous work, *The Souls of Black Folk*, women are virtually invisible, anonymous, or homogeneous in African American history, culture, and struggles. Examples of prominent African American men fill the pages of *The Souls of Black Folk*, with David Walker, Frederick Douglass, Charles Remond, and, most obviously, Alexander Crummell and Booker T. Washington receiving the lion's share of Du Bois's attention. To be clear, there are, in fact, scattered references to African American women throughout *The Souls of Black Folk*, but they are not given the depth of detail that men receive. This, in essence, leaves African American women's lives and struggles "veiled" in a book that purports to "lift the veil" so that the world can see the creative and complex black lives, thoughts, and cultural practices behind the veil and quarantined along the color-line. According to McCaskill,

> To talk of the women in *The Souls of Black Folk*, in fact, is to talk of very few women. When referencing African Americans collectively, Du Bois's gender of choice in the book is the masculine one. And when women do appear, the potential for their revolutionary involvement in political struggle is neutralized by their preordained functions as mothers, wives, daughters, and sisters. In these appearances, their corporate role seems largely that of serving as a metaphor for the orderly, moral African American home life that, Du Bois insisted, was a casualty of enslavement. To him, the black home stood in dire need of healing at the nineteenth century's end.[23]

Most Du Bois scholars who explore his contributions to black feminism generally agree that his early writings were "essentialist" and "reductive" with regard to African American women. However, many of these same critics often fervently insist that "The Damnation of Women" represents "an apparent exception" to Du Bois's otherwise "masculinist worldview." McCaskill contends that the essay was "written in resistance to the oppression of African American women" and in favor of their "equality with African American men, white men, and white women."[24] Indeed, in "The Damnation of Women," as he invoked the names of the Haitian revolutionaries Toussaint L'Ouverture and Jean Jacques Dessalines, Du Bois also called on Harriet Tubman, Sojourner Truth, and Mary Ann Shadd; quoted anonymously his contemporary Anna Julia

Cooper; and made veiled reference to Ida B. Wells.[25] Further, in an audacious turn of phrase, Du Bois placed the resistance activities of African American women on a par with those of African American men, going so far as to recall Sojourner Truth's classic query to Frederick Douglass, "Frederick, *is God dead?*," when the black male-feminist abolitionist, in a moment of deep desperation, declared that African Americans would have to fight for their freedom by force of arms. Douglass is reported to have stated: "It must come to blood; they [enslaved blacks] must fight for themselves, and redeem themselves, or it would never be done." Sojourner Truth was apparently troubled, according to Harriet Beecher Stowe and a host of white writers, by Douglass's radical tenor and questioned his faith in God, who – as Stowe's recounting of the story goes – Truth fervently believed would guide African Americans to an imminent victory over their enslavers and white supremacy.[26]

In recounting African American history, Du Bois increasingly cast black women in revolutionary roles, not only in "The Damnation of Women," but also in "The Freedom of Womanhood" from his 1924 book *The Gift of Black Folk*.[27] The struggle against African American enslavement and white supremacy was waged not simply by black men, but by black men *and* black women for all people of African ancestry and humanity as a whole. Du Bois reminded his readers that, although African American women, those "long-suffering victims" and "burdened sisters," were "sweetly feminine," "unswervingly loyal," "desperately earnest," and "instinctively pure in body and in soul," they were, even so, an "army" leading "not only a moral, but an economic revolution."[28] We witness here, once again, his recurring theme of highlighting the intersections of racism, sexism, and capitalism by engaging the lives and struggles of African American women, consequently contributing to both black feminist and intersectional thought.[29] Moreover, in his efforts to further emphasize the strength, resilience, and distinct socio-political world of African American women, Du Bois solemnly declared:

> No other women on earth could have emerged from the hell of force and temptation which once engulfed and still surrounds black women in America with half the modesty and womanliness that they retain. I have always felt like bowing myself before them in all abasement, searching to bring some tribute to these long-suffering victims, these burdened sisters of mine, whom the world, the wise, white world, loves to affront and ridicule and wantonly to insult.

I have known the women of many lands and nations – I have known and seen and lived beside them, but none have I known more sweetly feminine, more unswervingly loyal, more desperately earnest, and more instinctively pure in body and in soul than the daughters of my black mothers. This, then, – a little thing – to their memory and inspiration.[30]

Keeping in mind our above discussion of Du Bois's efforts to counter racist and sexist claims concerning black womanhood, note here how he highlighted the "wise, white world['s]" anti-black racist misogyny. The "wise, white world" includes both white men and white women. As a consequence, to speak of the "wise, white world['s]" anti-black racist misogyny is to speak of both white men and white women's hatred and domination of – or, at the least, their unceasing discrimination against – black women. In this instance, Du Bois's pro-feminist politics points to the ways *race is gendered* and *gender is raced*. This, in other words, is to say that his black women-centered social thought keeps a keen eye on the ways the combination of both white *and* male supremacy targets those persons who are black *and* female in a manner, and to a degree, very different from how it does those persons who are white and female or black and male. Additionally, emphasis should be placed on the fact that Du Bois's work here does not in any way attempt to deny the sexism that white women have been forced to endure, or diminish the anti-black racism that black men have been plagued with. Du Bois is not concerned here with denying others' oppression as much as he is with turning his readers' attention to African American women's multiple oppressions as a result of the intersections of racism *and* sexism *and* classism. Here we have come back to Du Bois's emphasis on the heterogeneity of African American lives and struggles addressed in *The Philadelphia Negro*.

Du Bois's focus in *The Philadelphia Negro* was on empirically and critically differentiating African American social classes, especially as they revolved around income, employment, and education.[31] In "The Damnation of Women," he seemed to be determined to draw distinctions between the lives and struggles of black women and of white women, as well as black women and black men. This is both politically and sociologically significant because, in making distinctions between black women's lives and struggles and those of either white women or black men, Du Bois not only demonstrated the ways in which *race is gendered* and *gender is raced* but, even more intellectually incendiary, he strongly stressed the ways

African American women constitute a *racially gendered class* whose lives and struggles are markedly different from the other women of their gender, and the men of their race. If we were to interject into this analysis the fact that both white women and black men can and often do exploit, oppress, and violate black women as a result of their respective privileged relationships with, and insidious embrace of, one or more of the major interlocking systems of oppression (i.e., racism, sexism, capitalism, and/or colonialism), then, we may be able to more clearly see why Du Bois's early intersectional social thought was simultaneously *inaugural, innovative,* and *insurgent.*[32] To be black in a white supremacist society, as Du Bois argued in *The Souls of Black Folk,* is indeed to be seen and approached more as a problem than as a person. Further, to be black in such a social world is to be perpetually plagued by that ever-unasked question that is seemingly on the tip of every tongue at every turn: "How does it feel to be a problem?"[33]

To be a woman in a male supremacist society, as Carole Pateman observed in *The Sexual Contract,* is to be seen and treated as a semi-citizen, if women are seen and treated as sometime-citizens at all.[34] It is an experience that affords few luxuries and little or no illusions about one's socially supposed place and "sex role," about men's power to discipline and punish women with impunity. However, to be a black woman in a white *and* male supremacist society, as Audre Lorde asserted in *Sister Outsider,* is to be seen, and ever approached, not as one who is humanly different, but as one who is sub-human – one who is humanly deviant and deficient.[35] Black women in white and male supremacist societies experience different, perhaps deeper, forms of racist and sexist domination and discrimination because they register as the antithesis, as the combined embodiment of the negation of both whiteness and maleness. To acknowledge anti-black racist misogyny, then, is to simply acknowledge, as Lorde did, "Some problems we share as women, some we do not."[36] It is to talk of that long-taboo topic in feminist theory and praxis revolving around the difference that race, racism, and anti-racist struggle historically have made, and continue currently to make, in the lives and struggles of non-white women, and African American women in particular.[37]

Du Bois's contributions to black feminist and intersectional thought are further distinguished by their emphasis on the political economy of racism and sexism in white and male supremacist capitalist societies. Early in his career, Du Bois noted the connections between capitalism, racism, and sexism. This is unique when one considers the rigid racist and sexist sociological framework that most social theorists (male and female) were operating out of at the turn of the twentieth century. Although in many respects quite crude by contemporary standards, Du Bois's discourse prefigured and provided a foundation for the study of race, gender, and class, as well as the critique of racism, sexism, and capitalism long touted by intersectionalists of the late twentieth and early twenty-first century. According to Cheryl Gilkes, Du Bois developed a "critical sociology," which "emphasized that gender, race, and class intersected in the lives of black women to foster an important critical perspective or standpoint."[38]

As the previous chapters on *The Philadelphia Negro*, *The Souls of Black Folk*, and "The Souls of White Folk" revealed, Du Bois utilized a variety of critical perspectives in his investigations of the Negro Problem. For instance, *The Souls of Black Folk* clearly conveys his lived-experience of anti-black racism, whereas, in *The Philadelphia Negro*, his interpretive elitism and bourgeois Eurocentrism unquestionably indicated that he was obviously out of touch with the the black masses' and black working class's lives and struggles. However, what is truly striking about Du Bois's evolving discourse is that it demonstrates that he was able to transcend a great deal of his early interpretive elitism and bourgeois Eurocentrism, to such an extent that he was eventually able to inaugurate intersectional social theory centered around the study of race, gender, and class and the critique of racism, sexism, and capitalism.

"No modern nation can shut the gates of opportunity in the face of its women, its peasants, its laborers, or its socially damned": Du Bois's African American women-centered and intersectional conception of democracy

Feminist sociologist Betsy Lucal asserts that "Had Du Bois ignored women in his work, he would not have been exceptional. The fact that women figure prominently in so much of his work sets him apart from his contemporaries, and, indeed, from not a small number of sociologists today."[39] Du Bois believed that women – and black women in particular – were (within white and male supremacist societies) a "subordinate group," who, by dint of hard labor and harsh living conditions, had developed a distinct and ever-intersecting race, gender, and class consciousness. With "All the virtues of her sex ... utterly ignored," the "primal black All-Mother of men," the "African mother," endured, on Du Bois's account, the "crushing weight of slavery" only to be re-subjugated in a world that claims to "worship both virgins and mothers," but "in the end despises motherhood and despoils virgins."[40] African American women, in the period after de jure American slavery, were flung into a world where they were dominated and discriminated against simultaneously because of their race *and* their gender. Their subordination is inherent – although implicit on many accounts – in the evolving social ontology of white and male supremacist US society. The chronic experience and effects of the interlocking and intersecting nature of racism, sexism, classism, and, as of late, heterosexism have led many black feminists to posit that African American women experience a reality that is distinctly different from the lives and struggles of those persons who are not black *and* female. Theories of "double," "triple," and "multiple" jeopardy abound but, curiously, rarely if ever have Du Bois's male feminism and innovative intersectional thought figured prominently in this discourse.[41]

From his early empirical studies through to his posthumously published autobiography, Du Bois spent the great bulk of his life and intellectual energy wrestling with various social "problems," different forms of domination and discrimination, and although he often missed the mark in his personal life with women, specifically with respect to his wife and daughter, there remains much that can be – and, perhaps, should be – salvaged from his long-overlooked innovative intersectional thought and contributions to black feminism.[42] To leave Du Bois to the traditional "great race man" or "pioneering" sociologist-of-race line of thinking is to throw the baby out with the bath water. The more radical and critical thing to do is to search for and salvage what we can from Du Bois's discourse that can aid us in our current endeavors to develop the concepts of racially gendered classes, black feminism, and intersectionality. This part of the chapter, then, is an earnest effort to build on and go beyond Du Bois's often unformed (and, at some points, seemingly uninformed) male feminism, as it is aimed at bringing his anti-sexist social thought into dialogue with the work of several key black feminists and intersectional social theorists who have popularized the interlocking and intersecting race–gender–class–sexuality paradigm within the world of contemporary intersectionalism.[43]

As with any social scientific method, there are things that are positive and others that are negative in Du Bois's discourse, which, of course, brings us to the question of dialectics. Indeed, a dialectical approach to Du Bois enables us to simultaneously acknowledge and critique the sexism he practiced at specific intervals in his private life, while appreciatively focusing on his production and promotion of male-feminist and other anti-sexist positions and policies in his public and political life. This dialectical approach also opens objective interpreters of Du Bois's discourse to the fact that he – as is common with many men struggling against their sexist socialization and internalization of sexism – may very well have had instances of sexist thought and behavior in both his public and private lives. As Warren importantly observed, "Theory and practice often cause problems for those under public scrutiny." Du Bois, she continued, "is no exception."[44] Similarly, Amy Helene Kirschke flatly asserted, "Du Bois was a known womanizer." However, "Despite this tension between patriarchal behavior and progressive philosophy, Du Bois's contribution to the struggle for women's emancipation," especially "with *The Crisis* as his vehicle, was considerable."[45] Kirschke continued:

> Du Bois stands as one of those rare African American men who severely criticized ... what he perceived as gaps of valor and integrity in the black male community. He was also exceptional in championing the black woman's right to personal freedom and social equity, and throughout his lifetime he supported women's rights in general. Du Bois supported the education of women, their right to vote and choose their own careers, and even their right not to have children, extending that privilege to the use of birth control. He also hoped that men would overcome the "freedom" they exercised to dehumanize and to plunder women.[46]

All of this is to say, were we to highlight Du Bois's sexism without accentuating his anti-sexism (or vice versa), we would be practicing and producing the very type of reductionism and one-dimensional interpretation and uncritical thought that inter-sectionality seeks to combat by offering ethical, epistemological, and radical political alternatives.[47] Because he has long been cast in the "great race man" cloak, it is difficult for many Du Bois scholars and critics to look at his life and work from multidimensional and interdisciplinary angles. A multidimensional and interdisciplinary interpretation of Du Bois's contributions to black feminism and early intersectionalism acknowledges that he was simultaneously, and quite incongruously, both a *public male feminist* and *private male-chauvinist*. In other words, Du Bois is not an ideal model for black male feminism (or male feminism more generally), but, unlike most other men of his epoch, he did devote some significant time, attention, and support to women's suffrage and women's liberation.[48]

Suffice to say, Du Bois is one of the few models we have of black male feminism after the deaths of Charles Lenox Remond in 1873 and Frederick Douglass in 1895. Although incredibly imperfect, Du Bois indeed does provide a bridge between nineteenth-century and twenty-first-century black male feminism.[49] Ultimately, it is important to accentuate those aspects of Du Bois's lifework that contribute to the development of the concept of racially gendered classes, black feminism, and intersectionality. That is to say, the concern here is with those elements of his discourse that critique domination and provide the promise of liberation. The Du Bois engaged here did not shy away from the forms of domination that women, and particularly African American women, experience as a result of white and male supremacy. Surely his essays such as "The Work of Negro Women in Society," "The Black Mother," "Hail Columbia!," "Woman Suffrage," "The Damnation of Women," "The Freedom of Womanhood," and "Sex and Racism," to name only a few, are sincere testimonies and somber testaments that affirm his claim in the last paragraph of "The Damnation of Women": "I honor the women of my race."[50]

Observing the fact that "women of African descent have struggled with the multiple realities of gender, racial, and economic or caste oppression," Joy James and Tracy Sharpley-Whiting, in a similar fashion to Cheryl Gilkes, contend that black women have "created … space for a more viable democracy."[51] Democracy is one of the most prevalent and pervasive themes in Du Bois's discourse, and he argued that it has not existed and will never exist so long as any human group – no matter how marginalized – or so-called "minority" is excluded from the civic decision-making processes of their respective national and international communities.[52] According to Nagueyalti Warren, "The issue of women's rights formed part of Du Bois's understanding of a democratic society. True democracy," Du Bois argued, "is inclusive not exclusive, and must be if it is to succeed."[53] Indeed, Du Bois included women when he spoke of "peasants," "laborers," and "socially damned" persons who must always be considered if the United States, or any nation for that matter, is to achieve anything remotely close to authentic democracy. For instance, in *Darkwater*, in the chapter entitled "Of the Ruling of Men," Du Bois asserted:

> Today we are gradually coming to realize that government by temporary coalition of small and diverse groups may easily become the most efficient method of expressing the will of man and of setting the human soul free.... [N]o nation, race, or sex, has a monopoly of ability or ideas ... no human group is so small as to deserve to be ignored as a part, and as an integral and respected part, of the mass of men ... above all, no group of twelve million black folk, even though they are at the physical mercy of a hundred million white majority, can be deprived of a voice in government and of the right to self-development without a blow at the very foundations of all democracy and all human uplift.... [N]o modern nation can shut the gates of opportunity in the face of its women, its peasants, its laborers, or its socially damned. How astounded the future world-citizen will be to know that as late as 1918 great and civilized nations were making desperate endeavor to confine the development of ability and individuality to one sex, – that is, to one-half of the nation; and he [or she] will probably learn that a similar effort to confine humanity to one race lasted a hundred years longer.[54]

We witness here an emphasis not only on racial oppression, but also on "sex" or gender domination, as well as a critique of many whites' and males' belief that they somehow have a "monopoly of ability or ideas." Du Bois directed his intellectual attention to the plight of African American women, and they are "an integral and respected part" of his beloved "black folk." In fact, the black woman, the "primal black All-Mother of men," could not and would not be held in check, neither by white nor by male supremacy, because, Du Bois surmised, she is leading both a "moral" and an "economic" revolution.[55] Although black women are often rendered invisible within the white male-dominated academic world of late-nineteenth- and early-twentieth-century America, Gilkes contends that "for Du Bois, black women represent a unique force for progressive change in the United States" because of the degree to which they experience and endure various forms of racial oppression, gender domination and discrimination, and economic exploitation.[56]

While most of the male social theorists of his age placed a greater emphasis on class theory, class formation, class consciousness, and the impact of political economy on culture and society, Du Bois innovatively engaged the intersections of class, race, *and* gender, utilizing black lived-experiences and black liberation theory as a paradigm for his social theories and conception of an ever-expanding, all-inclusive democracy. That is also to say, Du Bois's ever-evolving conception of an all-inclusive democracy was directly informed by his innovative intersectional social thought. Gilkes goes further to note that "Du Bois's vision pointed to a society that could confront, respect, and embrace the gifts of all."[57] He possessed a social imagination that did not limit itself to the issues of the white male working class, as was the custom in his day. Indeed, Du Bois audaciously sought to develop "a broad theory of history that concerned itself with the development of democracy and of American culture."[58] Going against the sociological grain of his time, Du Bois staunchly opposed the "subordination of the problems of gender and race in the development of sociological theory," Gilkes importantly observes.[59] Hence, here again, we see that Du Bois's sociological discourse is distinguished from that of classical European and European American sociologists, who by most accounts relegated race and gender, as well as racism and sexism, not merely to the sociological margin, but to intellectual oblivion. When race and gender did – or do – register in classical and contemporary Eurocentric and patriarchal sociological discourse, they are seen as social negatives that somehow, almost miraculously, fell from the sky, as though Europeans were not the architects of the concepts of race and racism (as we now experience and endure them), and as though men were not the masterminds behind gender domination and discrimination against women and other men who embrace and endorse what bell hooks calls "alternative masculinities" and "feminist manhood."[60]

It was precisely the "problems of gender and race" that Karl Marx, Emile Durkheim, and Max Weber – the "three names [that] rank above all others," according to esteemed British sociologist Anthony Giddens – either outright overlooked or downplayed in their "development of sociological theory."[61] Du Bois's social thought is distinguished by the fact that it sought solutions to the problems of racism and sexism while keeping a keen eye on the ways capitalism deforms, and ultimately destroys, the prospects for an authentically multiracial, multicultural, and gender justice-centered democracy. On the preoccupation with, and prevalence of, the "problem of class" in early modern social theory, Gilkes caustically comments, "Although issues of class, race, and gender ought to be addressed, most early social theory only focused on class and not on gender or race. In spite of its prominence in American society, the problem of race relations was not accorded the same theoretical importance as were issues centered on class, change, and social structure."[62]

Considering Du Bois's intense emphasis on both race and gender, it is not hard to see how his early intersectional sociology was seen to be suspect by sociology's early fraternity – that is, if or when his work was deemed to be "sociology" at all. This, however, leads us to call into question sociology's early, almost obsessive, interest in "class, change, and social structure," while it willfully overlooked the ways in which each of the aforementioned interconnected and intersected with race and gender – or, rather more specifically, racism and sexism. Questions concerning what kind of "change" early sociologists were seeking – and, further, "change" in the interest of which "class" – abound. In light of the many levels and shifting dynamics of the "social structure," we are also left wondering: which aspects of the "social structure" were the early sociologists seeking to "change," and in which class's interests?

Why is it that sociology's white "founding fathers" were unable to see what Du Bois's early intersectional sociology indicates that he so clearly saw and, even more, experienced and endured? It seems to be the case that what Du Bois identified as "social problems" were distinctly different from what white sociologists at the turn of the twentieth century deemed to be "social problems." From his early intersectional sociological perspective, "social problems" did not only emerge from the consequences of capitalism and class struggle, although he indeed did come to critically understand the importance of capitalism's "multiple" inextricable interconnections with racism and sexism.[63] The "social problems" revolving around race and racism *and* gender and sexism were equally important, from Du Bois's early intersectional sociological perspective, and they desperately demanded "solutions" right along with the "social problems" emerging from capitalism and class struggle. Indeed, in "The Damnation of Women," Du Bois succinctly said: "The uplift of women is, *next to* the problem of the color-line and the peace movement, our greatest modern cause."[64]

Here, when he employs the phrase "next to," Du Bois highlights how several "social problems" are not casually related simply because they are "social problems" in some free-floating general sense. Even more, he is emphasizing that they are intensely inextricable and unequivocally interrelated because they incessantly intersect and interconnect, influencing and informing (or, rather, *reforming*) each other, thus making their impact and effects as "social problems" that much more pervasive and profound, that much more diabolical and socially detrimental. The sentence that immediately follows the above quote from "The Damnation of Women" reads: "When, now, two of these movements – women and color – combine in one, the combination has deep meaning."[65] In view of his express emphasis on "two of these movements – women and color," it would seem, then, that we would not be stretching it too much to assert that the previously quoted sentence could be interpreted as Du Bois saying that the "uplift of women" and the "problem of the color-line" present social theorists with two of "our greatest modern cause[s]." And, what is more, when these two "great modern cause[s]" are "combined in one" – as they are in the lives and struggles of non-white women, and especially African American women – then the "combination has deep meaning" and, perhaps, even deeper discursive and intersectional sociological significance.

If we are willing to concede that Gilkes has assessed the history of sociology correctly when she contends that most early sociologists were preoccupied with, and primarily focused on, "class, change, and social structure," then the implications for the intersectional emphasis of Du Bois's sociological discourse needs no further explanation. Clearly, as the earlier chapter on *The Philadelphia Negro* demonstrated, Du Bois was no stranger to the sociology of social class, and, even within the world of the sociology of class, his work is distinguished by its emphasis on the inseparable interconnections of industrial, monopoly, corporate, and/or advanced-industrial capitalism with the rote racialization of, and impact of anti-black racism on, African American class formations and African American class struggles. Here, then, is precisely why Du Bois's sociology can be characterized as "early intersectional sociology" which, as far as one can tell, helped to establish the simultaneous study of race, gender, and class, and the simultaneous critique of racism, sexism, and capitalism, within the world of sociology before the close of the first quarter of the twentieth century.[66]

Emphasis on, and astute articulations of, intersectional sociology reemerged in the last quarter of the twentieth century, primarily under the guise of black feminist, Latina/Chicana feminist, and other non-white women's sociology. However, this reemergence all but left Du Bois's embryonic intersectional sociological discourse in the lurch. Angela Hattery and Earl Smith correctly contend that Du Bois "influenced the discipline of sociology to the extent that ... his work in the area of race, class and gender conceptually and cognitively," although long overlooked, demands that contemporary intersectional sociologists "recognize ... him, pulling him from the dustbin of American sociology for pioneering these theoretical arguments (and empirical studies)" and, even more so, acknowledge "the *contemporaneous* nature of his work."[67] The "contemporaneous nature" of Du Bois's discourse – and specifically his comparative and conjunctive analysis that combined the social scientific study of race, gender, and class with the systematic critique of racism, sexism, and capitalism – continues to distinguish his sociological discourse not simply from that of the large majority of the sociologists of his turbulent times, but also from that of the large majority of the sociologists of the twenty-first century.[68]

When and where Du Bois is engaged in sociology, his work is usually conceptually quarantined to the "Negro Question" – or, rather, the "Race Problem." The interpretation, reception, and re-articulation of his polymathic historical sociology, political sociology, rural sociology, urban sociology, sociology of culture, sociology of class, and sociology of gender are, thus, one-dimensionally reduced to and rendered as "sociology of race" or "black sociology," which ultimately translates into the academic ghettoization of Du Bois and his sociological discourse. Of course, this ghettoization makes it that much easier and "acceptable" for highbrow sociology professors and students of each and every human hue to ignore, exclude, or completely erase Du Bois from their sociological discourses. This means, then, that, because Du Bois has long been absent from most of the sociological curriculum, especially in the US, and also because, when and where his work is engaged, it is approached primarily and almost exclusively with regard to its contribution to the sociology of race, his innovative intersectional sociology has been rendered intellectually invisible, and he has never received the recognition he is due for inaugurating one of the most intellectually extraordinary and conceptually compelling critical paradigms in both the national and international history of sociology.

"The soul of womanhood": Du Bois on African American women's central role in the revolutions against racism, sexism, and capitalism

With all of the fanfare surrounding the centennial of *The Souls of Black Folk* in 2003, it is easy to lose sight of the fact that W. E. B.

Du Bois was so much more than an extremely eloquent "essayist" or "founding father" of the modern Civil Rights Movement.[69] Indeed, several sociological circles joined in the centenary commemorations, convening panels at professional symposia and commissioning distinguished lectures on Du Bois. However, Hattery and Smith contend that contemporary Du Boisian sociologists must move beyond repeatedly railing about how horribly Du Bois's discourse has been ignored or neglected within the world of sociology and begin to identify *why*, *how*, and *what*, in the most amazing intellectual history-making manner, he contributed to sociology. Staying stuck on Du Bois's "sociological negation" will never be enough and, in point of fact, it does not in any way provide answers to the aforementioned questions.[70] Hattery and Smith insistently interject: "Yet, what is not addressed is not so much the absence of Du Bois from mainstream sociology but rather, why is it that we need to know who he was and what he did?" Conversely, they continued, "it is not enough to repeat over and over the aforementioned but begin to situate that Du Bois made considerable contributions to the main canon of sociology similar in ways to the work of Max Weber, Karl Marx, and Emile Durkheim." Taking into consideration Du Bois and his discourse, Hattery and Smith concluded, "the real answer lays not so much in who he was but the lasting contributions of his work for understanding long-term, systematic, structured inequities that unfold along race, class, and gender lines."[71]

Sociologically, African American women's lives and struggles provided Du Bois with an almost ideal set of social variables through which to critically comprehend these inequities. Because of the socio-historical fact of their suffering, what black feminist sociologist Deborah King calls the "multiple jeopardy" of being black, female, poor, and perpetually hyper-sexualized – which is to say, black women to varying degrees simultaneously experience and endure racism, sexism, and the ravaging effects of economic exploitation, whether under capitalism or colonialism – Du Bois understood African American women to be the almost ideal agents of radical democratic social (and, later, radical democratic socialist) change.[72] In African American women and their lives and struggles, Du Bois found crucial subjects for social change and the spreading of radical democratic thought and practice. Although they are rarely referred to, Gilkes importantly asserts, "Du Bois's perspectives on African American women anticipated and influenced concepts and ideas we currently use to examine the intersection of gender, race, and class with reference to African American women."[73] Helping to corroborate the above contentions concerning Du Bois's inaugu-ration of intersectional sociology, she further explained, "his work is the earliest self-consciously sociological interpretation of the role of African American women as agents of social change," and, therefore, offers contemporary sociologists of gender in general, and black feminist sociologists in particular, a multi-perspectival and interdisciplinary model on which to build an openly insurgent anti-racist, anti-sexist, anti-capitalist, and anti-colonialist inter-sectional sociology.[74]

In fact, when Du Bois's work on women is taken together and juxtaposed with his research on race and class, African American women irrefutably emerge as integral parts of all three of the "great revolutions" he prophesied (e.g., in *Darkwater, The Gift of Black Folk, Dark Princess, Black Reconstruction, Black Folk: Then and Now, Color and Democracy,* and *The World and Africa*), which must take place if America (and the wider world) is to truly achieve democracy.[75] Observe below how each of the social "revolutions" to which he contended black women would be central emerged out of his overarching intersectional sociology: the first was the revolution against racism or the color-line; second was the revolution against sexism, and specifically patriarchy; and third, and finally, was the revolution against economic exploitation, which, from Du Bois's perspective, included both capitalism and colonialism. Here, we see most clearly how Du Bois sought to confront and contest the major problems of his epoch (and, even now, ours): racism, sexism, capitalism, and colonialism.

Of the three "great revolutions," first there was the revolt of the masses of non-white folk against racism, racial colonialism, and the global color-line. This, of course, translated itself in Du Bois's discourse into his anti-racist and anti-colonialist writings in *The Moon, The Horizon, The Crisis, Phylon,* and the *National Guardian,* amongst other publications, public intellectualism, and political activism. African American women were cast in a "messianic" or "prophetic" role in the revolution against racial domination and discrimination because Du Bois believed that their sufferings "provided them with a legitimate voice of challenge."[76] Who knew then in 1920, and who would know now in 2020 – perhaps more so than most other classes of citizens – the deficiencies of US democracy than those persons simultaneously experiencing white and male supremacy, as well as economic super-exploitation?[77] Prefiguring Patricia Hill Collins's conception of "subjugated knowledge," Du Bois attempted to highlight the "hidden" and/

or "suppressed" knowledge produced by black women as they confronted, combated, and often contradicted both white and male supremacy, as well as the conundrums of capitalism.[78]

The second "great revolution" to which African American women would be integral, according to Du Bois, especially in "The Damnation of Women" and "The Freedom of Womanhood," was the revolution of the "freeing" of women – which is to say, "women's liberation." In his 1915 classic essay "Woman Suffrage," he unequivocally asserted: "The actual work of the world today depends more largely upon women than upon men." Consequently, he continued with weighted words, "this man-ruled world faces an astonishing dilemma. . . . The meaning of the twentieth century is the freeing of the individual soul; the soul longest in slavery and still in the most disgusting and indefensible slavery is the soul of womanhood."[79] He contended that it was the "new revolutionary ideals" of women, and especially African American women, "which must in time have vast influence on the thought and action of this land [i.e., the United States]."[80]

In fact, taken by themselves, "The Damnation of Women" and "The Freedom of Womanhood" make it virtually impossible to deny Du Bois's – again, however contradictory and controversial – relationship with late-nineteenth and early-twentieth-century black feminist theory and praxis. Without question, the Black Women's Club Movement's central organization, the National Association of Colored Women (NACW), not only provided Du Bois with a paradigm and point of departure with which to develop his own distinct brand of male feminism and inaugurate intersectional sociology, but also ultimately enabled him to link his increasingly insurgent intersectional sociology with radical political praxis: first, with his leadership in the Niagara Movement (the precursor to the NAACP), and then, second, with his leadership in the NAACP itself.[81] All of this helps to highlight, once again, that "Du Bois believed in the importance of an activist social science for the growth and development of democracy," as Gilkes correctly contends.[82] As has been witnessed throughout this chapter, Du Bois understood women to be special contributors to not only women's decolonization and women's liberation but, even more, to human liberation and democratic social transformation.

The last of the "three great revolutions" in which Du Bois maintained that African American women were to play a pivotal role was the revolution against economic exploitation, particularly contemporary capitalism. Du Bois asserted that the "emancipation of man is the emancipation of labor and the emancipation of labor is the freeing of that basic majority of workers who are yellow, brown, and black."[83] Moreover, in "slavery," in "concubinage," as cooks, nurses, and washerwomen, Du Bois recognized the significance of African American women as workers, passionately stating in "The Freedom of Womanhood" that the issue of "economic independence is ... the central fact in the struggle of women for equality. In the earlier days the slave woman was found to be economically as efficient as the man."[84] Then, historically moving from the past to the present, he reiterated the significance of black women as workers and the ways in which their work disrupted the psychopathic sanctions of the white supremacist patriarchal capitalist social world: "In our modern industrial organization the work of women is being found as valuable as that of men.... The Negro woman as laborer, as seamstress, as servant and cook, has come into competition with the white male laborer and with the white woman worker." Furthermore, directly hitting the heart of the matter, he stated that the "fact that she could and did replace the white man as laborer, artisan and servant, showed the possibility of the white woman doing the same thing, and led to it." In fact, he thundered in conclusion, the "usual sentimental arguments against women at work were not brought forward in the case of Negro womanhood."[85] With these often-overlooked words, Du Bois revealed that black women workers were racially gendered in ways that essentially meant that their race trumped their gender in the white supremacist patriarchal capitalist public sphere, while their centuries-spanning endurance of anti-black racist rape and other forms of white supremacist sexual violence as "concubines" and the like illustrated the ways their gender trumped their race in the white supremacist patriarchal capitalist private sphere.[86]

In addition, Du Bois's historical sociological discourse here also inverts the conventional white feminist revisionist histories in which white women are incessantly seen as the gender-conscious "wonder women" and "women warriors" leading the gender-unconscious and sexism-submissive black (and other non-white) women to critical gender or feminist consciousness. Quite the contrary, Du Bois historically documented that it was African American women who were arguably the first women to be an integral part of the US workforce en masse, and that it was black women who paved the way for other women to be seen and taken seriously as workers. Moreover, this last point helps to highlight how black women's lives and struggles challenge not only white supremacist patriarchal notions of "a woman's place," but, more specifically, many black men's, white women's, and other non-white women's misconceptions about "a woman's place."

Du Bois's contributions to black feminist sociology point to the historical fact that black women are attempting to grasp and grapple with distinctly different social and political issues when compared with their white counterparts, although he openly acknowledged that both groups of women are discriminated against because of their gender. Race, racism, and anti-racist struggle historically made, and currently make, distinct differences in the life-worlds, life-struggles, and liberation theory and praxis of African American women, and this is especially true when coupled with their simultaneous struggles for gender justice and an end to economic exploitation. To put it another way, gender *and* racial domination and discrimination, and the theory and praxis developed to combat these oppressions, have historically served, and continue currently to serve, as central determining factors in African American women's lives and struggles, and it is this stubborn socio-historical fact, combined with the contradictions of capitalism and colonialism, that has routinely put many black feminists at loggerheads with the inexcusable racial lethargy and lacunae of white feminists and their brand of feminism.

In many ways, black women's lives and struggles are unique when one critically considers that they have been not only relegated to the margins within feminist theory, women's studies, and the wider Women's Liberation Movement, but also frequently ignored or rendered invisible in African American studies, the Civil Rights Movement, and the Black Power Movement.[87] In "Grounding with My Sisters: Patriarchy and the Exploitation of Black Women," Manning Marable discusses the double dilemma of African American women both *within* and *without* their race, and *within* and *without* their gender:

> Black social history, as it has been written to date, has been profoundly patriarchal. The sexist critical framework of American white history has been accepted by black male scholars; the reconstruction of our past, the reclamation of our history from the ruins, has been an enterprise wherein women have been too long segregated. Obligatory references are generally made to those "outstanding sisters" who gave some special contribution to the liberation of the "black man." Even these token footnotes probably do more harm than good, because they reinforce the false belief that the most oppressed victim

of white racial tyranny has been *the black man*. ... From the dawn of the slave trade until today, U.S. capitalism was both racist and sexist. The super-exploitation of black women became a permanent feature in American social and economic life, because sisters were assaulted simultaneously as workers, as blacks, and as women.[88]

As we have witnessed throughout this chapter, Du Bois's insurgent intersectional sociological framework was one of the first to critically engage African American women's simultaneous social statuses "as workers, as blacks, and as women." He increasingly focused on African American women's roles in the "economic revolution," stating: "black women toil and toil hard," and they "are a group of workers, fighting for their daily bread like men; independent and approaching economic freedom."[89] It is not enough for black liberationists to struggle against anti-black racism and white supremacy. It is not enough for women's liberationists to struggle against patriarchy or male supremacy. And it is not enough for Marxists and other radicals on the left to struggle against capitalist exploitation. What is needed is a critical comparative and conjunctive historical, cultural, sociological, political, and economic framework that takes into consideration each of the aforementioned forms of domination and discrimination. For Du Bois, as a critical social theorist and radical political activist, a real revolutionist has the onerous task of critiquing society as a whole, not simply the parts of it that most inhibit and encumber the theorist's particular race, gender, and class. In "The Damnation of Women" and "The Freedom of Womanhood," among other articles and essays, Du Bois turned his readers' attention to the plight of African American women, thus putting into principled practice his admonition that a truly critical social theorist critique society as a whole, not simply selected parts of it which most hinder and harm the theorist and their closest kith and kin.

With all of the foregoing in mind, we now turn our attention away from Du Bois's critique of patriarchy and contributions to black feminism and intersectionality to his critique of capitalism and contributions to black Marxism and democratic socialism. When we examine Du Bois's Marxist studies and critique of capitalism, we, literally, witness him moving beyond his "closest kith and kin" (i.e., black folk in the US) and stepping onto the international stage to raise the plight of continental and diasporan Africa and workers around the world. Indeed, as observed throughout this book, Du Bois understands capitalism and colonialism to be inextricable, and his emphasis on the connections between these overlapping exploitative systems is most pronounced when we chart and critically engage the origins and evolution of his pioneering anti-racist Marxism. Consequently, the fifth and final chapter will examine Du Bois's development of black Marxism: beginning with his embrace of genteel socialism, which advocated reformism and gradual social transformation, and going through to his evolution into a committed Marxist internationalist who believed that only world revolution could topple racism, capitalism, and colonialism.

5

Black Reconstruction: *Critique of Capitalism, Contributions to Black Marxism, and Discourse on Democratic Socialism*

Introduction: From Black Reformism to Black Radicalism

In a rare 1957 television interview with Al Morgan, a world-weary 89-year-old W. E. B. Du Bois nonchalantly stated, "I am certainly not a conservative. I should call myself a Socialist, although that isn't a very definite term."[1] Du Bois went further to clarify what he meant by the indefinite term: "I mean I believe in the welfare state. I believe that business should be carried on not for private profit but for public welfare. I believe in many steps which are usually associated with socialism."[2] Du Bois's interest in socialism and Marxism can be traced back to his graduate studies at the University of Berlin. However, he did not begin to seriously study socialism until the Russian Revolution of 1917. His interest in socialism and Marxism intensified during the 1920s, and especially in the 1930s as a consequence of the Great Depression. Du Bois traveled to Russia (then known as the Soviet Union) in 1926, and from the mid-1920s through to the end of the 1930s he entered into an intense radical political and economic phase of his thought that continued until the end of his life in 1963.

The culmination of Du Bois's Marxist studies was his 1935 book *Black Reconstruction in America, 1860–1880.*[3] As will be seen below, *Black Reconstruction* is widely considered Du Bois's "manifesto" of the pivotal role that black workers, both in slavery and in freedom, have played in the development of American capitalism. The book argues that African Americans practiced self-emancipation during the Civil War (1861–65) and participated in "one of the most extraordinary experiments of Marxism" during the Reconstruction era (1865–77). *Black Reconstruction* represents Du Bois's most detailed attempt to develop an economic history and political sociology of the connections between African American enslavement, US capitalism and global imperialism, and how black working-class struggle played a vanguard role in challenging them all. Lastly, the book is remarkable because it exposed the racist historiography of African American enslavement, the Civil War, and Reconstruction that dominated scholarship from the post-Reconstruction era through to the Great Depression years.

Although frequently glossed over, W. E. B. Du Bois's pioneering critique of colonialism was inextricably linked to his critique of capitalism. In some senses, it could be argued that, as he developed his simultaneously socio-historic and politico-economic analyses, beginning with race and racism and quickly connecting them to colonialism, Du Bois eventually added capitalism to his anti-imperialist agenda as a major source of oppression and exploitation to be eliminated.[4] On the one hand, one of the many things that distinguish his criticisms of capitalism from his criticisms of colonialism involves the fact that, from his optic, capitalism and colonialism are two very different – albeit intimately interrelated – oppressive and exploitative systems that require specificity in approaching them analytically. On the other hand, another major distinguishing marker of Du Bois's critique of capitalism that he put to use in the black liberation struggle drew on the fact that some whites – that is to say, some members of the ruling racial class – also understood capitalism to be an oppressive and exploitative system and had developed anti-capitalist critical theory and radical political praxis traditions. This was even though, as Du Bois observed early, most white critics of capitalism focused almost exclusively on capitalism's political and economic exploitative aspects without giving concerted critical attention to how it intersected with and exacerbated racial oppression (and colonial domination). This led Du Bois at the outset of his critique of capitalism to simultaneously critique capitalism *and* many of the white critics of capitalism.[5]

The white critics of capitalism were critical of it for very different reasons than those of their "colored" comrades (to use the parlance of the period). Du Bois was one of the first non-white radical theorists to register this difference. As several interpreters of Du Bois have observed, he had a critical and dialectical relationship with the white critics of capitalism, especially Marxist socialist and communist thought and practice. According to Adolph Reed, in *W. E. B. Du Bois and American Political Thought*, "everyone agrees that Du Bois died a socialist, but few agree on when he became one or on what kind of socialist he was."[6]

In *W. E. B. Du Bois: Negro Leader in a Time of Crisis*, Francis Broderick explained that Du Bois's thought may be difficult to periodize in the manner that many intellectual historians are accustomed to because "His ideas changed constantly, but the major changes came gradually, with a considerable overlap."[7] This is an important point because it speaks to the evolving radical quality and critical character of Du Bois's thought. Consequently, Broderick's comments in this regard deserve further quotation:

> Writing month after month on current events, he [Du Bois] did not, of course, abruptly end one period of intellectual change and begin another. He might drop a hint, then wait twenty years before picking it up for further development. His praise of self-sufficient, segregated Negro communities came at the flood tide of the Niagara Movement. He was making advances to socialism in 1907, although in early 1908 he affirmed his attachment to the principles of the Republican party. Africa had an almost mystical fascination for him even on his twenty-fifth birthday, but thirty years elapsed before the fascination produced a program of action. Even as the hope for alliance with workers and colored men dominated his thought in the 1930s, a minor theme, self-sufficiency for the Negro community, was rising in a crescendo which by the early 1930s would make it dominant. Conversely, as new ideas came to prominence after the World War, the old ones did not disappear: the essence of his lecture "Race Relations in the United States," for the American Academy of Political and Social Science in 1928, could have been written twenty-five years before. His ideas changed constantly, but the major changes came gradually, with a considerable overlap.[8]

Du Bois's "socialism," to use this term loosely, may have never been as scientific, dogmatic, and/or orthodox Marxist as many intellectual historians have claimed – or would like to claim. As he matured, both personally and professionally, his thought took on a chameleonic character, crisscrossing back and forth between the chasms of race and class. His thought often exhibited internal tensions, sometimes appearing race-centered, and at other times seeming overly concerned with class, labor, and economic justice issues. In addition, the complexity and multidimensionality of his thought gave it a contradictory and often confusing character,

which his critique of sexism – also a major item on his anti-imperialist agenda right alongside the critique of racism, colonialism, and
capitalism – exacerbated. Therefore, it is important to distinguish
Du Bois's criticisms of capitalism from those of the white critics
of capitalism, especially white Marxists, because his criticisms
harbored an acute sensitivity to, and critical employment of, black
radical thought aimed at the ways capitalist oppression intersects
and interconnects with racial, colonial, and gender domination
and exploitation. Consequently, this chapter elucidates several of
the key themes of Du Bois's critique of capitalism, contributions to
black Marxism, and discourse on democratic socialism, with special
attention being given to his most noted work in this area, *Black
Reconstruction*.

Du Bois's inchoate critique of capitalism

Du Bois's critique of capitalism was not clear-cut or laid out in an
easily accessible manner, but rather was interspersed throughout
his oeuvre and most often surfaced as a result of his critiques of
racism and colonialism, which ultimately spawned his discourse
on democratic socialism.[9] As early as 1901, 6 years prior to his
so-called "socialist turn" in "Negro and Socialism" in 1907, and
16 years before the Russian Revolution of 1917, he argued that the
maxim "from each according to his ability – to each according to
his needs" embodied the ideal of modern society.[10] His primary
problem with capitalism stemmed from what he understood to be
its emphasis on gross individual gain and personal greed – in other
words, private profit at any cost. As an economic system, capitalism
privileged the wants and whims of the rich minority over the
authentic human needs of the poor majority. The situation is made
even more complex and compounded by the political economy of
race and racism.[11]

Du Bois's initial criticisms of capitalism were not radical but,
rather, reformist.[12] His concept of socialism could be characterized
as "evolutionary" as opposed to "revolutionary," which made it a
major point of contention between him and young "New Negro"
and Harlem Renaissance radicals.[13] For instance, in his 1921 classic,
"The Class Struggle," published in *The Crisis*, Du Bois stated:

> The NAACP has been accused of not being a "revolutionary"
> body. This is quite true. We do not believe in revolution. We expect

revolutionary changes in many parts of this life and this world, but we expect these changes to come mainly through reason, human sympathy and the education of children, and not by murder. We know that there have been times when organized murder seemed the only way out of wrong, but we believe those times have been very few, the cost of the remedy excessive, the results as terrible as beneficent, and we gravely doubt if in the future there will be any real recurrent necessity for such upheaval.[14]

According to A. Philip Randolph and Chandler Owen, the editors of the black socialist magazine *The Messenger*, Du Bois's "anti-revolutionary" socialist thought was that of the "Old Crowd Negro," and it revealed "Du Bois's ignorance of [Marxist] theory and his inability to advise the Negro in the most critical period of the world's history."[15] Randolph and Owen, representing themselves as "New Negro" radicals, mercilessly criticized Du Bois's early socialism for its emphasis on moderate and moralistic gradual social reform as opposed to all-out social, political, and economic revolution.[16] In "Du Bois on Revolution: A Reply," originally published in 1921, they argued that Du Bois misunderstood revolution because he appeared to almost completely associate it with violence, or "organized murder," as he put it above.[17] Revolutions need not entail violence, *The Messenger* retorted, as the examples of the Copernican revolution and the revolutions in economic and sociological thought of the nineteenth century (*à la* John Stuart Mill, Adam Smith, Herbert Spencer, August Comte, and Richard Ely) demonstrated. Du Bois, from *The Messenger* editors' point of view, simply did not take seriously the fact that "every notable and worth-while advance in human history has been achieved by revolution, either intellectual, political or economic."[18]

There was much truth to many of Randolph and Owen's criticisms of Du Bois's early socialism. However, because of the longevity and incessantly evolving nature of his Marxism, *The Messenger*'s criticisms are time-sensitive and should not be applied to the whole of Du Bois's work geared toward critiquing capitalism and developing democratic socialism. Manning Marable observed that, although Randolph and Owen were initially regarded as the "Lenin and Trotsky" of Harlem, their revolutionary socialism was short-lived.[19] Owen, Marable reported, "became embittered by the racism in the Socialist party and in 1923 withdrew from radical politics."[20] Randolph continued to edit *The Messenger*, although it took a decidedly "more moderate political tone."[21] Of course,

Randolph went on to become one of the most acclaimed civil rights leaders in US history, leading and organizing the March on Washington with one of the unsung heroes of the Civil Rights Movement, Bayard Rustin.[22] One of Randolph's more noted biographers, Paula Pfeffer, in *A. Philip Randolph: Pioneer of the Civil Rights Movement*, remarked: "Randolph had begun his career as a radical by denouncing Du Bois's conservatism, but by the time of his death, Du Bois had become far more radical than Randolph."[23]

Randolph and Owen's criticisms of Du Bois's socialism help to highlight the important but long ignored fact that his conception of socialism changed just as twentieth-century capitalism and his relationship with Marxism changed. As Marable pointed out, even when Du Bois joined the Socialist Party in 1911, it "did not mark any significant turn to radicalism."[24] Wilson Jeremiah Moses went further to argue that Du Bois's "early years with *The Crisis* fall into the period when Du Bois toyed with the idea of non-revolutionary white-collar socialism of the American domestic variety.... Even as late as 1912, at the age of forty-four, Du Bois had not become a committed radical, but was still an optimistic Progressive."[25] Marable, Moses, and Reed each note that Du Bois's conception of socialism, for a long period of time, was in line with that of the reformist British Labour Party, which he applauded time and again throughout the pages of *The Crisis*.[26]

In *W. E. B. Du Bois: The Quest for the Abolition of the Color-Line*, Zhang Juguo observed that it was Du Bois's four visits to the Soviet Union in 1926, 1936, 1949, and 1958, and his visits to other socialist countries, such as Czechoslovakia, East Germany, and China, that quickened, broadened, and "deepened his understanding of socialism."[27] After his 1926 visit to the Soviet Union, Du Bois clearly took a greater interest in the more radical aspects of socialism, although he repeatedly asserted that the Russian Revolution was not the rule. However, he was convinced that Russia "had chosen the only way open to her at the time."[28] He realized early on that there was no blueprint for bringing socialism into being, and that what might work in one country may not work in another.

Partly as a result of the economic depression of the 1930s, and in some degree owing to African Americans' incessant political disenfranchisement and economic exploitation, Du Bois began to seriously engage socialism on his own terms during the last three decades of his career (*circa* 1930–60). As a result, he developed one of the first race-based and racism-conscious critiques of capitalism employing a Marxist methodological orientation.[29] In his burgeoning anti-bourgeois and anti-racist view, capitalism was not simply (as many of the white Marxists would have it) a system of economic exploitation, but also a "racial polity" – which is to say, a system of racial domination *and* economic exploitation.[30] Race *and* class struggle combined to create the key political and economic dimensions characteristic of black existence in a simultaneously racist and capitalist society. Moreover, because he found Marxism inadequate for the tasks of critically theorizing race and racism in both capitalist and colonialist societies, Du Bois created his own – and some of the first – race/class concepts and categories of analysis.[31]

"One of the most extraordinary experiments of Marxism that the world, before the Russian Revolution, had seen": *Black Reconstruction* and the emergence of black Marxism

Along with studying Marxism, in the 1930s Du Bois began to intensely study the history of American capitalism. Ultimately, his simultaneous studies of both Marxism and US economic history centered on the pivotal role that the triad of African American enslavement, the Civil War, and Reconstruction played in the evolution of American capitalism and the United States' emergence as a global imperial power. In *Black Reconstruction*, Du Bois magnificently reinterpreted the drama surrounding the end of slavery, the Civil War, and Reconstruction, casting black laborers in leading roles. Applying his burgeoning Marxism to US history, from Du Bois's point of view it was the "black worker, as founding stone of a new economic system in the nineteenth century and for the modern world, who brought civil war in America. He was its underlying cause, in spite of every effort to base the strife upon union and national power."[32] African American enslavement both defined and deformed American democracy. For Du Bois, the contradiction was clear: "From the day of its birth, the anomaly of slavery plagued a nation which asserted the equality of all men, and sought to derive powers of government from the consent of the governed." However, he continued, "Within sound of the voices of those who said this lived more than half a million Black slaves."[33]

After the American Revolution (*circa* 1765–83), the enslavement of African Americans significantly declined in the North. In the South, however, it increased markedly and held sway for nearly 250 years (*circa* 1619–1865). Enslaved blacks' labor was the primary source of wealth for the dominant class in the South, those whom Du Bois dubbed the "planter class" – essentially, the Southern plantation owners. Enslaved blacks' grueling work on Southern plantations produced millions of pounds of cotton, tobacco, rice, corn, and wheat, as a result bringing in billions of dollars in profit for the planter class. The planter class's enormous profits guaranteed that the slavocracy (a government composed of, or dominated by, slave owners and plantation owners), even though it essentially died in the North and was replaced with an emerging wage labor system, would live on for the foreseeable future in the South. These vast plantation profits fueled capitalist expansion in the US and also, it should be emphasized, eventually became a cornerstone of the emerging global capitalist economy. One of the many things that attracted Du Bois to Karl Marx was Marx's acknowledgment of African American enslavement's central role not only in the evolution of American capitalism, but also in the development of global capitalism. For example, commenting on the centrality of enslaved blacks' unprecedented cotton production and its importance for the Industrial Revolution (*circa* 1760–1840), Marx perceptively wrote:

> [S]lavery is as much the pivot upon which our present-day industri-alism turns as are machinery, credit, etc. Without slavery there would be no cotton, without cotton there would be no modern industry. It is slavery which has given value to the colonies, it is the colonies which have created world trade, and world trade is the necessary condition for large-scale machine industry. Consequently, prior to the slave trade, the colonies sent very few products to the Old World [i.e., Europe], and did not noticeably change the face of the world. Slavery is therefore an economic category of paramount importance.[34]

Taking Marx very seriously when he wrote "Slavery is ... an economic category of paramount importance," Du Bois's *Black Reconstruction* was written with Marx's admonition borne solemnly in mind. More than that of any other Marxist of his epoch, Du Bois's Marxism took Marx's dictum regarding the "paramount impor-tance" of slavery as its primary point of departure. This, indeed, was unorthodox. Where most Marxists of his time turned to Europe and primarily focused on white workers, Du Bois turned to America and primarily focused on black workers. It was Du Bois's modification of Marxism, his adaptation of it to speak to the lives and struggles of both enslaved and emancipated black workers, and his application of it to key moments in African American history, culture, and struggle, that constitutes what has come to be called "black Marxism."[35] In other words, Du Bois's *African-Americanization of Marxism*, his development of a distinct brand of Marxism that synthesizes key elements of anti-racism and anti-colonialism with Marx's thought and the discourse it gave rise to, has evolved into a distinguishable form of Marxism that is specifically focused on the political economy of enslaved and emancipated black folk's lives and struggles.

Seemingly picking up where Marx left off in the quote above, Du Bois's *Black Reconstruction* highlights the role both enslaved and emancipated black labor played in the Industrial Revolution, the Civil War, and Reconstruction. Exposing the political and economic implications of slavery for the evolution of capitalism in the US and imperialist expansion around the globe, Du Bois underscored that:

> [T]he black workers of America bent at the bottom of a growing pyramid of commerce and industry; and they not only could not be spared, if this new economic organization was to expand, but rather they became the cause of new political demands and alignments, of new dreams of power and visions of empire. ... their work called for widening stretches of new, rich, black soil – in Florida, in Louisiana, in Mexico; even in Kansas. This land, added to cheap labor, and labor easily regulated and distributed, made profits so high that a whole system of culture arose in the South, with a new leisure and social philosophy. Black labor became the foundation stone not only of the Southern social structure, but of Northern manufacture and commerce, of the English factory system, of European commerce, of buying and selling on a world-wide scale; new cities were built on the results of black labor, and a new labor problem, involving all white labor, arose both in Europe and America.[36]

Black Reconstruction demonstrates that enslaved blacks were not only at the bottom of a racial hierarchy, but also "at the bottom of a growing pyramid of commerce and industry," an economic order that essentially placed plantation owners on the top, poor whites in the middle, and blacks – whether enslaved or emancipated – at the bottom. After years of studying Marxism and developing critiques of American capitalism, Du Bois advanced a new and revolutionary framework for understanding the end of slavery, the Civil War, and Reconstruction. Notably, his Marxism drew as much from black nationalism and Pan-Africanism as it did from European and

European American intellectual traditions, such as Fabianism and Pragmatism.[37]

Prior to *Black Reconstruction*, conventional Civil War and Reconstruction historiography stressed the benevolence of whites, especially Abraham Lincoln, and typically turned on racist stereotypes about African Americans' inability to think for themselves and free themselves. Completely going against racist interpretations of this period in American history, Du Bois radically reinterpreted it as the first time that the majority of the black working class self-organized and practiced self-emancipation. For instance, *Black Reconstruction* revealed not only that African Americans ran away from plantations during the Civil War, but also that they ultimately provided "200,000 Federal soldiers whose evident ability to fight decided the war."[38] Du Bois argued that African Americans deserting the plantations and joining the Union Army constituted a "general strike." His "general strike" thesis is actually quite simple, as Guy Emerson Mount observed: "Slaves are workers. As workers, slaves constantly struggled with their masters not only over their working conditions but over their legal and social status as well. The end game for any slave insurgency was not just to own the means of production but to own one's very self."[39]

During the Reconstruction era, African Americans politicized and organized themselves and quickly came to participate in government, simultaneously upsetting the US racial hierarchy and class order. *Black Reconstruction* illustrates that black-led state governments redistributed land, doled out resources, and established the first social services and public school system in American history. Du Bois contended that these African American-administered state governments and welfare programs were in essence an "experiment of Marxism." He asserted: "As the Negro laborers organized separately, there came slowly to realization the fact that here was not only separate organization but a separation in leading ideas; because among Negroes, and particularly in the South, there was being put into force one of the most extraordinary experiments of Marxism that the world, before the Russian Revolution, had seen."[40]

When Du Bois points to enslaved African Americans as workers (as opposed to merely docile "slaves"), and their self-politicization, self-emancipation, and self-government as "one of the most extraordinary experiments of Marxism that the world, before the Russian revolution, had seen," he is hinting at his use of the Russian Revolution as a framework for understanding the relationship between slavery and capitalism. According to Cedric Robinson, in *Black Marxism: The Making of the Black Radical Tradition*, the "processes of the Russian Revolution were a framework for his [Du Bois's] interpretation of Reconstruction because it, too, had begun among an agrarian, peasant people. It was a characteristic shared by all the revolutions that Du Bois linked in significance to the American Civil War and its Reconstruction: that is, France, Spain, India, and China."[41] Du Bois innovatively conceived of enslaved black workers and roughly 100,000 poor whites as setting into motion the "revolutionary dynamics" that culminated in the "experiments of Marxism" that characterized the Reconstruction years. Robinson elaborated:

> [I]n the midst of the Civil War, it was these two peoples, the black and the white workers, who had mounted the rebellions, the "General Strike," which had turned loose the revolutionary dynamics that Du Bois would describe as "the most extraordinary experiments of Marxism that the world, before the Russian Revolution, had seen." One hundred thousand poor whites had deserted the Confederate armies and perhaps a half million Black workers had abandoned the plantations. It was the same pattern, indeed, that would come to fruition in Russia. Like the American slaves and the poor whites, in the midst of war the Russian peasantry would desert their armies in the field. Their rebellion, too, marked the beginnings of revolution.[42]

In Du Bois's Marxist analysis of the Civil War and Reconstruction, there was a pitched battle between two distinctly American adversaries. On one side, he contended, was the American proletariat (workers or working-class folk): the enslaved, the formerly enslaved (i.e., freedmen and freedwomen), and poor whites. On the other side was the American bourgeoisie (the capitalists who own and control most of the US's wealth and means of production): Southern plantation owners and Northern industrialists. For Du Bois, the great tragedy of Reconstruction is that the interracial working class that came together to topple American slavery was ultimately conquered by the predatory and avaricious nature of American capitalism. In 1877, Southern plantation owners and Northern industrialists essentially decided to bury the hatchet in the interest of maintaining their wealth and class dominance. Even if they could not see eye to eye on the "Negro question," after more than a decade of bickering back and forth and the devastating economic depression between 1873 and 1877, Southern plantation owners and Northern industrialists were certainly in agreement that, in order for capitalism to not only survive but expand, it needed to open up the lucrative markets of the South, which had been closed as a consequence of the Civil War.[43]

Although they may have only lasted for a short amount of time (*circa* 1861–77), Du Bois was convinced that the Civil War and Reconstruction "experiments of Marxism," African American self-emancipation, and instances of interracial working-class solidarity contributed much to Marxism and the history of national and international revolution. "The unending tragedy of Reconstruction is the utter inability of the American mind to grasp its real significance, its national and worldwide implications," Du Bois thundered; "We are still too blind and infatuated to conceive of the emancipation of the laboring class in half the nation as a revolution comparable to the upheavals in France in the past, and in Russia, Spain, India and China today."[44]

Du Bois's emphasis on the revolutionary implications of Reconstruction should be stressed, as should the way he compares Reconstruction with previous or, at the time, ongoing international revolutions. This clearly demonstrates the influence of Marxist internationalism on his evolving discourse. Du Bois argued that the breakdown of Reconstruction was important because it helped to resuscitate capitalism, which had been placed on life support as a consequence of the Civil War and its catastrophic economic aftermath. The collapse of Reconstruction was also significant, he asserted, because it enabled the emergence of US imperialism from the late nineteenth century through to the twentieth. Consequently, a key contention of *Black Reconstruction* is that enslaved black workers, from 1619 to 1865, provided what Marx, above, called a "pivot" in the development of both American capitalism and global imperialism. According to Du Bois, the black worker in slavery and in freedom symbolizes:

> That dark and vast sea of human labor in China and India, the South Seas and all Africa; in the West Indies and Central America and in the United States – that great majority of mankind, on whose bent and broken backs rest today the founding stones of modern industry – shares a common destiny; it is despised and rejected by race and color; paid a wage below the level of decent living; driven, beaten, prisoned and enslaved in all but name; spawning the world's raw material and luxury – cotton, wool, coffee, tea, cocoa, palm oil, fibers, spices, rubber, silks, lumber, copper, gold, diamonds, leather – how shall we end the list and where? All these are gathered up at prices lowest of the low, manufactured, transformed and transported at

fabulous gain; and the resultant wealth is distributed and displayed and made the basis of world power and universal dominion and armed arrogance in London and Paris, Berlin and Rome, New York and Rio de Janeiro.[45]

Once again, Du Bois's embrace of Marxist internationalism is on display, as he essentially recasts Marx's "primitive accumulation" thesis and applies it to the origins and evolution of the black working class in the US.[46] By connecting the black working-class struggle in the US to the struggles of racially colonized workers globally, Du Bois not only reveals that the African American working class is an integral part of "that great majority of mankind, on whose bent and broken backs rest today the founding stones of modern industry," but also that many elements of Marxism can be adapted and applied to black workers in slavery and in freedom. In *Black Reconstruction*, Du Bois audaciously put both capitalists and Marxists on notice that racialization and colonization are central to modern labor and economic exploitation, not only in America, but throughout the world – indeed, anywhere anyone has been racially colonized and "paid a wage below the level of decent living; driven, beaten, prisoned and enslaved in all but name."

From Du Bois's perspective, mainstream Marxists were right in their critique of capitalism. However, he believed, mainstream Marxists were wrong in either overlooking or downplaying the fact that the "great majority" of modern workers are wrestling with not only capitalism, but also racism and colonialism. "Here is the real modern labor problem. Here is the kernel of the problem of Religion and Democracy, of Humanity," Du Bois declared; "Words and futile gestures avail nothing." He ardently continued: "Out of the exploitation of the dark proletariat comes the Surplus Value filched from human beasts which, in cultured lands, the Machine and harnessed Power veil and conceal. The emancipation of man is the emancipation of labor and the emancipation of labor is the freeing of that basic majority of workers who are yellow, brown and black."[47]

Even as he insightfully adapted and applied Marxism to the struggles of the black working class in the US, Du Bois's own "experiments in Marxism" (to slightly paraphrase) reveal several contradictions in his *African-Americanization of Marxism* and efforts to develop a Marxist methodology in the interest of black folk. Similar to Marx, Du Bois understood the Civil War as a war with the potential to liberate both black and white workers. Marx asserted:

In the United States of America, every independent workers' movement was paralyzed as long as slavery disfigured a part of the republic. Labor in a white skin cannot emancipate itself where it is branded in a black skin. However, a new life immediately arose from the death of slavery. The first fruit of the American Civil War was the eight hours' agitation, which ran from the Atlantic to the Pacific, from New England to California, with the seven-league boots of the locomotive.[48]

No matter how fervently Du Bois believed Marx's dictum that "Labor in a white skin cannot emancipate itself where it is branded in a black skin," he acknowledged that white workers in the US, "while they received a low wage, were compensated in part by a sort of public and psychological wage" – what David Roediger, building on Du Bois's *Black Reconstruction* thesis, called the "wages of whiteness."[49] Du Bois explained:

It must be remembered that the white group of laborers, while they received a low wage, were compensated in part by a sort of public and psychological wage. They were given public deference and titles of courtesy because they were white. They were admitted freely with all classes of white people to public functions, public parks, and the best schools. The police were drawn from their ranks, and the courts, dependent upon their votes, treated them with such leniency as to encourage lawlessness. Their vote selected public officials, and while this had small effect upon the economic situation, it had great effect upon their personal treatment and the deference shown them. White schoolhouses were the best in the community, and conspicuously placed, and they cost anywhere from twice to ten times as much per capita as the colored schools. The newspapers specialized on news that flattered the poor whites and almost utterly ignored the Negro except in crime and ridicule.[50]

In essence, during Reconstruction, even though poor whites received a meager material wage, as a consequence of the post-war continuation of white supremacy, they acquired a "psychological wage" simply for being white and upholding the racial hierarchy of white superiority and black inferiority. Regardless of the obvious economic exploitation of white workers, their enmity was aimed at both the Southern plantation owners and, initially, enslaved blacks, and later emancipated blacks. *Black Reconstruction* details the ways in which black enslavement defined and deformed Southern society to the extent that even those whites who did not "own" enslaved blacks were reliant on the slavocracy for their daily bread and bare necessities. Above, Du Bois noted that the police force in the South was primarily populated by working-class whites, and he also underscored that this class also made up the large majority of "slave catchers, slave drivers and overseers." Indeed, "They were the men called in upon all occasions by the masters whenever any fiendish outrage was to be committed upon the slave."[51] Sadly, Du Bois shared, "Gradually the whole white South became an armed and commissioned camp to keep Negroes in slavery and to kill the black rebel."[52]

Throughout *Black Reconstruction* (especially in the chapters "The White Worker," "The Transubstantiation of a Poor White," and "The White Proletariat in Alabama, Georgia, and Florida"), Du Bois explained that the psychological benefit white workers were given on the basis of their whiteness in many ways disguised the material deficit that the Black Codes, Jim Crow laws, and other forms of racial segregation reinforced not simply for black workers, but for white workers as well. Consequently, both Marx and Du Bois acknowledged that the Civil War failed to emancipate and unite the US working class.[53] Nonetheless, it is important to emphasize that Du Bois's interpretation of the black working class and some parts of the white working class as active agents in their own liberation illustrates his clear commitment to social transformation from the bottom-up, if not in fact something like "socialism from below."[54]

The picture that Du Bois paints of "fugitive slaves" fleeing plantations as a "general strike" was an unorthodox – but not completely erroneous – adaptation and application of Marx's analysis of labor self-activity.[55] Enslaved blacks' "yearning for freedom found its climax during the American Civil War," Mount shared, where "slaves increasingly ran away, took up arms against their masters, and intentionally sabotaged and disrupted global cotton production. These actions were not accidents. They were a form of politics." These political acts of the enslaved actually fit squarely within Marx's analysis of labor self-activity because they in fact "emanated from a class conscious slave community."[56] Further elaborating on the ways the emancipatory actions of the enslaved can be comprehended within Marx's theory of labor self-activity, Mount continued:

> For Du Bois, the general strike forced the hand of President Lincoln while turning a war to save the Union into a war to end slavery. In this way, the American Civil War should not be euphemistically romanti-cized as a "war between the states" but instead re-understood as the

most massive slave revolt in the history of the New World. Slaves freed themselves. It was a revolution – one that came and went. "A splendid failure."[57]

When Du Bois writes that the Civil War was a "splendid failure," he puts on display one of the many contradictions of his attempt to adapt and apply Marxism to African American enslavement and the Civil War.[58] The fact of the matter is that the Union government in the North, dominated by industrial capitalist interests, was never in solidarity with either the black or white working classes, and, therefore, was never an emancipatory force working in the best interests of the American proletariat. Consequently, when the industrial capitalists of the North triumphed over the plantation-owning capitalists of the South, their victory essentially sealed a deal that turned the Civil War into a "bourgeois revolution." Why? Because, even though the Civil War was primarily fought by Northern and Southern, black and white working-class folk, ultimately the ruling classes of each respective region (i.e., industrial factory owners in the North and plantation owners in the South) were able to advance and extend capitalism and bourgeois hegemony. With this in mind, it is possible to make connections between Du Bois's concept of African Americans' "experiments of Marxism," which he used to characterize black worker self-activity during the Civil War and the Reconstruction era, and the Communist International's "Black Belt" thesis (*circa* 1928–34), which emphasized the importance of "Negro work" and black self-determination for American Marxism, the American labor movement, and world revolution.[59]

The juxtaposition of Du Bois's "experiments of Marxism" argument and the Communist International's "Black Belt" thesis is important because it clearly demonstrates the influence of Marxist internationalism on Du Bois's developing thought and the ways he, literally, *modified* Marxism to speak to the lives and struggles of both enslaved and emancipated blacks in the US. "Many in the American Left hoped that a worldwide socialist revolution would follow the 1917 Bolshevik Revolution," Denise Lynn reported. Increasingly, throughout the 1920s and 1930s, Du Bois gradually gravitated toward the left and grew to deeply desire "a worldwide socialist revolution." However, "When no revolution materialized, the Soviet Union, in an attempt to keep the revolutionary fervor alive, challenged Communists overseas to push for revolutionary change in their own countries."[60] Lynn offered further insight:

For Black Americans, it was the Communist International's (Comintern) adoption of the Black Belt Nation thesis in 1928 and international communism's pledge to fulfill the "Marxist proposition" that "no nation can be free if it oppresses other nations" that articulated the socialist promise. The Black Belt thesis defined Blacks living in the American South as an oppressed nation and argued that as a nation they had a right to self-determination. This meant that the Comintern and the U.S. Communist Party (CPUSA) recognized Black Nationalism as a part of the communist revolutionary commitment.[61]

In *Black Reconstruction*, Du Bois modified and applied elements of the Comintern's "Black Belt" thesis to Civil War and Reconstruction historiography. He demonstrated both enslaved and emancipated blacks' centrality to, and agency in, the Civil War and Reconstruction. Even more, he showed that enslaved black folk during the Civil War and emancipated black folk during Reconstruction had come to many of the conclusions of the "Marxist proposition" long before the Russian Revolution of 1917 and the Comintern's official adoption of the "Black Belt" thesis in 1928. This is significant because it illustrates both the influence of Marxist internationalism on Du Bois and the innovative ways he challenged his Marxist comrades to take African Americans' distinct history, culture, and struggle more seriously. *Black Reconstruction* turns its readers' attention to the specific nature and nuances of enslaved black folk fighting for their freedom during the Civil War, and, once emancipated, freedmen and freedwomen's ongoing struggles with racism, capitalism, and distinctly American forms of racial colonialism during the Reconstruction era.

Nonetheless, the connections between Du Bois's "experiments of Marxism" argument and the Comintern's "Black Belt" thesis are admittedly, at best, tenuous. Whether enslaved or emancipated, black workers' lives and struggles did not quickly or easily correspond to either thesis. What Du Bois identified as black worker self-activity during the Civil War and Reconstruction may in fact correlate with the Comintern's conception of the revolutionary potential of black self-determination in the 1920s and 1930s. Even so, the Comintern's "Black Belt" thesis seems to presuppose workers (in a very general sense) struggling in either a capitalist or colonialist context, not the kind of combined racial capitalist and racial colonialist context that both enslaved and emancipated African American workers were in during the Civil War and Reconstruction years. Black workers' lives and struggles were definitely in greater alignment with those colonized workers around the world who were "despised and rejected by race and color" and "paid a wage below the level of decent living." However, a crucial point must be taken into consideration here: no matter how racially colonized their lives, both enslaved and emancipated black workers were waging their working-class struggle from within the belly of one of the greatest simultaneously racist, capitalist, and colonialist beasts in modern history – the United States of America. This is to say, key elements of Du Bois's "experiments of Marxism" argument are, similar to the Comintern's "Black Belt" thesis, untenable when the vicissitudes of American racism, capitalism, and colonialism, as well as the emergence of American global imperialism, are taken into serious consideration.

Consequently, *Black Reconstruction* lays bare many of Du Bois's judgments and misjudgments based on his evolving Marxism. The book also provides insight into his developing conception of revolution and which groups have either overlooked or untapped revolutionary potential. First, over time, Du Bois reevaluated the African American working class and, instead of being led based on a top-down leadership model by the "Talented Tenth" (as he argued in 1903), he came to acknowledge and strongly advocate black working-class folk's capacity to play a bottom-up vanguard role in the struggles against racism, capitalism, and colonialism.[62] Second, Du Bois's contention that the collapse of Reconstruction opened the way for even more unbridled forms of capitalist and imperialist expansion was obviously correct, as was his assertion that the end of Reconstruction would haunt American and world history for decades, if not centuries, to come. Third, Du Bois's "wages of whiteness" thesis in *Black Reconstruction*, where he underscored the psychological benefits, social status, and access to political power that white workers receive as a result of their allegiance to the white bourgeoisie and white supremacy, clearly demonstrated his revolutionary understanding of Marx's declaration: "Labor in a white skin cannot emancipate itself where it is branded in a black skin." In other words, in Du Bois's conception of revolution, black and white workers unite and rise together, or they are divided and conquered and, consequently, fall apart, as they did at Reconstruction's end. Fourth, *Black Reconstruction* – especially the concluding chapter of the book, "The Propaganda of History," which was a scathing critique of white bourgeois histories of African American enslavement, the Civil War, and Reconstruction – made it widely known that Du Bois completely rejected the white bourgeois historiography and methodology he had been trained in at Harvard and the University of Berlin. Finally, *Black Reconstruction* announced to all the world that Du Bois was no longer a genteel socialist who advocated reformism and gradual social transformation, but a committed black Marxist internationalist who believed that only world revolution could bring racism, capitalism, and colonialism to their knees.

On ruling races and ruling classes: Du Bois's unorthodox, independent anti-racist Marxism

Black Reconstruction was obviously a major turning point in Du Bois's intellectual and political life. It represents his gravitation toward Marxism and, eventually, revolutionary activism, sometimes under the guise of socialism, and later communism. After *Black Reconstruction* and his "Marxist turn" of the 1920s and 1930s, Du Bois continued to modify Marxism to speak to the special needs of racially colonized workers, particularly in Africa and Asia.[63] Much like his Marxism of the 1920s and 1930s, Du Bois's Marxist politics and pronouncements of the 1940s and 1950s teeter-totter between progressive judgments and regressive misjudgments. While the imperialist aspects of colonialism were undeniable from Du Bois's perspective – perhaps, ironically, because of his Marxist studies – he believed that capitalism had certain beneficial elements. However, because of the anti-black racist character of capital in the white supremacist world system, whites benefited greatly and inordinately from capitalism. In 1944, seemingly building on his "wages of whiteness" thesis from *Black Reconstruction*, Du Bois asserted:

> Capitalism was a great and beneficent method of satisfying human wants, without which the world would have lingered on the edge of starvation. But like all invention, the results depend upon how it is used and for whose benefit. Capitalism has benefited mankind, but not in equal proportions. It has enormously raised the standard of living in Europe and even more in North America. But in the parts of the world where human toil and natural resources have made the greatest contribution to the accumulation of wealth, such parts of the earth, curiously enough, have benefited least from the new commerce and industry. This is shown by the plight of Africa and India today. To be sure Africans and Indians have benefited from modern capital. In education, limited though it be; in curbing of disease, slow and incomplete as it is; in the beginning of the use of

machines and labor technique; and in the spread of law and order, both Negroes and Hindus have greatly benefited; but as compared with what might have been done; and what in justice and right should have been accomplished, the result is not only pitiful, but so wrong and dangerous as already to have helped cause two of the most destructive wars in human history, and is today threatening further human death and disaster.[64]

Du Bois's critique of capitalism moved well beyond the mainstream Marxists' two-class critique and class struggle thesis. In his Marxist framework, there were not only classes but also various races, and the white race was the "ruling class" – were we to refer back to Marx's class theory – *and* the ruling race.[65] For Du Bois, as we have witnessed in our discussion of *Black Reconstruction* above, it was not as simple as the bourgeoisie and the proletariat fighting it out until the finish. There was also the obdurate fact of race and racism, and even more, as his comments above emphasize, the racialization of colonialism and the racialization of capitalism. That is to say, the primary focus of Du Bois's brand of Marxism was *racial* colonialism and *racial* capitalism.[66]

Marx and Engels asserted in *The Communist Manifesto*, "The ruling ideas of each age have ever been the ideas of its ruling class."[67] Du Bois continually questioned: So, what happens when the "ruling class" is for the most part racist? And what happens when more than white workers compose the proletariat? Along with many orthodox Marxists, Du Bois believed that capitalism had helped to modernize and rationalize the economy.[68] However, in contradistinction to his white Marxist comrades, he asserted that there was a racist dimension to the modernization and rationalization associated with capitalism. In addition, as we witnessed in the previous chapter, he also came to understand capitalist modernization and rationalization to have a sexist (and particularly a patriarchal) dimension.

From Du Bois's point of view, capitalism is inextricable from the rise of racism. Therefore, an exclusively Marxist or class analysis only engaged part of the race/class problem. What he and countless others in the black Marxist tradition sought by coupling anti-racism and critical race theory with Marxism was to comprehensively understand and develop solutions to both sides of the race/class equation, which is to say, to the problems of racism and capitalism. Perhaps Cornel West's contentions in *Keeping Faith: Philosophy and Race in America* best captures the position of many black Marxists and other race/class theorists: "I hold that Marxist theory as a methodological orientation remains indispensable – although ultimately inadequate – in grasping distinctive features of African American oppression.... Marxist theory still may provide the best explanatory account for certain phenomena, but it also may remain inadequate for other phenomena – notably here, the complex of racism in the modern West."[69] The black Marxist tradition has consistently echoed West's view, although not without reservation and serious criticism.[70]

Marxism may be "indispensable" when it comes to the critique of capitalism but, as West argued in "Black Strivings in a Twilight Civilization":

> For those of us interested in the relation of white supremacy to modernity (African slavery in the New World and European imperial domination of most of the rest of the world) or the consequences of the construct of "race" during the Age of Europe (1492–1945), the scholarly and literary works of Du Bois are *indispensable*. For those of us obsessed with alleviating black social misery, the political texts of Du Bois are insightful and inspiring. In this sense, Du Bois is the brook of fire through which we all must pass in order to gain access to the intellectual and political weaponry needed to sustain the radical democratic tradition in our time.[71]

According to West, Marx is "indispensable" for the critique of capitalism, where Du Bois is "indispensable" for the critique of racism. But, even further, as West emphasized in *The American Evasion of Philosophy*, Du Bois was also an innovator in the Marxist tradition.[72] He was not only a pioneer race theorist, but also a pioneer racial class theorist. His work prefigured and proposed issues that remain on the radical political and critical theoretical agenda. He challenged white Marxists to take seriously the centrality of race and racism to capitalism and European imperialist expansion.[73] White Marxists regularly shot back that race consciousness is "false consciousness" and a capitalist or bourgeois invention created to divide the workers.

Part of the problem with Du Bois's critique of capitalism involves his contention that capitalism was inequitably creating an enormous amount of wealth and power that was being unjustly distributed on a roughly "whites only" (or, at the least, "wealthy whites only") basis. This was compounded by his search for a solution to both the race and class aspects of this issue. White Marxists, focusing almost exclusively on the class dimension of the problem, found their solution in the proletariat – that is to say, the white working class. Du Bois dismissed the majority of the white proletariat, querying: "Why should we assume on the part of unlettered and suppressed masses of white workers, a clearness of thought, a sense of human brotherhood, that is sadly lacking in the most educated [white] classes?"[74] Du Bois never adequately addressed the question of *who* the revolutionary social agents would be that would crush capitalism and usher in democratic socialism. Obviously the "experiments of Marxism" and interracial working-class solidarity he detailed in *Black Reconstruction* were short-lived and, ultimately, a "splendid failure," as he put it. In addition – and of the utmost importance here – is the question of *how* the transition from capitalism to democratic socialism would take place. To be fair to Du Bois, these questions continue to haunt the whole of the black Marxist tradition, if not the Marxist tradition more generally.

It could be that there are no ideal agents of revolutionary social change. Considering the vicissitudes of capitalism, one of the things that anti-capitalist theorists and activists have to bear in mind is that a social faction that may have revolutionary potential in one era may not in the next. This means, then, that as capitalism grows and changes, so too must anti-capitalist theory. This is where we come back to Du Bois's evolving critical relationship with Marxist theory. He not only criticized Marxism, but also revised and reconstructed the Marxian tradition by providing new theories, concepts, and categories of analysis – such as race, the critique of racism, and anti-racist theory, as well as the concerted critique of colonialism, and anti-colonial theory – that extend and expand Marxism's original intellectual arena and political program. Cedric Robinson's remarks in this regard are extremely insightful: "Du Bois committed himself to the development of a theory of history, which by its emphasis on mass action was both a critique of the ideologies of American socialist movements and a revision of Marx's theory of revolution and class struggle."[75] Further, Robinson continued, Du Bois "possessed no obligation to Marxist or Leninist dogma, nor to the vagaries of historical analysis and interpretation that characterized American communist thought."[76]

All of this is to say that, when Du Bois advanced democratic socialism, or communism as he did at the end of his life, he did so from a position independent of mainstream Marxism and Marxist party politics, and often from a black nationalist and Pan-Africanist optic that stands outside the Marxist tradition altogether. It is in this sense that Moses declared, "Even when he urged Communism, the aging Du Bois did so on black nationalistic rather than on Marxist grounds."[77] Du Bois's concept of democratic socialism highlights and accents several aspects of classical and contemporary social, political, and economic reality that Marx and most of his disciples neglected or downplayed in their respective discourses. Du Bois's discourse on democratic socialism provides these assertions with greater weight and gravity.

The radicalization of democracy and the democratization of socialism: Du Bois's discourse on democratic socialism

As early as his 1907 essay "Negro and Socialism," Du Bois detected and detailed deficiencies in the Marxist tradition which included, among other things, a silence on and/or an inattention to: race, racism, and anti-racist struggle; colonialism and anti-colonial struggle; and the ways in which *both* capitalism and colonialism exacerbate not simply the economic exploitation of non-whites, but continue (both physical and psychological) colonization beyond the realm of political economy.[78] Du Bois, therefore, laboring long and critically with Marxian theory and methodology, deconstructed them and developed his own original radical democratic socialist theory that: simultaneously built on his pioneering work as a critical race theorist, Pan-Africanist, and radical anti-colonialist; called for the radical transformation of US society and the power relations of the world; was deeply concerned about and committed to world peace and demanded disarmament; and advocated for the liberation of all racially colonized, politically oppressed, and economically exploited people.[79]

Du Bois was well aware of the fact that anyone in the citadel of super-capitalism, the United States, who openly embraced socialism or Marxism in any of its manifestations would quickly become a social and political pariah. But, against a barrage of black bourgeois and white conservative criticism, he sought democratic socialism and a methodical and meticulous understanding of Marxism. In point of fact, Du Bois did not believe that the Russian communists had a monopoly on Marxism any more than he believed that the Marxists put a patent on the critique of capitalism. Marxism was merely one of many tools in Du Bois's ever-evolving critical framework. Just as the meaning of socialism and Marxism changed as a result of revolutionary praxis and re-theorization, so too did Du Bois's relationship with, and critical appreciation or rejection of, certain aspects of Marxism change. It is in this sense that Du Bois can be viewed as a critic of both capitalism *and* Marxism.[80]

In one of his later essays on socialism, "The Negro and Socialism," which was published in 1958, Du Bois argued that a socialist society is a society where there exists the "central idea that men must work for a living, but that the result of their work must not mainly be to support privileged persons" – persons who as a result of the labor and economic exploitation of the "colored" masses and working classes have an exponential amount of power and privilege.[81] It is a society where the "welfare of the mass of people should be the main object of government," a society where the government is "controlled by the governed" – which is to say, it is fundamentally a democratic society.[82] In such a society, Du Bois declared, the "mass of people, increasing in intelligence, with incomes sufficient to live a good and healthy life, should control all government, and ... they would be able to do this by the spread of science and scientific technique, access to truth, the use of reason, and freedom of thought and of creative impulse in art and literature."[83]

Calculating "seventy-five to ninety percent" of the earth's population to be racially colonized people living in what he called the "colonies proper: America, Africa, and Asia," Du Bois was critically conscious of the fact that, if indeed socialism purported to concern itself principally with "the mass" of "the governed" having a critical and decisive voice in their government, then non-whites should have prominent positions in national and international affairs and policy-making.[84] It could be no other way, he asserted, or else non-whites ultimately would be led to the "last red alternative of revolt, revenge and war."[85] Where revolution was something he once shied away from, and where war was something that he utterly despised, Du Bois now openly considered both as options for bringing democratic socialism into being. Long gone was the talk of a reformist, gradual transition from capitalism to socialism. Additionally, here we also see a significant change in Du Bois's conception of socialism and his strategies and tactics for the realization of a democratic socialist society.[86]

For centuries, capitalism has had non-whites in its clutches. Consequently, from Du Bois's point of view, the "colored" and colonized were justified in their fight against it. Their fight would free not only the racially colonized, but also economically exploited white workers as well – a concept carried over from

Black Reconstruction. Du Bois reasoned: "The footsteps of the long oppressed and staggering masses are not always straight and sure, but their mistakes can never cause the misery and distress which the factory system caused in Europe, colonial imperialism caused in Asia and Africa, and which slavery, lynching, disenfranchisement, and Jim Crow legislation have caused in the United States."[87] Du Bois stated in 1944 that in order to fully realize democratic socialism, there must be "Freedom." By "Freedom," he meant the *"full economic, political and social equality"* of all people *"in thought, expression and action, with no discrimination based on race or color."*[88] "Freedom" is fundamental to democratic socialism, and without the "full economic, political and social equality" of all citizens within a particular society, democratic socialism remains an unrealized project of historical, cultural, social, political, and economic change.

African Americans "were not" and have never been socialists *en masse*, Du Bois contended in 1960, "nor did they know what communism was or was doing. But they knew that Negro education must be better; that Negroes must have better opportunity to work and receive a wage which would let them enjoy a decent standard of life."[89] Consequently, socialism, being a "democratic program," could not "contemplate the complete subordination of one race to another."[90] It was to be a "program" or "project" of world revolution that sought ultimately to establish "world democracy" so that there might be "world peace."[91] Du Bois queried, "without democracy, what hope is there of Peace?"[92]

The "essence of democracy," according to Du Bois, "demands freedom for personal tastes and preferences so long as no social injury results."[93] This is important to emphasize because, in Du Bois's conception of democracy, it was not merely a political project, but a cultural one as well.[94] He explained:

> [T]he vaster possibility and the real promise of democracy is adding to human capacities and culture from hitherto untapped sources of cultural variety and power. Democracy is tapping the great possibilities of mankind from unused and unsuspected reservoirs of human greatness. Instead of envying and seeking desperately outer and foreign sources of civilization ... in these magnificent mountains a genius and variety of human culture, which once released from poverty, ignorance and disease, will help guide the world. Once the human soul is thus freed, then and only then is peace possible. There will be no need to fight for food, for healthy homes, for free speech; for these will not depend on force, but increasingly on knowledge, reason and art.[95]

As long as the "human soul" remained in bondage, so long would the world exist on the brink of "war after war."[96] Under capitalism and colonialism, the vast majority of human beings have "for the most part no voice in government."[97] Under these systems, it is only the "blood-sucking whites" who "rule and receive large income while others," mostly the "dark" or "native" proletariat, "work and live in poverty."[98] Moreover, capitalism and colonialism, interpreted as two sides of the same coin and two of the greatest impediments to "world democracy," had to be eradicated on the grounds that, since their inception, they have consistently caused the great mass of human beings, who are (it should be reiterated) "colored," to exist in various states and stages of "slavery, cultural disintegration, disease, death, and war."[99] Furthermore, democracy, which for Du Bois was fundamentally predicated on "free discussion," required at minimum the "equal treatment [of] the colored races of the world."[100]

As stated above, a prerequisite for Du Bois's conception of democracy is "freedom," and the "real freedom toward which the soul of man has always striven" is, of course, the "right to be different, to be individual and pursue personal aims and ideals."[101] Long before postmodernist discourse and debate on the politics of difference, Du Bois asserted that the "richness of a culture ... lies in differentiation." He contended that "Difference" did not necessarily equal "Dangerous," and that once the bare necessities of "food, shelter, and ... security" were met, then "human friendship and intermingling ... based on broad and catholic reasoning" could lead to "happier ... individual and ... richer ... social" lives.[102] He importantly continued:

> Once the problem of subsistence is met and order is secured, there comes the great moment of civilization: the development of individual personality; the right of variation; the richness of a culture that lies in differentiation. In the activities of such a world, men are not compelled to be white in order to be free: they can be black, yellow or red; they can mingle or stay separate. The free mind, the untrammeled taste can revel. In only a section and a small section of the total life is discrimination inadmissible and that is where my freedom stops yours and your taste hurts me. Gradually such a free world will learn that not in exclusiveness and isolation lies inspiration and joy, but that the very variety is the reservoir of invaluable experience and emotion. This crowning of equalitarian democracy in artistic freedom of difference is the real next step of culture.

The hope of civilization lies not in exclusion, but in inclusion of all human elements; we find the richness of humanity not in the Social Register, but in the City Directory; not in great aristocracies, chosen people and superior races, but in the throngs of disinherited and underfed men. Not the lifting of the lowly, but the unchaining of the unawakened mighty, will reveal the possibilities of genius, gift and miracle, in mountainous treasure-trove, which hitherto civilization has scarcely touched; and yet boasted blatantly and even glorified in its poverty. In world-wide equality of human development is the answer to every meticulous taste and each rare personality.[103]

Du Bois's later-life radical democratic theory eschewed the reformism and elitism of his "Talented Tenth" thesis – what Moses called the "conservatism of his intellectual origins." Rather, Du Bois based his radical democratic theory on the "inclusion of all human elements," the "richness of humanity" – not on the "great aristocracies, chosen people and superior races," but the "throngs of disinherited and underfed men."[104] Du Bois as radical democratic theorist, particularly in his later years, looked not to the elite, as he once did, but to "disinherited" and "underfed" human beings to bring about the radical socialist transformation of society. In his view, a capitalist society, a so-called "developed society," is to a certain extent a colonized society because it is a society where everyday life and common culture are not only defined and deformed by the avarice of the ruling class, but inextricable from the exploitation of the racially colonized.[105]

Always and everywhere, colonization, like Pandora's box once opened, seeps into every sphere of the lives and struggles of both the colonized and the colonizer. In other words, capitalism is inextricable from colonialism and creates, according to Du Bois, a world of "race war," "racial friction," and "disastrous contradiction."[106] Only in a "free world" where the "problem of subsistence is met and order is secured" can human beings arrive at the "great moment of civilization." This "moment," representing perhaps *the* highpoint in human history in Du Bois's thought, would foster the "development of individual personality," and these "new" individuals, free from the constant pursuit of their basic needs and capitalist greed – similar to Frantz Fanon's "new men" who speak a "new language" to express their "new humanity" – would pride themselves on the "right of variation."[107] In such a world, Du Bois declared, human beings "are not compelled to be white in order to be free." The "free world" Du Bois envisioned is a world that puts the premium on the potential of humble, hard-working, ordinary people – folk Fanon referred to as the "wretched of the earth."

Conquered, colonized, "colored" people must be willing to struggle for liberation and higher levels of human life, and if they are not, they will never know, or have the possibility of, the "practice of freedom," which for Du Bois rested on *a radicalization of democracy* and *a democratization of socialism*.[108] Du Bois cautiously offered a caveat: "No group of privileged slave-owners is easily and willingly going to recognize their former slaves as men."[109] This means, then, that "former slaves" have as one of their central life-tasks the reclamation and rehabilitation of their denied humanity.

As the "majority of men do not usually act in accord with reason, but follow social pressures, inherited customs and long-established, often subconscious, patterns of action," Du Bois believed that "race prejudice ... will linger long and may even increase."[110] He charged the racially colonized, and the "black race" in particular, with a special duty to *not* – as Fanon admonished – imitate European civilization and culture in "obscene caricature."[111] On the contrary, Du Bois believed that "It is the duty of the black race to maintain its cultural advance, not for itself alone, but for the emancipation of mankind, the realization of democracy and the progress of civilization."[112] Civilization is to progress, and democracy is to be realized (or, rather, *radicalized*), only insofar as the "masses" of human beings gain "social control" of the "methods of producing goods and of distributing wealth and services." Moreover, he importantly continued, the "freedom which this abolition of poverty will involve, will be freedom of thought and not freedom for private profit-making."[113]

"Espous[ing] the cause of opponents of Wall Street and the Pentagon": Du Bois and the despotic communism of Joseph Stalin and Mao Tse-tung

Ironically, considering his steadfast emphasis on the radicalization of democracy and the democratization of socialism, Du Bois made several significant misjudgments in his efforts to modify Marxism in the interests of black and other racially colonized folk. A major mistake was what appeared to many to be his uncritical support of two of America's Cold War nemeses: Russia and China. To understand Du Bois's support for Russia and China, it is important to bear in mind that, between his initial exposure to the Social Democratic

Party in Berlin during his time there in the 1890s and his insistence in the 1930s, 1940s, and 1950s that socialism was the answer to several key problems around the world, Du Bois's late-life socialism was in many ways the culmination of his critiques of racism, dedication to decolonization, and commitment to the complete destruction of capitalism. Aligning himself with the leader of the Soviet Union, Joseph Stalin, and the leader of communist China, Mao Tse-tung, was in many ways tantamount to Du Bois embracing the enemies of his life-long enemies: American racism, American capitalism, and American global imperialism.[114]

In other words, Lewis asserted, Du Bois "believed that the enemies of his enemies were his friends in Africa and Asia," and "neither communism's doctrinal rigidities nor the Soviet Union's 1956 rampages in Eastern Europe would shake Du Bois's commitment to world socialism."[115] In a sense recasting the pitched battle between the bourgeoisie and the proletariat that Marx and Engels famously outlined in *The Communist Manifesto*, Du Bois envisioned American capitalism as representative of the aspirations of the global bourgeoisie and Russian and Chinese communism as representative of the aspirations of the global proletariat.[116] "As a battle to the death had been joined between the two superpowers, he [Du Bois] saw himself being compelled by the logic of his racial and economic priorities to espouse the cause of opponents of Wall Street and the Pentagon, even when such advocacy corrupted other ideals of intellectual honesty and humanism," Lewis lamented.[117]

With regard to the Soviet Union, part of Du Bois's allegiance to Russian communism may have much to do with the fact that he was convinced that the United States was quickly becoming the world's leading imperialist power. Stalin and the Soviets repeatedly proclaimed their support for colonial independence, which was the exact opposite of America's (and Europe's) position on the "colonial question." Perhaps another reason Du Bois was duped into increasingly supporting the Soviets was because they outright condemned American racism and developed the "doctrine of Negro Soviets in the Deep South." At the Sixth Congress of the Communist International in 1928, Lewis shared, the "American Negro was defined as a special case – a 'peculiarity ... not only in view of the prominent *racial distinctions*' but as an 'oppressed nation' whose eventual self-determination in the Black Belt would be followed by integration into the working-class and final liberation as a constituent of the triumphant proletariat." Although he seems to have never fully accepted the Black Belt thesis, Lewis continued, "a troubled Du Bois conceded, neither the Democratic or Republican parties had made as concerted an effort to enroll Negroes as the CPUSA [Communist Party USA] or to place them in prominent administrative and elective positions."[118]

A final reason Du Bois idealized the Soviet Union was because he did not experience racism on his various trips there in 1926, 1936, 1949, and 1958, which seemed to confirm the Soviets' ostensible commitment to anti-racism. This is a point that should be emphasized. If, indeed, the Russian communists had created an anti-capitalist society seemingly free from racism, then that would mean that two of the major interlocking systems of oppression – racism and capitalism – had been eradicated. This, obviously, excited Du Bois and led him to believe that Russian communism might offer real alternatives to American racism and American capitalism. Of course, Du Bois could not have been more wrong. The Soviet Union was not the paragon of anti-racism or communism it appeared to be based on his highly orchestrated brief visits and long-distance studies. But, being bullheaded and embittered by his ill-treatment in America in the Cold War 1940s and 1950s, Du Bois saw what he wanted to see, and eventually Stalinism became an expression of communism in his mind, as detailed in his 325-page manuscript, "Russia and America: An Interpretation," which was rejected for publication by Harcourt, Brace & Company in 1950.[119]

Du Bois's growing support for socialism and communism caused the US government to take note of his increasingly outspoken radical political views and activities. The more he felt he was being hushed and harassed because of his commitment to socialism, the more he drifted to the left and voiced his support for communist leaders like Joseph Stalin and Mao Tse-tung. The situation became so bad that Du Bois was ultimately indicted as an agent of the Soviet Union in 1951, due to his contributions to the Peace Information Center, a radical pacifist organization. His indictment led to his passport being revoked and him being "blacklisted." His "blacklisting" caused him to take even more audacious stands against the rampant anti-communism sweeping across the United States in the 1950s and 1960s. Consequently, he not only openly supported Stalin and the Soviets, but also added his support for Mao and the Chinese Communist Revolution of 1949. Undoubtedly, Du Bois felt ideologically imprisoned by the United States government, which proudly proclaimed to the world that America was an open democratic society with freedom of religion, speech, press, assembly, and the right to petition the government, but vilified, censured, and silenced serious critics of American democracy.[120]

Without a doubt, Du Bois was right to challenge the government's "blacklisting." However, he was wrong to hitch his horse to Stalin and Stalinism. No matter how magnificent we may find elements of Du Bois's democratic socialism, there simply is no getting around his inattention to Stalin's commandeering and corruption of the principles of Marxism, as well as the numerous abuses of Stalinism. For example, Du Bois defensively pointed to the high rate of voter participation in the Soviet Union as proof that it was democratic. Unfortunately, he did not note that the Communist Party was basically the only party Russians could vote for. Regarding Stalin's destruction of the small farm system (the *kulaks*), which caused the Soviet famine of 1932–3 and which subsequently led to the deaths of approximately 7.5 million people, Du Bois blithely justified it because it ultimately advanced the Russian Revolution. Even more problematic, Du Bois defended Stalin's 1936–8 "show trials," which were essentially "purges" of his political opponents, by accepting the Stalinist contention that those expelled were "enemies of the state" who had betrayed the revolution. The typically critical Du Bois basically uncritically accepted the blatant lies Stalin told to defend his tyrannical regime and reign of terror, which had little or nothing to do with actual Marxism.[121]

As well as uncritically supporting Stalinism, Du Bois also supported Mao Tse-tung and the Chinese Communist Revolution of 1949, which eventually adopted the Stalinist corruption of communism that C. L. R. James called "state capitalism."[122] Mao's conception of communism was essentially modeled on Stalinism, and even though he most often made his ideas sound Marxist, Maoism was actually a crude combination of the imperial ideology of Qin Shi Huang, the first emperor of China, and Stalinism. Similar to Stalinism, Maoism has an equally long list of crimes committed in the name of communism that Du Bois imprudently either overlooked or unwittingly accepted. For instance, as soon as they came to power in 1949, the Communist Party of China made China a single-party state. Like Stalin's "Great Purges," the Chinese Community Party denied free speech, restricted political dissent, and repressed workers' efforts to organize against the state. When Du Bois visited China in 1959, his itinerary was carefully orchestrated by the Chinese leadership. Even though what Mao promoted as the "Great Leap Forward" was a miserable failure which led to the deadliest famine in history and the deaths of approximately 25 to 45 million people between 1958 and 1962, Du Bois and Shirley Graham Du Bois saw no evidence of it during their two-month visit in early 1959. Lewis emphasized, "As they moved about Beijing in their ceremonial cocoon, Du Bois and Graham Du Bois knew absolutely nothing of the catastrophe inflicted upon the Chinese people by their omnipotent ruler."[123] The Chinese government wanted to demonstrate the industrial advancement and social harmony that the revolution fostered and, as a result, provided Du Bois with a carefully guided tour of more than 5,000 miles through Shanghai, Canton (now Guangzhou), Chengdu, Chungking, and Nanjing. He had a four-hour meeting with Mao and the Prime Minister of China, Zhou Enlai, where he was wined and dined and afterward whisked from one staged scene of an idyllic communist society to another.[124]

It is difficult to reconcile how Du Bois, who spent much of his long life preoccupied with democracy and the rights of the downtrodden and disenfranchised, could embrace the autocratic and totalitarian regimes of Stalin and Mao. According to Bill Mullen, Du Bois's support for Russia and China may have more to do with his tendency to "find only good in socialist revolutions," which itself was "a sign of how far the Cold War and his own internal exile [and 'blacklisting'] in the U.S. had shaped his political perspective."[125] Kate Baldwin cautions us to keep in mind that Du Bois's "commitment to the Soviet Union must be seen as linked to a philosophy of history and an investment in the legacy of intellectual countertraditions." She insightfully explained:

> Du Bois's work, then, poses a challenge: to tread the fine line between overidentifying Du Bois with the ruin of the Soviet empire – and hence assigning to his idealism a necessarily "tragic" fate – and underidentifying or not fully appreciating the ways in which Du Bois allied himself with the Soviet Union through a consciousness of outsider status and thus as a counter to what he insisted were the monolithic goals of a post-World War II Americanization. Given the innumerable accounts of the past tyrannies, bloodshed, and corruption of the Soviet system that continue to pour out of the ex-Soviet state, this is a difficult though necessary task. In resisting an easy triumphalism, a space must be carved out wherein the commitment of Du Bois to the Soviet Union can be acknowledged without condemning his vision. The affective sweep and inspirational power of the explanatory framework offered him by Marxism and the Soviet model needs to be appreciated as one that appealed to both the unquestionable depth of his intellectual

prowess and correlated to his unflagging commitment to global liberation, decolonization, and peace movements, as well as to his opposition to militarism, corporate tyranny, social inequality, and racial segregation.[126]

In his unpublished "Russia and America" manuscript, Du Bois revealingly wrote: "Whether or not Russian Communism is a success is beside the point; the point is, are the ideals of human uplift as conceived by Karl Marx and Nicholai Lenin ideals which ought to be realized? If so, how can they best be realized?" Furthermore, Du Bois went on, "Even if Communism as tried in Russia had completely failed, it was a splendid effort, a magnificent vision."[127] Du Bois seemed to be more interested in the "magnificent vision[s]" and the realization of the ideals of Marx and Lenin than with the actual strategies and tactics their followers utilized to implement their visions and ideals. This, indeed, is incredibly problematic, if not an error of epic proportions when we turn to what Stalin and Mao did in the name of Marxism and Leninism, but it does not in any way diminish the magnificence of Marx's and Lenin's communist ideals and visions according to Du Bois. Speaking directly to this issue, and building on Baldwin's contentions above, Eric Porter bluntly stated that "Du Bois might have praised Stalin ... but he was not a Stalinist in any systematic way." In fact, "Reading him as such relegates to the background his engagement with an array of issues that exceeded his pro-communist or pro-Soviet positions." What is more, and bringing Du Bois's alignment with Maoism into the mix, Porter continued:

> contrary to the claim that Du Bois's affinity for Stalin and later Mao was merely the telos of his authoritarian streak, we can consider instead how his longstanding ruminations on race, war, peace, and imperialism were given new sustenance by similar critiques voiced by the Soviet Union and communist parties more generally. Increasingly invested in the necessity of some kind of socialist response to problems of racism, poverty, and disease engendered by unequal capitalist economic relationships, Du Bois refused the negatively productive political role to which the Soviet Union was consigned during the Cold War. He instead insisted that, despite its problems, the Soviet Union should serve as a source, at a symbolic level at least, for conceptualizing fairer economic relationships and a more just social order.[128]

Taking all of this into consideration, an honest assessment of Du Bois's dedication to Stalinism and Maoism reveals that, while he obviously endeavored to present the principles of socialism and the need for socialist revolution around the world, this presentation was severely undermined by his inattention to, or uncritical acceptance of, elements of both Stalinist and Maoist propaganda and state repression. Without a doubt, the starvations, persecutions, and mass executions committed by the Stalinist and Maoist regimes went against the radical humanism at the heart of Du Bois's best work.[129] As discussed above regarding his conception of democratic socialism, Du Bois believed in a version of socialism that was decidedly democratic and that would place power in the hands of the mass of people, who are working-class, whether we turn to Africa, Asia, Europe, the Caribbean, or the Americas.

Du Bois's failure to adequately assess and critically address Stalin's and Mao's corruption of communism and many misdeeds in the name of Marxism contributed to ruining the reputation of communism and Marxism. Throughout his life, many looked to Du Bois for critical leadership and intellectual inspiration in the fight against oppression, but unfortunately, by aligning himself with Stalinism and Maoism, he failed and led many astray. Indeed, this may help us understand some of the reasons communism continues to be denounced as an outdated and oppressive ideology throughout the capitalist world, where the masses are in desperate need of tools to combat and ultimately topple capitalism. To be fair to Du Bois, he was "sincere in his determined profession of Socialist ideals," Lewis noted. He continued, Du Bois "found himself intellectually and temperamentally predisposed to condone the economic critique and social vision of Marx and Engels while reserving a troubled judgment on the tactics of Lenin, Trotsky, and Josef Stalin," and Mao Tse-tung.[130] Even when we take into consideration his "troubled judgment" and unfortunate forays into Stalinism and Maoism, Du Bois's democratic socialism provides us with much that may aid us in our ongoing struggles to bring into being a truly democratic and socialist society. In other words, even as we correctly criticize Du Bois for being misled by, and mute on, the atrocities Stalin and Mao committed in the name of communism, we should not allow his patently poor judgment regarding Russian and Chinese despotic communism to stop us from critically exploring and salvaging the best of his radical politics and vision of democratic socialism.

Du Bois was committed to socialism before Stalin and Mao came to power, and the socialist legacy he left continues to inspire long after the fall of the Stalinist and Maoist regimes. Simply said,

Du Bois's socialist principles are worth reconsidering precisely because, when engaged on their own terms, they are authentic socialist principles in that they revolve around a radical form of democracy and worker self-activity that is the antithesis of the tyrannical communism espoused and enacted by Stalin and Mao. Even as he mouthed support for Stalin and Mao, Du Bois continued to blaze his own independent Marxist path. For instance, Du Bois's Marxist independence can be detected in the fact that he wrote over 100 articles for the left-wing independent weekly the *National Guardian* between 1948 and 1961. He also published several pieces in independent Marxist magazines such as *New Masses*, *Masses & Mainstream*, the *Monthly Review*, and *American Socialist* during the 1940s and 1950s. Consequently, his commitment to democratic socialism should not be completely disqualified because of the many contradictions and misjudgments he made regarding Stalin's and Mao's rogue states claiming to be communist. Du Bois spent nearly his entire life searching for solutions to problems, and in the last half of his long life he strongly believed that capitalism was a major problem and that democratic socialism was a prime solution to the problem of capitalism. Admittedly, he made many mistakes along the way, but in 1958 he solemnly stated that socialism demands: "No more war; cease preparation for war and atomic bomb testing; stop universal military service; justice to labor with fair taxation; abolish the racial and color-line; peaceful co-existence with socialist states; [and] recognition of a citizens' right to vote for Socialism."[131] This means that much of what Du Bois ultimately understood to be, and espoused as, socialism was anathema to Stalinism and Maoism.

Du Bois's discourse on democratic socialism, perhaps above all else, is distinguished by its incessant emphasis on anti-racism. This is a point that should be underscored because it differentiates Du Bois's socialism and later communism not only from that of Stalin and Mao, but also from that of Marx, Lenin, and Trotsky, who all made occasional passing mention and scattered references to racism but did not consistently develop detailed analyses and anti-racist Marxist programs of action like Du Bois did. It was not simply capitalism and class struggle that impeded the democratization and implementation of socialism, but racism, sexism, and colonialism as well. Where he began his adventure in socialism toying with its most conservative, reformist, and gradualist strains, historical happenings on the world scene and the acute and increasing economic exploitation of blacks and other non-whites in racial capitalist and racial colonialist societies led him to couple his longstanding anti-racism and anti-colonialism with Marxism. As a consequence, Du Bois developed some of the first race/class theory and criticisms of both capitalism and Marxism from a black radical frame of reference. Indeed, it was his development of a distinct black radical frame of reference in the period after he published more noted early works – such as *The Philadelphia Negro* in 1899, *The Souls of Black Folk* in 1903, and "The Talented Tenth" also in 1903 – that ultimately enabled Du Bois to declare near the end of his life in 1957: "I am certainly not a conservative. I should call myself a Socialist, although that isn't a very definite term."[132]

Conclusion: Du Bois's Legacy

As we have witnessed, W. E. B. Du Bois made several seminal contributions to history, sociology, politics, and economics. His work in these areas is usually engaged exclusively for the ways it contributes to racial history, racial politics, and the sociology of race. However, this book has discursively deconstructed the longstanding reductionist tendency which seems to always and everywhere relegate Du Bois to racial studies, as though he did not make significant contributions to the study and critique of sexism, capitalism, and colonialism, among other interlocking systems of oppression. Undoubtedly, as discussed in the chapters on *The Souls of Black Folk* and "The Souls of White Folk," Du Bois was one of the first social scientists and critical theorists of race. But, as the chapters on *The Philadelphia Negro*, "The Damnation of Women," and *Black Reconstruction* revealed, he should also be considered a pioneering interdisciplinary scholar who contributed to several academic disciplines and intellectual traditions, such as: history, sociology, political science, economics, Marxism, black feminism, intersectionality and, of course, African American studies.[1]

Throughout this study, we have come to understand that Du Bois was an early interdisciplinary scholar whose history-based and culture-centered theory consistently identified key socio-political problems and utilized a wide range of scholarship from various disciplines in an effort to produce solutions to those problems. The "problems" that Du Bois's thought sought to grasp and grapple with went well beyond the realm of race and racism, and often encompassed other enigmatic issues, such as sexism, colonialism, capitalism, and American imperialism, which all remain on the radical political agenda. Although his work is most frequently read for its contributions to the critique of racism – and white supremacy, specifically – Du Bois actually understood racism to be one of many interlocking oppressive systems that threaten not only the "souls of black folk," but also the heart and soul of humanity. As Du Bois developed his discourse, various themes and theories were either embraced or rejected based on particular historical and cultural conditions.

By taking a conceptual (as opposed to the conventional chronological) approach to Du Bois's writings, we have been able to highlight some of the significant developments in his thought that speak to ongoing and important issues revolving around race, gender, and class. Instead of viewing changes in his thought as signs of confusion, vacillation, or intellectual inertia, emphasis has been placed on the subtle logic of the modifications Du Bois made in his thinking by placing it in the context of black history, culture, and struggle, as well as world history, culture, and struggle. Similar to several other intellectual-activists, Du Bois oriented his political theory toward what he perceived as the most progressive political struggles (or, lack thereof) at a particular historical moment and, thus, articulated possibilities and potentialities specific to his epoch and social reality, rather than putting forward a blueprint for future social change or an architecture for emancipation in an epoch to come.[2]

This means that, no matter how prescient Du Bois may have been, "we are on our own" and must find solutions to contemporary problems by trial and error just as he did during his day.[3] However, it does not mean that we should abandon those aspects of Du Bois's thought that may aid us in our efforts to develop a truly democratic society – one free from the racism, sexism, capitalism, and colonialism Du Bois spent the great bulk of his life critiquing and combating. In other words, there is no need to reinvent the wheel. We can and should build on the best of the work Du Bois began long ago, which is precisely what he hoped anyone who objectively read his work would do. For instance, in his "Last Message," written in 1957 but not published until his death in 1963, he solemnly said:

> I have loved my work, I have loved people and my play, but always I have been uplifted by the thought that what I have done well will live long and justify my life; that what I have done ill or never

finished can now be handed on to others for endless days to be finished, perhaps better than I could have done.[4]

Du Bois sought to comprehend, critique, and offer alternatives to the contradictions of the culture, economics, politics, and society of his era. Therefore, his discourse is always in need of adaptation to the new times, to the twenty-first century and beyond, because its basic concepts and categories are time-sensitive and situation-specific and tethered to the major issues of the twentieth century. That is to say, the basic concepts and categories of Du Bois's discourse are historical; and history, to put it plainly, has never bowed to the wishes and whims of any human being or human group. Hence, history is always unfolding and playing itself out in new and unimagined ways. Du Bois's discourse, then, being a form of historical and cultural critique, must be modified, extended, and expanded to speak to our time and our problems. We must take him seriously when he stated that he wants us to build on and go beyond what he did "ill or never finished." His work needs to be adapted and reinterpreted if it is to remain receptive to the various ways the world is changing and if it is to actually assist us in transforming contemporary culture, economics, politics, and society.

Du Bois the reformist, Du Bois the radical, Du Bois the revolutionary

In summary, the tensions noted in the previous chapters point to and produce an extremely uneasy combination of interpretations and criticisms of Du Bois that defy simple synopsis. Consequently, many of Du Bois's critics have previously downplayed and diminished the real brilliance of his work by failing to grasp its antinomies, and they have, therefore, put forward a divided and distorted Du Bois, who is either, for example, a Pan-Africanist *or* Europhile, a black nationalist *or* radical internationalist, a social scientist *or* propagandist, a race man *or* radical women's rights man, a bourgeois individualist *or* dogmatic Marxist collectivist. Each of the aforementioned superficial ascriptions falls short of capturing the complex and chameleonic character of Du Bois's ever-evolving discourse and the difficulties involved in interpreting it.

Many dismiss Du Bois and charge his work with being dense and contradictory because it employs a wide range of theory from several different disciplines. Even so, others are attracted to his work because it is intensely interdisciplinary, rich in both originality and radicality, and boldly crosses so many academic and political boundaries. No matter what one's ultimate attitude toward Du Bois, the fact that his thought and texts continue to cause contemporary controversies, and that they have been discussed and debated across the disciplines for over a century, in some degree points to the ongoing relevance of his scholarship. Hence, the dialectic of attraction and repulsion in Du Bois studies can partly be attributed to the ambiguities inherent in his thought and the intellectual and political anxieties of many of the interpreters of his work. How could someone so bourgeois and elitist early in his life evolve into a revolutionary Marxist and democratic socialist by the end of his life? How can a University of Berlin- and Harvard University-trained social scientist become one of the most iconic propagandists and polemicists of his generation? How can someone be simultaneously a black nationalist and a radical Marxist internationalist? Indeed, as this book has detailed, Du Bois was all of these things, and so much more.

Whatever the deficiencies of his thought and the problems with his approach to critical issues confronting black and other oppressed people, Du Bois forces his readers to think deeply, to criticize thoroughly, and, ultimately, to move beyond the imperialist views and values of the established order. Many critics have made solid criticisms of some aspect of Du Bois's thought but, when taken together and analyzed objectively, his lifework and intellectual legacy are impressive and inspiring, as is his loyalty to some of the most radical thought and political praxes in black and world history. His impact and influence have been widespread, not only cutting across academic disciplines, but setting aglow several social movements and political programs.

Where some theorists dogmatically hold views simply because they are intellectually in vogue or politically popular, Du Bois's work draws from a diverse array of often eclectic and enigmatic sources and, therefore, offers no closed system or absolute truths. His thought was constantly open and routinely responsive to changing historical and cultural conditions, both nationally and internationally. There are several, sometimes stunning, transformations in his thought that are in most instances attempts to answer conundrums created by changing historical, cultural, social, political, and economic conditions. In conclusion, then, it is Du Bois's evolution from reformist to radical to revolutionary that undoubtedly attracts so many people from various political persuasions – from conservative and liberal to radical and revolutionary backgrounds – to his lifework and legacy. This means that all of us, perhaps, can find something of value in Du Bois's discourse, including his mistakes, which have many crucial lessons and special truths to teach. Whether one identifies with Du Bois the reformist, or Du Bois the radical, or Du Bois the revolutionary, it is the intellectual openness and evolving nature of his project, the richness and wide range and reach of his ideas, and the absence of any finished system or body of clearly defined truths that constitutes both the continuing fascination with, and critical importance of, W. E. B. Du Bois and his discourse.

Notes

Introduction: Du Bois's Lifework

1 For the award-winning volumes widely considered the definitive discussions of Du Bois's polymathic life and work, see David Levering Lewis, *W. E. B. Du Bois: Biography of a Race, 1868–1919* (New York: Henry Holt, 1993); David Levering Lewis, *W. E. B. Du Bois: The Fight for Equality and the American Century, 1919–1963* (New York: Henry Holt, 2000); David Levering Lewis, *W. E. B. Du Bois: A Biography* (New York: Henry Holt, 2009).
2 W. E. B. Du Bois, "The Talented Tenth," in *The Negro Problem: A Series of Articles by Representative American Negroes of Today*, ed. Booker T. Washington (New York: J. Pott & Company, 1903), 31–75; W. E. B. Du Bois, *The Souls of Black Folk* (Chicago: A. C. McClurg & Co., 1903).
3 For selections of Du Bois's work in *The Crisis*, see W. E. B. Du Bois, *The Emerging Thought of W. E. B. Du Bois: Essays and Editorials from* The Crisis, ed. Henry Lee Moon (New York: Simon & Schuster, 1972); W. E. B. Du Bois, *W. E. B. Du Bois:* The Crisis *Writings*, ed. Daniel Walden (Greenwich, CT: Fawcett, 1972); W. E. B. Du Bois, *Selections from* The Crisis, *Vol. 1*, ed. Herbert Aptheker (Millwood, NY: Kraus-Thomson, 1983); W. E. B. Du Bois, *Selections from* The Crisis, *Vol. 2*, ed. Herbert Aptheker (Millwood, NY: Kraus-Thomson, 1983).
4 W. E. B. Du Bois, *Black Reconstruction in America, 1860–1880* (New York: Harcourt, Brace & Co., 1935).
5 W. E. B. Du Bois, *In Battle for Peace: The Story of My 83rd Birthday* (New York: Masses & Mainstream, 1952).
6 W. E. B. Du Bois, *The Autobiography of W. E. B. Du Bois: A Soliloquy on Viewing My Life from the Last Decade of Its First Century* (New York: International Publishers, 1968), 64.

7 Lewis, *W. E. B. Du Bois: Biography of a Race*, 23.
8 Ibid., 29. On Du Bois's childhood and adolescence, see Amy Bass, *Those About Him Remained Silent: The Battle Over W. E. B. Du Bois* (Minneapolis: University of Minnesota Press, 2009), 1–22, 83–108; Lewis, *W. E. B. Du Bois: Biography of a Race*, 11–55.
9 Lewis, *W. E. B. Du Bois: Biography of a Race*, 29.
10 W. E. B. Du Bois, *The Reminiscences of W. E. B. Du Bois: An Oral History* [transcript of a series of tape-recorded interviews with W. E. B. Du Bois conducted by William T. Ingersoll for the Oral History Research Office of Columbia University in New York City, May 5–June 6, 1960] (Glen Rock, NJ: Microfilming Corporation of America, 1972), 5. See also Du Bois, *The Souls of Black Folk*, 2–3, and chapter 3, "*The Souls of Black Folk*: Critique of Racism and Contributions to Critical Race Studies," in this volume.
11 W. E. B. Du Bois, *Darkwater: Voices from Within the Veil* (New York: Harcourt, Brace and Howe, 1920), 12–13; Du Bois, *The Autobiography of W. E. B. Du Bois*, 102; Lewis, *W. E. B. Du Bois: Biography of a Race*, 53.
12 For further discussion of Du Bois's relationship with Max Weber, see Nahum D. Chandler, "The Possible Form of an Interlocution: W. E. B. Du Bois and Max Weber in Correspondence, 1904–1905," *CR: The New Centennial Review* 6, no. 3 (2006): 193–239; Kazuhisa Honda, "Max Weber and W. E. B. Du Bois on the Color-Line," *Annual Review of Sociology* 28 (2015): 35–9; Thomas M. Kemple, "Weber / Simmel / Du Bois: Musical Thirds of Classical Sociology," *Journal of Classical Sociology* 9, no. 2 (2009): 187–207; Aldon D. Morris, "Max Weber Meets Du Bois," in Aldon D. Morris, *The Scholar Denied: W. E. B. Du Bois and the Birth of Modern Sociology* (Berkeley: University of California Press, 2015), 149–67.
13 W. E. B. Du Bois, "The Suppression of the African Slave Trade to the United States of America, 1638–1870" (Ph.D. dissertation, Department of History, Harvard University, 1895); Lewis, *W. E. B. Du Bois: Biography of a Race*, 160–1.
14 W. E. B. Du Bois, *The Suppression of the African Slave Trade to the United States of America, 1638–1870* (New York: Longmans, Green & Company, 1896).
15 For further discussion of the evolution of Du Bois's relationship with Africa and anti-colonialism, see W. E. B. Du Bois, *W. E. B. Du Bois on Africa*, ed. Eugene F. Provenzo and Edmund Abaka (Walnut Creek, CA: Left Coast Press, 2012). See also Babacar M'Baye, "Africa, Race, and Culture in the Narratives of W. E. B. Du Bois," *Philosophia Africana* 7, no. 2 (2004): 33–46; Wilson Jeremiah Moses, *Afrotopia: The Roots of African American Popular History* (Cambridge University Press, 1998), 136–208; Eric Porter, "Imagining Africa, Remaking the World: W. E. B. Du Bois's History for the Future," *Rethinking History* 13, no. 4 (2009): 479–98; Eric Porter, *The Problem of the Future World: W. E. B. Du Bois*

and the Race Concept at Midcentury (Durham: Duke University Press, 2010), 103–44; Earl Smith, "Du Bois and Africa, 1933–1963," *Ufahamu: A Journal of African Studies* 8, no. 2 (1978): 4–33.

16 For more detailed discussion of Du Bois's contributions to the origins and evolution of intersectionality, see chapter 4, "'The Damnation of Women': Critique of Patriarchy, Contributions to Black Feminism, and Early Intersectionality," in this volume.

17 Lewis, *W. E. B. Du Bois: Biography of a Race*, 55–178.

18 W. E. B. Du Bois, *The Philadelphia Negro: A Social Study* (Philadelphia: University of Pennsylvania Press, 1899).

19 Du Bois, *The Autobiography of W. E. B. Du Bois*, 197. See also Lewis, *W. E. B. Du Bois: Biography of a Race*, 150–92.

20 W. E. B. Du Bois, ed., *Some Efforts of American Negroes for Their Own Social Betterment* (Atlanta University Press, 1898); W. E. B. Du Bois, ed., *The Negro in Business* (Atlanta University Press, 1899); W. E. B. Du Bois, ed., *The College-Bred Negro* (Atlanta University Press, 1900); W. E. B. Du Bois, ed., *The Negro Common School* (Atlanta University Press, 1901); W. E. B. Du Bois, ed., *The Negro Artisan* (Atlanta University Press, 1902); W. E. B. Du Bois, ed., *The Negro Church* (Atlanta University Press, 1903); W. E. B. Du Bois, ed., *Some Notes on Negro Crime, Particularly in Georgia* (Atlanta University Press, 1904); W. E. B. Du Bois, ed., *A Select Bibliography of the Negro American* (Atlanta University Press, 1905); W. E. B. Du Bois, ed., *The Health and Physique of the Negro American* (Atlanta University Press, 1906); W. E. B. Du Bois, ed., *Economic Co-operation among Negro Americans* (Atlanta University Press, 1907); W. E. B. Du Bois, ed., *The Negro American Family* (Atlanta University Press, 1908). W. E. B. Du Bois, ed., *Efforts for Social Betterment among Negro Americans* (Atlanta University Press, 1909); W. E. B. Du Bois, ed., *The College-Bred Negro American* (Atlanta University Press, 1910); W. E. B. Du Bois, ed., *The Common School and the Negro American* (Atlanta University Press, 1911); W. E. B. Du Bois, ed., *The Negro American Artisan* (Atlanta University Press, 1912); W. E. B. Du Bois, ed., *Morals and Manners among Negro Americans* (Atlanta University Press, 1914).

21 Lewis R. Gordon, "Du Bois's Humanistic Philosophy of Human Sciences," *Annals of the American Academy of Political and Social Science* 568, no. 1 (2000): 278.

22 Elijah Anderson, "Introduction to the 1996 Edition of *The Philadelphia Negro*," in W. E. B. Du Bois, *The Philadelphia Negro: A Social Study* (Philadelphia: University of Pennsylvania Press, 1996), xiv.

23 Lewis, *W. E. B. Du Bois: The Fight for Equality and the American Century*, 571.

24 Ibid., 570.

1 *The Philadelphia Negro*: Early Work and the Inauguration of American Sociology

1 W. E. B. Du Bois, "The Negroes of Farmville, Virginia: A Social Study," *Bulletin of the Department of Labor* 3, no. 14 (1898): 1–38; W. E. B. Du Bois, *The Philadelphia Negro: A Social Study* (Philadelphia: University of Pennsylvania Press, 1899).

2 David Levering Lewis, *W. E. B. Du Bois: Biography of a Race, 1868–1919* (New York: Henry Holt, 1993), 190.

3 Elijah Anderson, "Introduction to the 1996 Edition of *The Philadelphia Negro*," in W. E. B. Du Bois, *The Philadelphia Negro: A Social Study* (Philadelphia: University of Pennsylvania Press, 1996), xix.

4 Lewis, *W. E. B. Du Bois: Biography of a Race*, 188–9.

5 Du Bois, *The Philadelphia Negro*, 8.

6 Ibid., 4.

7 W. E. B. Du Bois, *Dusk of Dawn: An Essay Toward an Autobiography of a Race Concept* (New York: Harcourt, Brace & Co., 1940), 59.

8 W. E. B. Du Bois, *The Autobiography of W. E. B. Du Bois: A Soliloquy on Viewing My Life from the Last Decade of Its First Century* (New York: International Publishers, 1968), 198.

9 W. E. B. Du Bois, "The Study of the Negro Problems," *Annals of the American Academy of Political and Social Science* 11 (1898): 12.

10 Du Bois, *The Philadelphia Negro*, 98, 141, 147, 193.

11 See John Brueggemann, "A Century after *The Philadelphia Negro*: Reflections on Urban Ethnography and Race in America," *Journal of Contemporary Ethnography* 26, no. 3 (1997): 364–74; Lynn C. Burbridge, "W. E. B. Du Bois as Economic Analyst: Reflections on the 100th Anniversary of *The Philadelphia Negro*," *Review of Black Political Economy* 26, no. 3 (1999): 13–31; Marcus Anthony Hunter, "Black Philly after *The Philadelphia Negro*," *Contexts* 13, no. 1 (2014): 26–31; Marcus Anthony Hunter, *Black Citymakers: How* The Philadelphia Negro *Changed Urban America* (New York: Oxford University Press, 2013); Kevin Loughran, "*The Philadelphia Negro* and the Canon of Classical Urban Theory," *Du Bois Review: Social Science Research on Race* 12, no. 2 (2015): 249–67.

12 Aldon Morris, "Social Movement Theory: Lessons from the Sociology of W. E. B. Du Bois," *Mobilization: An International Quarterly* 24, no. 2 (2019): 125–36; Aldon Morris and Amin Ghaziani, "Du Boisian Sociology: A Watershed of Professional and Public Sociology," *Souls* 7, nos. 3–4 (2005): 47–54; Melissa F. Weiner, "Decolonial Sociology: W. E. B. Du Bois's Foundational Theoretical and Methodological Contributions," *Sociology Compass* 12, no. 8 (2018): https://doi.org/10.1111/soc4.12601.

13 Pierre Saint-Arnaud, *African American Pioneers of Sociology: A Critical History* (University of Toronto Press, 2009), 140.

14　Du Bois, *The Philadelphia Negro*, 322–67. See also Du Bois, "The Negroes of Farmville, Virginia," 23–38.

15　Elijah Anderson, "The Emerging Philadelphia African American Class Structure," *Annals of the American Academy of Political and Social Science* 568, no. 1 (2000): 54–77.

16　W. E. B. Du Bois, *Black Reconstruction in America, 1860–1880* (New York: Harcourt, Brace & Co., 1935). Also, see chapter 5, "*Black Reconstruction*: Critique of Capitalism, Contributions to Black Marxism, and Discourse on Democratic Socialism," in this volume.

17　Douglas S. Massey and Nancy A. Denton, *American Apartheid: Segregation and the Making of the Underclass* (Cambridge, MA: Harvard University Press, 1993). See also Douglas A. Blackmon, *Slavery by Another Name: The Re-Enslavement of Black Americans from the Civil War to World War II* (New York: Anchor, 2009).

18　Du Bois, *The Philadelphia Negro*, 5.

19　Ibid., 393. See Du Bois, *The Autobiography of W. E. B. Du Bois*, 194–204.

20　Du Bois, *The Philadelphia Negro*, 5.

21　Ibid., 5.

22　David W. Blight, "W. E. B. Du Bois and the Struggle for American Historical Memory," in *History and Memory in African American Culture*, ed. Geneviève Fabre and Robert G. O'Meally (Oxford University Press, 1994), 45–71; Robert Gregg, "Giant Steps: W. E. B. Du Bois and the Historical Enterprise," in *W. E. B. Du Bois, Race, and the City: The Philadelphia Negro and Its Legacy*, ed. Michael B. Katz and Thomas J. Sugrue (Philadelphia: University of Pennsylvania Press, 1998), 77–100; Gerald Horne, *W. E. B. Du Bois: A Biography* (Westport, CT: Greenwood Press, 2009); Hunter, *Black Citymakers*; Lewis, *W. E. B. Du Bois: Biography of a Race*; Manning Marable, *W. E. B. Du Bois: Black Radical Democrat* (Boston: Twayne, 1986); Aldon Morris, *The Scholar Denied: W. E. B. Du Bois and the Birth of Modern Sociology* (Oakland: University of California Press, 2015).

23　Lewis, *W. E. B. Du Bois: Biography of a Race*, 202–3.

24　Du Bois, "The Study of the Negro Problems," 18.

25　Gregg, "Giant Steps," 77–100.

26　Du Bois, *The Philadelphia Negro*, 386–7.

27　Allen F. Davis and Mark H. Haller, eds., *The Peoples of Philadelphia: A History of Ethnic Groups and Lower-Class Life, 1790–1940* (Philadelphia: Temple University Press, 1973); Theodore Hershberg, ed., *Philadelphia: Work, Space, Family, and Group Experience in the 19th Century: Essays Toward an Interdisciplinary History of the City* (New York: Oxford University Press, 1981); Philip Scranton, *Work Sights: Industrial Philadelphia, 1890–1950* (Philadelphia: Temple University Press, 1986); Sam B. Warner, *Urban Growth in America: Philadelphia, 1774–1930* (Ann Arbor: University of Michigan Press, 1984).

28　Du Bois, *The Philadelphia Negro*, 11.

29 Prior to Du Bois's foray into African American class formation, there was Joseph Willson's 1841 study *Sketches of the Higher Classes of Colored Society in Philadelphia*, which was recently retitled and republished in 2000 as *The Elite of Our People: Joseph Willson's Sketches of the Black Upper-Class in Antebellum Philadelphia* (ed. Julie Winch [University Park: Pennsylvania State University Press, 2000]). However, Du Bois, it would seem, still holds the distinction of offering us the first extended analysis of African American class formation, insofar as his work, however elitist, attempted to paint portraits of not only the African American upper class, but also the black middle class, working class, and "submerged tenth" class, as well as to strike at African American class conflict. See also Du Bois, *The Philadelphia Negro*, 309–21.

30 Lewis, *W. E. B. Du Bois: Biography of a Race*, 209.

31 Marcus Anthony Hunter, "W. E. B. Du Bois and Black Heterogeneity: How *The Philadelphia Negro* Shaped American Sociology," *American Sociologist* 46, no. 2 (2015): 225.

32 Du Bois, *The Philadelphia Negro*, 310–11.

33 Ibid., 309.

34 Ibid., 310–11.

35 Ibid., 311.

36 Ibid.

37 Ibid.

38 Anderson, "The Emerging Philadelphia African American Class Structure," 63–74; Hunter, "W. E. B. Du Bois and Black Heterogeneity," 226–7.

39 Du Bois, *The Philadelphia Negro*, 322–67, esp. 322–55.

40 Saint-Arnaud, *African American Pioneers of Sociology*, 135.

41 Du Bois, *The Philadelphia Negro*, 322–67. See also Bruce Laurie, *Working People of Philadelphia, 1800–1850* (Philadelphia: Temple University Press, 1980); Walter Licht, *Getting Work: Philadelphia, 1840–1950* (Cambridge, MA: Harvard University Press, 1992); Scranton and Licht, *Work Sights*.

42 Du Bois, *The Philadelphia Negro*, 347.

43 Ibid., 310, 316–17.

44 On the long-established and oft-noted backward-thinking of the black bourgeoisie, see E. Franklin Frazier, *The Black Bourgeoisie: The Rise of a New Middle-Class in the United States* (New York: Collier, 1957), 130–73.

45 Du Bois, *The Philadelphia Negro*, 10–46, 318–21. See also Weiner, "Decolonial Sociology."

46 Du Bois, *The Philadelphia Negro*, 315–17.

47 Ibid., 317.

48 Ibid., 311–21.

49 Ibid., 317.

50 For more detailed discussion of Du Bois's 1903 theory of the "Talented Tenth" and its evolution into his often-overlooked 1948 doctrine of the "Guiding Hundredth," see Reiland Rabaka, *Du Bois's Dialectics: Black*

Radical Politics and the Reconstruction of Critical Social Theory (Lanham, MD: Rowman & Littlefield, 2008), 93–118.

51 On the sociological negation of Du Bois and his discourse, see Dan S. Green and Edwin D. Driver, "W. E. B. Du Bois: A Case in the Sociology of Sociological Negation," *Phylon* 37, no. 4 (1976): 308–33; Reiland Rabaka, *Against Epistemic Apartheid: W. E. B. Du Bois and the Disciplinary Decadence of Sociology* (Lanham, MD: Rowman & Littlefield, 2010); Earl Wright, "Why Black People Tend To Shout! An Earnest Attempt to Explain the Sociological Negation of the Atlanta Sociological Laboratory Despite its Possible Unpleasantness," *Sociological Spectrum* 22, no. 3 (2002): 335–61.

52 Mindy M. Saari, "W. E. B. Du Bois and the Sociology of the African American Family," *Sociation Today* 7, no. 1 (2009): 1–23, www.ncsociology.org/sociationtoday/dubois/fam.htm.

53 Du Bois, *The Philadelphia Negro*, 311–12.

54 Ibid., 314. See also Du Bois, "The Negroes of Farmville, Virginia," 22–3.

55 Du Bois, *The Philadelphia Negro*, 66–7. For further discussion of the African American family, see Andrew Billingsley, *Black Families in White America* (New York: Simon & Schuster, 1988); Andrew Billingsley, *Climbing Jacob's Ladder: The Enduring Legacy of African American Families* (New York: Simon & Schuster, 1992); Donna L. Franklin and Angela D. James, *Ensuring Inequality: The Structural Transformation of the African American Family* (Oxford University Press, 1997); Herbert G. Gutman, *The Black Family in Slavery and Freedom, 1750–1925* (New York: Vintage Books 1977); Angela J. Hattery and Earl Smith, *African American Families* (Los Angeles: Sage, 2007); Leanor Boulin Johnson and Robert Staples, *Black Families at the Crossroads: Challenges and Prospects* (San Francisco: Jossey-Bass, 2005); Jacqueline Jones, *Labor of Love, Labor of Sorrow: Black Women, Work, and the Family, from Slavery to the Present* (New York: Basic Books, 2010); Harriette Pipes McAdoo, *Black Families* (Thousand Oaks, CA: Sage, 2007); Stewart Emory Tolnay, *The Bottom Rung: African American Family Life on Southern Farms* (Urbana: University of Illinois Press, 1999).

56 Du Bois, *The Philadelphia Negro*, 66–7.

57 Ibid., 67–8.

58 Ibid., 68.

59 On the myth of the welfare queen, see Ange-Marie Hancock, *The Politics of Disgust: The Public Identity of the Welfare Queen* (New York University Press, 2004); Josh Levin, *The Queen: The Forgotten Life Behind an American Myth* (New York: Little, Brown and Company, 2019); Stephen Pimpare, *Ghettos, Tramps, and Welfare Queens: Down and Out on the Silver Screen* (Oxford University Press, 2017); David Zucchino, *Myth of the Welfare Queen* (New York: Simon & Schuster, 1999).

60 Du Bois, *The Philadelphia Negro*, 72.

61 For further discussion of middle-class African American women's

sexuality, see Patricia Hill Collins, *Black Sexual Politics: African Americans, Gender, and the New Racism* (New York: Routledge, 2005); Brittney C. Cooper, *Beyond Respectability: The Intellectual Thought of Race Women* (Urbana: University of Illinois Press, 2017); Evelynn M. Hammond, "Toward A Genealogy of Black Female Sexuality: The Problematic of Silence," in *Feminist Genealogies, Colonial Legacies, Democratic Futures*, ed. M. Jacqui Alexander and Chandra Talpade Mohanty (New York: Routledge, 1997), 170–81; Saidiya Hartman, *Wayward Lives, Beautiful Experiments: Intimate Histories of Social Upheaval* (New York: Norton, 2019); Treva B. Lindsey, *Colored No More: Reinventing Black Womanhood in Washington, D.C.* (Urbana: University of Illinois Press, 2017); Lisa B. Thompson, *Beyond the Black Lady: Sexuality and the New African American Middle-Class* (Urbana: University of Illinois Press, 2012).

62 For further discussion of middle-class African American men's sexuality, and black masculinity more generally, see Darlene Clark Hine and Earnestine Jenkins, eds., *A Question of Manhood: A Reader in U.S. Black Men's History and Masculinity, Volume 1* (Bloomington: Indiana University Press, 1999); Darlene Clark Hine and Earnestine Jenkins, eds., *A Question of Manhood: A Reader in U.S. Black Men's History and Masculinity, Volume 2* (Bloomington: Indiana University Press, 2001); Ronald L. Jackson and Mark C. Hopson, eds., *Masculinity in the Black Imagination: The Politics of Communicating Race and Manhood* (New York: Peter Lang, 2013); Athena D. Mutua, ed., *Progressive Black Masculinities?* (New York: Routledge, 2006); Riché Richardson, *Black Masculinity and the U.S. South: From Uncle Tom to Gangsta* (Athens: University of Georgia Press, 2007); Marlon Bryan Ross, *Manning the Race: Reforming Black Men in the Jim Crow Era* (New York University Press, 2004); Robert Staples, "Masculinity and Race: The Dual Dilemma of Black Men," *Journal of Social Issues* 34, no. 1 (1978): 169–83; Martin Anthony Summers, *Manliness and its Discontents: The Black Middle-Class and the Transformation of Masculinity, 1900–1930* (Chapel Hill: University of North Carolina Press, 2004).

63 For further discussion of intersectionality – or, rather, intersectionalism – see Anna Carastathis, *Intersectionality: Origins, Contestations, Horizons* (Lincoln: University of Nebraska Press, 2016); Patricia Hill Collins, *Intersectionality as Critical Social Theory* (Durham: Duke University Press, 2019); Patricia Hill Collins and Sirma Bilge, *Intersectionality* (Cambridge: Polity, 2016); Kimberlé Crenshaw, *On Intersectionality: Essential Writings* (New York: New Press, 2019); Ange-Marie Hancock, *Intersectionality: An Intellectual History* (Oxford University Press, 2016); Jennifer C. Nash, *Black Feminism Reimagined: After Intersectionality* (Durham: Duke University Press, 2019); Mary Romero, *Introducing Intersectionality* (Cambridge: Polity, 2018).

64 Du Bois, *The Philadelphia Negro*, 67.

65 Ibid., 68, 70.

66 Ibid., 98.

67 Ibid., 71–2.

68 See Daina Ramey Berry and Leslie M. Harris, eds., *Sexuality and Slavery: Reclaiming Intimate Histories in the Americas* (Athens: University of Georgia Press, 2018); Gutman, *The Black Family in Slavery and Freedom*; Jones, *Labor of Love, Labor of Sorrow*; Stephanie E. Jones-Rogers, *They Were Her Property: White Women as Slave Owners in the American South* (New Haven: Yale University Press, 2019); Jessica Millward, *Finding Charity's Folk: Enslaved and Free Black Women in Maryland* (Athens: University of Georgia Press, 2015).

69 Remco Heesen, Liam Kofi Bright, and Andrew Zucker, "Vindicating Methodological Triangulation," *Synthese: An International Journal for Epistemology, Methodology and Philosophy of Science* 196, no. 8 (2019): 3067–81; Morris, *The Scholar Denied*, 19–54; Weiner, "Decolonial Sociology."

70 See Du Bois, *The Philadelphia Negro*, 66–72, 164–96, 235–86.

71 Ibid., 235–86.

72 Ibid., 310–11.

73 Dan S. Green and Robert A. Wortham, "The Sociological Insight of W. E. B. Du Bois," *Sociological Inquiry* 88, no. 1 (2018): 56–78; Morris, *The Scholar Denied*, 15–55; Adolph L. Reed, *W. E. B. Du Bois and American Political Thought: Fabianism and the Color-Line* (Oxford University Press, 1997), 27–41; Robert A. Wortham, "W. E. B. Du Bois and Demography: Early Explorations," *Sociation Today* 7, no. 1 (2009): 1–27; Earl Wright, *The First American School of Sociology: W. E. B. Du Bois and the Atlanta Sociological Laboratory* (London: Routledge, 2016), 73–9; Shamoon Zamir, *Dark Voices: W. E. B. Du Bois and American Thought, 1888–1903* (University of Chicago Press, 1995), 68–109.

74 Dorcas Davis Boles, June Gary Hopps, Obie Clayton, and Shena Leverett Brown, "The Dance Between Addams and Du Bois: Collaboration and Controversy in a Consequential 20th Century Relationship," *Phylon* 53, no. 2 (2016): 34–53; Francis L. Broderick, "German Influence on the Scholarship of W. E. B. DuBois," *Phylon* 19, no. 4 (1958): 367–71; Mary Jo Deegan, "W. E. B. Du Bois and the Women of Hull-House, 1895–1899," *American Sociologist* 19, no. 4 (1988): 301–11; Loughran, "*The Philadelphia Negro* and the Canon of Classical Urban Theory," 249–67; Shannon O'Connor, "Methodological Triangulation and the Social Studies of Charles Booth, Jane Addams, and W. E. B. Du Bois," *Sociation Today* 7, no. 1 (2009): 1–21; Alexander G. Weheliye, "Diagrammatics as Physiognomy: W. E. B. Du Bois's Graphic Modernities," *CR: The New Centennial Review* 15, no. 2 (2015): 23–58.

75 Tufuku Zuberi [a.k.a. Antonio McDaniel], "The 'Philadelphia Negro' Then and Now: Implications for Empirical Research," in *W. E. B. Du Bois, Race, and the City*, ed. Katz and Sugrue, 155–94.

76 Du Bois, *The Autobiography of W. E. B. Du Bois*, 198.

77 Jane Addams, *Hull House Maps and Papers* (New York: Crowell Publishing, 1895); Charles Booth, *Life and Labor of the People in London*, 17 vols. (London: Macmillan, 1889–1902).

78 Phil Zuckerman, "Introduction to the Social Theory of W. E. B. Du Bois," in W. E. B. Du Bois, *The Social Theory of W. E. B. Du Bois*, ed. Phil Zuckerman (Thousand Oaks, CA: Sage, 2004), 6.

79 Martin Bulmer, "W. E. B. Du Bois as a Social Investigator: *The Philadelphia Negro*, 1899," in *The Social Survey in Historical Perspective, 1880–1940*, ed. Martin Bulmer, Kevin Bales, and Kathryn Kish Sklar (Cambridge University Press, 1991), 174. For more detailed discussion of Florence Kelley and her work, see Leigh B. Bienen, *Florence Kelley and the Children: Factory Inspector in 1890s Chicago* (Chicago: Open Books, 2014); Josephine Goldmark, *Impatient Crusader: Florence Kelley's Life Story* (Urbana: University of Illinois Press, 1953); Kathryn Kish Sklar, *Florence Kelley and the Nation's Work: The Rise of Women's Political Culture, 1830–1900* (New Haven: Yale University Press, 1997). It is important to observe that the influential social reformer Florence Kelley eventually became one of Du Bois's colleagues and a co-founder of the NAACP, which was established on February 12, 1909 by a diverse group of dissidents, which included Du Bois, Kelley, Ida B. Wells, Archibald Grimké, Henry Moscowitz, Mary White Ovington, Oswald Garrison Villard, and William English Walling.

80 On the assertion that Du Bois virtually single-handedly inaugurated empirical sociology in the United States, see Barrington Steven Edwards, "W. E. B. Du Bois Between Worlds: Berlin, Empirical Social Research, and the Race Question," *Du Bois Review: Social Science Research on Race* 3, no. 2 (2006): 395–424; Joseph Jakubek and Spencer D. Wood, "Emancipatory Empiricism: The Rural Sociology of W. E. B. Du Bois," *Sociology of Race and Ethnicity* 4, no. 1 (2018): 14–34; Hynek Jerabek, "W. E. B. Du Bois on the History of Empirical Social Research," *Ethnic and Racial Studies* 39, no. 8 (2016): 1391–7; Morris, *The Scholar Denied*, 1–54; Robert W. Williams, "The Early Social Science of W. E. B. Du Bois," *Du Bois Review: Social Science Research on Race* 3, no. 2 (2006): 365–94; Robert A. Wortham, "The Early Sociological Legacy of W. E. B. Du Bois," in *Diverse Histories of American Sociology*, ed. Anthony J. Blasi (Boston: Brill, 2005), 74–95; Earl Wright, "The Atlanta Sociological Laboratory, 1896–-1924: A Historical Account of the First American School of Sociology," *Western Journal of Black Studies* 23, no. 3 (2002): 165–74; Wright, *The First American School of Sociology*, 15–70; Earl Wright, "Using the Master's Tools: The Atlanta Sociological Laboratory and American Sociology, 1896–1924," *Sociological Spectrum* 22, no. 1 (2002): 15–40; Zuberi, "The 'Philadelphia Negro' Then and Now."

81 Bulmer, "W. E. B. Du Bois as a Social Investigator," 174.

82 See Hunter, "W. E. B. Du Bois and Black Heterogeneity," 219–33.

83   Du Bois, "The Study of the Negro Problems," 12.
84   Audre Lorde, "The Master's Tools Will Never Dismantle the Master's House," in Audre Lorde, *Sister Outsider: Essays and Speeches by Audre Lorde* (Freedom, CA: The Crossing Press Feminist Series, 1984), 110–13.
85   Mia Bay, "'The World Was Thinking Wrong About Race': *The Philadelphia Negro* and Nineteenth-Century Science," in *W. E. B. Du Bois, Race, and the City*, ed. Katz and Sugrue, 41.
86   Ibid., 41–2.
87   Kevin K. Gaines, "Urban Pathology and the Limits of Social Research: W. E. B. Du Bois's *The Philadelphia Negro*," in Kevin K. Gaines, *Uplifting the Race: Black Leadership, Politics, and Culture in the Twentieth Century* (Chapel Hill: University of North Carolina Press, 1996), 171–8.
88   Du Bois, *The Philadelphia Negro*, 351, 66.
89   Gaines, "Urban Pathology and the Limits of Social Research," 152–78; cf. Hunter, "W. E. B. Du Bois and Black Heterogeneity," 219–33.

2 *The Souls of Black Folk*: Critique of Racism and Contributions to Critical Race Studies

1   Earl Wright, *The First American School of Sociology: W. E. B. Du Bois and the Atlanta Sociological Laboratory* (London: Routledge, 2016).
2   W. E. B. Du Bois, *The Souls of Black Folk* (Chicago: A. C. McClurg & Co., 1903).
3   Stephanie J. Shaw, *W. E. B. Du Bois and* The Souls of Black Folk (Chapel Hill: University of North Carolina Press, 2013).
4   Brent Hayes Edwards, "Introduction," in W. E. B. Du Bois, *The Souls of Black Folk*, ed. Brent Hayes Edwards (Oxford University Press, 2007), xxi, emphasis in original.
5   Du Bois, *The Souls of Black Folk*, vii.
6   Ibid., 63.
7   Ibid., 63–6.
8   Ibid., 71–2.
9   Ibid., 251.
10   Arnold Rampersad, *The Art and Imagination of W. E. B. Du Bois* (New York: Schocken, 1990), 70–2.
11   Du Bois, *The Souls of Black Folk*, vii.
12   Ibid., vii.
13   Ibid., 1.
14   Ibid., vii.
15   Ibid., 4.
16   Ibid., 59.
17   Ibid., vii.
18   Ibid., 4.

19 Robert Stepto, *From Behind the Veil: A Study of Afro-American Narrative* (Urbana: University of Illinois Press, 1979), 53.
20 Du Bois, *The Souls of Black Folk*, viii.
21 For further discussion of Du Bois's theory of the Veil, see Judith R. Blau and Eric S. Brown, "Du Bois and Diasporic Identity: The Veil and the Unveiling Project," *Sociological Theory* 19, no. 2 (2001): 219–33; Stanley Brodwin, "The Veil Transcended: Form and Meaning in W. E. B. Du Bois's *The Souls of Black Folk*," *Journal of Black Studies* 2, no. 3 (1972): 303–22; Lynn England and W. Keith Warner, "W. E. B. Du Bois: Reform, Will, and the Veil," *Social Forces* 91, no. 3 (2013): 955–73; Harriet Fertik and Mathias Hanses, "Above the Veil: Revisiting the Classicism of W. E. B. Du Bois," *International Journal of the Classical Tradition* 26, no. 1 (2019): 1–9; Charles Lemert, "A Classic from the Other Side of the Veil: Du Bois's *The Souls of Black Folk*," *Sociological Quarterly* 35, no. 3 (1994): 383–96; Cynthia D. Schrager, "Both Sides of the Veil: Race, Science, and Mysticism in W. E. B. Du Bois," *American Quarterly* 48, no. 4 (1996): 551–86; John Sheehy, "The Mirror and the Veil: The Passing Novel and the Quest for American Racial Identity," *African American Review* 33, no. 3 (1999): 401–15; Stepto, *From Behind the Veil*; Gordon O. Taylor, "Voices from the Veil: Black American Autobiography," *Georgia Review* 35, no. 2 (1981): 341–61; Howard Winant, "Dialectics of the Veil," in Howard Winant, *The New Politics Of Race: Globalism, Difference, Justice* (Minneapolis: University of Minnesota Press, 2004), 25–38.
22 Du Bois, *The Souls of Black Folk*, 108, 202, 258.
23 Ibid., vii.
24 Ibid., 181, 202. See Brodwin, "The Veil Transcended"; Schrager, "Both Sides of the Veil"; Stepto, *From Behind the Veil*, 52–94.
25 Du Bois, *The Souls of Black Folk*, vii.
26 Ibid., vii.
27 Ibid., viii.
28 W. E. B. Du Bois, *The Philadelphia Negro: A Social Study* (Philadelphia: University of Pennsylvania Press, 1899), 309. See also Marcus Anthony Hunter, "W. E. B. Du Bois and Black Heterogeneity: How *The Philadelphia Negro* Shaped American Sociology," *American Sociologist* 46, no. 2 (2015): 219–33.
29 Rampersad, *The Art and Imagination of W. E. B. Du Bois*, 74.
30 For further discussion of Du Bois's distinct humanism, see Lewis R. Gordon, "Du Bois's Humanistic Philosophy of Human Sciences," *Annals of the American Academy of Political and Social Science* 568, no. 1 (2000): 265–80; Patrice Rankine, "Afterlife: Du Bois, Classical Humanism, and the Matter of Black Lives," *International Journal of the Classical Tradition* 26, no. 1 (2019): 86–96; Gary Wilder, "Reading Du Bois's Revelation: Radical Humanism and Black Atlantic Criticism," in *The Postcolonial Contemporary: Political Imaginaries for the Global Present*, ed. Jini Kim

Watson and Gary Wilder (New York: Fordham University Press, 2018), 95–125.

31 For further discussion of Du Bois's concept of the color-line, see Alexander Anievas, Nivi Manchanda, and Robbie Shilliam, "Confronting the Global Color-Line: An Introduction," in *Race and Racism in International Relations*, ed. Alexander Anievas, Nivi Manchanda, and Robbie Shilliam (London: Routledge, 2014), 13–28; Kwame Anthony Appiah, "The Race in the Modern World: The Problem of the Color-Line," *Foreign Affairs* 94, no. 2 (2015): 1–8; Russ Castronovo, "Beauty Along the Color-Line: Lynching, Aesthetics, and the *Crisis*," *PMLA* 121, no. 5 (2006): 1443–59; W. E. B. Du Bois, *The Problem of the Color-Line at the Turn of the Twentieth Century: The Essential Early Essays*, ed. Nahum Dimitri Chandler (New York: Fordham University Press, 2015); W. E. B. Du Bois, *W. E. B. Du Bois on Asia: Crossing the World Color-Line*, ed. Bill V. Mullen and Cathryn Watson (Jackson: University Press of Mississippi, 2005); Kazuhisa Honda, "Max Weber and W. E. B. Du Bois on the Color-Line," *Annual Review of Sociology* 28 (2015): 35–9; Maulana Karenga, "Du Bois and the Question of the Color-Line: Race and Class in the Age of Globalization," *Socialism and Democracy* 17, no. 1 (2003): 141–60; Frank M. Kirkland, "The Problem of the Color-Line: Normative or Empirical, Evolving or Non-Evolving," *Philosophia Africana* 7, no. 1 (2004): 57–82; Bill V. Mullen, *W. E. B. Du Bois: Revolutionary across the Color-Line* (London: Pluto Press, 2016); Alina Müller, *The Problem of the Color-Line in Du Bois's* The Souls of Black Folk (Munich: GRIN Verlag, 2015); Adolph L. Reed, *W. E. B. Du Bois and American Political Thought: Fabianism and the Color-Line* (Oxford University Press, 1997); Shawn Michelle Smith, *Photography on the Color-Line: W. E. B. Du Bois, Race, and Visual Culture* (Durham: Duke University Press, 2005); Eric J. Sundquist, *To Wake the Nations: Race in the Making of American Literature* (Cambridge, MA: Harvard University Press, 1993), 540–25; Miriam F. Williams, "Tracing W. E. B. Du Bois's 'Color-Line' in Government Regulations," *Journal of Technical Writing and Communication* 36, no. 2 (2006): 141–65; Zhang Juguo, *W. E. B. Du Bois: The Quest for the Abolition of the Color-Line* (London: Routledge, 2002).

32 W. E. B. Du Bois, *The Autobiography of W. E. B. Du Bois: A Soliloquy on Viewing My Life from the Last Decade of Its First Century* (New York: International Publishers, 1968), 222.

33 W. E. B. Du Bois, "The Souls of Black Folk," *Independent* 57, November 17, 1904, 1152.

34 David Levering Lewis, *W. E. B. Du Bois: Biography of a Race, 1868–1919* (New York: Henry Holt, 1993), 278.

35 Ibid.

36 Ibid., 279.

37 Robert A. Wortham, "The Sociological Souls of Black Folk," in W. E. B.

Du Bois, *The Sociological Souls of Black Folk: Essays by W. E. B. Du Bois*, ed. Robert A. Wortham (Lanham, MD: Lexington Books, 2011), xiii–xlv.

38 Du Bois, *The Souls of Black Folk*, 9.
39 Ibid., 9.
40 Du Bois, *The Problem of the Color-Line at the Turn of the Twentieth Century*.
41 Rayford W. Logan, *The Negro in American Life and Thought, the Nadir, 1877–1901* (New York: Dial Press, 1954).
42 Müller, *The Problem of the Color-Line in Du Bois's* The Souls of Black Folk.
43 Du Bois, *The Souls of Black Folk*, 231.
44 Ibid., 229–30.
45 Ibid., 242.
46 Ibid., 243.
47 Ibid., 243.
48 Jonathon S. Kahn, *Divine Discontent: The Religious Imagination of W. E. B. Du Bois* (Oxford University Press, 2009), 60–4.
49 Du Bois, *The Souls of Black Folk*, 1–2.
50 W. E. B. Du Bois, "Of Mr. Booker T. Washington and Others," in Du Bois, *The Souls of Black Folk*, 41–59.
51 Du Bois, *The Souls of Black Folk*, 13.
52 Ibid., 52.
53 W. E. B. Du Bois, *Darkwater: Voices from Within the Veil* (New York: Harcourt, Brace and Howe, 1920); W. E. B. Du Bois, *Dark Princess: A Romance* (New York: Harcourt, Brace & Co., 1928); W. E. B. Du Bois, *Color and Democracy: Colonies and Peace* (New York: Harcourt, Brace & Co., 1945); W. E. B. Du Bois, *The World and Africa* (New York: Viking Press, 1947).
54 For more detailed discussion of double-consciousness, see Sandra Adell, *Double-Consciousness / Double Bind: Theoretical Issues in Twentieth-Century Black Literature* (Urbana: Illinois University Press, 1994); David W. Blight, "Up from 'Twoness': Frederick Douglass and the Meaning of W. E. B. Du Bois's Concept of Double-Consciousness," *Canadian Review of American Studies* 21, no. 3 (1990): 301–20; Joseph Evans, *Lifting the Veil over Eurocentrism: The Du Boisian Hermeneutic of Double-Consciousness* (Trenton, NJ: Africa World Press, 2014); Paul Gilroy, *The Black Atlantic: Modernity and Double-Consciousness* (Cambridge, MA: Harvard University Press, 1993); Robert Gooding-Williams, *In the Shadow of Du Bois: Afro-Modern Political Thought in America* (Cambridge, MA: Harvard University Press, 2009), 66–95; Frank M. Kirkland, "On Du Bois's Notion of Double-Consciousness," *Philosophy Compass* 8, no. 2 (2013): 137–48; Paul C. Mocombe, *The Soul-less Souls of Black Folk: A Sociological Reconsideration of Black Consciousness as Du Boisian Double-Consciousness* (Lanham, MD: University Press of America, 2008); Reiland Rabaka, "The Discourse on Double-Consciousness," in *Keywords for African American Studies*, ed. Erica R. Edwards, Roderick A.

Ferguson, and Jeffrey O. G. Ogbar (New York University Press, 2018), 75–8; Anthony Reed, "Alightings of Poetry: The Dialectics of Voice and Silence in W. E. B. Du Bois's Narrative of Double-Consciousness," in *A Political Companion to W. E. B. Du Bois*, ed. Nick Bromell (Lexington: University Press of Kentucky, 2018), 85–100; Anne Warfield Rawls, "'Race' as an Interaction Order Phenomenon: W. E. B. Du Bois's 'Double-Consciousness' Thesis Revisited," *Sociological Theory* 18, no. 2 (2000): 241–74.

55 Emmanuel C. Eze, "On Double-Consciousness," *Callaloo* 34, no. 3 (2011): 877–98; Kirkland, "On Du Bois's Notion of Double-Consciousness"; Nasar Meer, "W. E. B. Du Bois, Double-Consciousness and the 'Spirit' of Recognition," *Sociological Review* 67, no. 1 (2019): 47–62.

56 Du Bois, *The Souls of Black Folk*, 7. See also Sundquist, *To Wake the Nations*, 457–539.

57 For further discussion of Du Bois's work on black women, see chapter 4, "'The Damnation of Women': Critique of Patriarchy, Contributions to Black Feminism, and Early Intersectionality," in this volume.

58 Du Bois, *The Souls of Black Folk*, 3–4.

59 Sandra L. Barnes, "A Sociological Examination of W. E. B. Du Bois's *The Souls of Black Folk*," *The North Star: A Journal of African American Religious History* 7, no. 2 (2003): 1–6; José Itzigsohn and Karida Brown, "Sociology and the Theory of Double-Consciousness: W. E. B. Du Bois's Phenomenology of Racialized Subjectivity," *Du Bois Review: Social Science Research on Race* 12, no. 2 (2015): 231–48; Wortham, "The Sociological Souls of Black Folk."

60 Dickson D. Bruce, "W. E. B. Du Bois and the Idea of Double-Consciousness," *American Literature* 64, no. 2 (1992): 299–309; Robert Gooding-Williams, "Philosophy of History and Social Critique in *The Souls of Black Folk*," *Information (International Social Science Council)* 26, no. 1 (1987): 99–114.

61 Du Bois, *The Souls of Black Folk*, 3–4, 202.

62 Tomás Almaguer, *Racial Fault Lines: The Historical Origins of White Supremacy in California* (Berkeley: University of California Press, 1994).

63 Bruce, "W. E. B. Du Bois and the Idea of Double-Consciousness"; Itzigsohn and Brown, "Sociology and the Theory of Double-Consciousness"; Meer, "W. E. B. Du Bois, Double-Consciousness and the 'Spirit' of Recognition."

64 For further discussion of Du Bois's theory of second-sight, see Julio Cammarota, "The Praxis of Ethnic Studies: Transforming Second-Sight into Critical Consciousness," *Race, Ethnicity, and Education* 19, no. 2 (2016): 233–51; Gooding-Williams, *In the Shadow of Du Bois*, 70–86; Shannon Mariotti, "On the Passing of the First-Born Son: Emerson's 'Focal Distancing,' Du Bois's 'Second-Sight,' and Disruptive Particularity," *Political Theory* 37, no. 3 (2009): 351–74; Gladys L. Mitchell-Walthour and Elizabeth Hordge-Freeman, "Introduction: In

Pursuit of Du Bois's 'Second-Sight' through Diasporic Dialogues," in *Race and the Politics of Knowledge Production: Diaspora and Black Transnational Scholarship in the United States and Brazil*, ed. Gladys L. Mitchell-Walthour and Elizabeth Hordge-Freeman (New York: Palgrave Macmillan, 2016), 1–11; James W. Perkinson, "The Gift/ Curse of 'Second Sight,'" in James W. Perkinson, *Shamanism, Racism, and Hip Hop Culture: Essays on White Supremacy and Black Subversion* (New York: Palgrave Macmillan, 2005), 45–83; Schrager, "Both Sides of the Veil"; Shaw, *W. E. B. Du Bois*, 15–18; Shawn Michelle Smith, "Second-Sight: Du Bois and the Black Masculine Gaze," in *Next to the Color-Line: Gender, Sexuality, and W. E. B. Du Bois*, ed. Susan Gillman and Alys E. Weinbaum (Minneapolis: University of Minnesota Press, 2007), 350–77; Eugene Victor Wolfenstein, *A Gift of the Spirit: Reading The Souls of Black Folk* (Ithaca: Cornell University Press, 2007), 9–10.

65 Du Bois, *The Souls of Black Folk*, 1–12. See also Kahn, *Divine Discontent*, 49–70; Shaw, *W. E. B. Du Bois*, 15–36.

66 Du Bois, *The Souls of Black Folk*, 3–4.

67 David W. Blight and Robert Gooding-Williams, "Introduction to *The Souls of Black Folk* – The Strange Meaning of Being Black: Du Bois's American Tragedy," in W. E. B. Du Bois, *The Souls of Black Folk*, ed. David W. Blight and Robert Gooding-Williams (Boston: Bedford Books, 1997), 10–16.

68 Lewis, *W. E. B. Du Bois: Biography of a Race*, 280.

69 Du Bois, *The Souls of Black Folk*, 262–3.

70 For further discussion of Du Bois's gift theory, see W. E. B. Du Bois, *The Gift of Black Folk: The Negroes in the Making of America* (Boston: Stratford, 1924); Gooding-Williams, *In the Shadow of Du Bois*, 130–61; Stepto, *From Behind the Veil*, 52–94; Shannon Sullivan, "Remembering the Gift: W. E. B. Du Bois on the Unconscious and Economic Operations of Racism," *Transactions of the Charles S. Peirce Society* 39, no. 2 (2003): 205–25; Wolfenstein, *A Gift of the Spirit*.

71 On whites' historic and hegemonic racial classifications and ethno-cultural categorizations, which denote which *human beings* count as "human," "sub-human," and/or "non-human" within the white supremacist world, see Charles W. Mills, *The Racial Contract* (Ithaca: Cornell University Press, 1997), 41–90.

3 "The Souls of White Folk": Critique of White Supremacy and Contributions to Critical White Studies

1 The final version of the "The Souls of White Folk" published in *Darkwater* in 1920 was a substantially revised essay based on two of Du Bois's previously published missives: W. E. B. Du Bois, "The Souls of White Folk," *The Independent* 69, August 18, 1910, 339–42;

and W. E. B. Du Bois, "Of the Culture of White Folk," *Journal of Race Development* 7, no. 4 (1917): 434–47. See W. E. B. Du Bois, "The Souls of White Folk," in W. E. B. Du Bois, *Darkwater: Voices from Within the Veil* (New York: Harcourt, Brace and Howe, 1920), 29–52 (all references to "The Souls of White Folk" hereafter are to the final version of the essay published in *Darkwater*). See also Mike Hill, "'Souls Undressed': The Rise and Fall of the New Whiteness Studies," *Review of Education/ Pedagogy/Cultural Studies* 20, no. 3 (1998): 229–39; Matthew W. Hughey and W. Carson Byrd, "The Souls of White Folk Beyond Formation and Structure: Bound to Identity," *Ethnic and Racial Studies* 36, no. 6 (2013): 974–81; Zeus Leonardo, "The Souls of White Folk: Critical Pedagogy, Whiteness Studies, and Globalization Discourse," *Race, Ethnicity, and Education* 5, no. 1 (2002): 29–50; Veronica T. Watson, *The Souls of White Folk: African American Writers Theorize Whiteness* (Jackson: University Press of Mississippi, 2013).

2 W. E. B. Du Bois, *Black Reconstruction in America, 1860–1880* (New York: Harcourt, Brace & Co., 1935), 17–31, 487–525. See also James Edward Ford, "The Imperial Miracle: *Black Reconstruction* and the End(s) of Whiteness," in *A Political Companion to W. E. B. Du Bois*, ed. Nick Bromell (Lexington: University Press of Kentucky, 2018), 101–20; Lisa J. McLeod, "Transubstantiation of Andrew Johnson: White Epistemic Failure in Du Bois's *Black Reconstruction*," *Phylon* 51, no. 1 (2014): 88–101; Ella Myers, "Beyond the Psychological Wage: Du Bois on White Dominion," *Political Theory* 47, no. 1 (2019): 6–31; David R. Roediger, *The Wages of Whiteness: Race and the Making of the American Working-Class* (London: Verso, 1991).

3 Keith Byerman, "W. E. B. Du Bois and the Construction of Whiteness," in *The Souls of Black Folk: One Hundred Years Later*, ed. Dolan Hubbard (Columbia: University of Missouri Press, 2003), 161. See also George Yancy, "W. E. B. Du Bois on Whiteness and the Pathology of Black Double-Consciousness," *APA Newsletters: Philosophy and the Black Experience* 4, no. 1 (2004): 9–22.

4 Byerman, "W. E. B. Du Bois and the Construction of Whiteness," 161.

5 David S. Owen, "Whiteness in Du Bois's *The Souls of Black Folk*," *Philosophia Africana* 10, no. 2 (2007): 108.

6 Ibid.

7 Ibid.

8 W. E. B. Du Bois, *The Souls of Black Folk* (Chicago: A. C. McClurg & Co., 1903), viii, 1.

9 Frederick Douglass, *Narrative of the Life of Frederick Douglass* (Boston: Anti-Slavery Office Press, 1845); William Wells Brown, *Narrative of William W. Brown, A Fugitive Slave* (Boston: Anti-Slavery Office Press, 1847); Booker T. Washington, *Up from Slavery* (Garden City, NY: Doubleday, Page & Co., 1901).

10 W. E. B. Du Bois, *The Suppression of the African Slave Trade to the United*

States of America, 1638–1870 (New York: Longmans, Green & Company, 1896).

11 Yancy, "W. E. B. Du Bois on Whiteness and the Pathology of Black Double-Consciousness," 10–13.

12 Owen, "Whiteness in Du Bois's *The Souls of Black Folk*," 109, emphasis in original.

13 Ibid.; Byerman, "W. E. B. Du Bois and the Construction of Whiteness," 162.

14 Byerman, "W. E. B. Du Bois and the Construction of Whiteness," 162. See also Du Bois, *The Souls of Black Folk*, vii–viii.

15 For further discussion of subaltern studies, see Vinayak Chaturvedi, ed., *Mapping Subaltern Studies and the Postcolonial* (London: Verso, 2012); Ranajit Guha, ed., *A Subaltern Studies Reader, 1986–1995* (Minneapolis: University of Minnesota Press, 1997); Rosalind C. Morris, ed., *Can the Subaltern Speak? Reflections on the History of an Idea* (New York: Columbia University Press, 2010).

16 Du Bois, *The Souls of Black Folk*, 1.

17 Byerman, "W. E. B. Du Bois and the Construction of Whiteness," 163, emphasis in original.

18 Ibid., 162–3.

19 Du Bois, *The Souls of Black Folk*, vii.

20 Byerman, "W. E. B. Du Bois and the Construction of Whiteness," 164, all emphasis in original.

21 Owen, "Whiteness in Du Bois's *The Souls of Black Folk*," 110.

22 Du Bois, *The Souls of Black Folk*, 3.

23 Ibid., 2.

24 Dominic J. Capeci and Jack C. Knight, "Reckoning with Violence: W. E. B. Du Bois and the 1906 Atlanta Race Riot," *Journal of Southern History* 62, no. 4 (1996): 727–66.

25 Du Bois, *The Souls of Black Folk*, vii–viii.

26 Ibid., viii.

27 Ibid., 2.

28 David Levering Lewis, *W. E. B. Du Bois: Biography of a Race, 1868–1919* (New York: Henry Holt, 1993), 32–7.

29 Ernest Allen, "'Ever Feeling One's Twoness': 'Double Ideals' and 'Double-Consciousness' in *The Souls of Black Folk*," *Critique of Anthropology* 12, no. 3 (1992): 261–75; Dickson D. Bruce, "W. E. B. Du Bois and the Idea of Double-Consciousness," *American Literature* 64, no. 2 (1992): 299–309; Frank M. Kirkland, "On Du Bois's Notion of Double-Consciousness," *Philosophy Compass* 8, no. 2 (2013): 137–48.

30 Du Bois, *The Souls of Black Folk*, 3.

31 Judith R. Blau and Eric S. Brown, "Du Bois and Diasporic Identity: The Veil and the Unveiling Project," *Sociological Theory* 19, no. 2 (2001): 219–33; Stanley Brodwin, "The Veil Transcended: Form and Meaning in W. E. B. Du Bois's *The Souls of Black Folk*," *Journal of Black Studies*

2, no. 3 (1972): 303–22; Howard Winant, "Dialectics of the Veil," in Howard Winant, *The New Politics Of Race: Globalism, Difference, Justice* (Minneapolis: University of Minnesota Press, 2004), 25–38.

32 Myers, "Beyond the Psychological Wage."

33 W. E. B. Du Bois, *The Problem of the Color-Line at the Turn of the Twentieth Century: The Essential Early Essays*, ed. Nahum Dimitri Chandler (New York: Fordham University Press, 2015); W. E. B. Du Bois, *W. E. B. Du Bois on Asia: Crossing the World Color-Line*, ed. Bill V. Mullen and Cathryn Watson (Jackson: University Press of Mississippi, 2005). See also Maulana Karenga, "Du Bois and the Question of the Color-Line: Race and Class in the Age of Globalization," *Socialism and Democracy* 17, no. 1 (2003): 141–60; Frank M. Kirkland, "The Problem of the Color-Line: Normative or Empirical, Evolving or Non-Evolving," *Philosophia Africana* 7, no. 1 (2004): 57–82; Miriam F. Williams, "Tracing W. E. B. Du Bois's 'Color-Line' in Government Regulations," *Journal of Technical Writing and Communication* 36, no. 2 (2006): 141–65; Kirt H. Wilson, "Towards a Discursive Theory of Racial Identity: *The Souls of Black Folk* as a Response to Nineteenth-Century Biological Determinism," *Western Journal of Communication* 63, no. 2 (1999): 193–215; Zhang Juguo, *W. E. B. Du Bois: The Quest for the Abolition of the Color-Line* (London: Routledge, 2002).

34 Henry Louis Gates, "Introduction to *The Souls of Black Folk*," in W. E. B. Du Bois, *The Souls of Black Folk* (New York: Bantam Books, 1989), vii–xxix; Henry Louis Gates and Terri Hume Oliver, "Preface to *The Souls of Black Folk*," in W. E. B. Du Bois, *The Souls of Black Folk: Authoritative Text, Contexts, Criticism* (New York: Norton, 1999), ix–xxxv; Melvin L. Rogers, "The People, Rhetoric, and Affect: On the Political Force of Du Bois's *The Souls of Black Folk*," *American Political Science Review* 106, no. 1 (2012): 188–203; Stephanie J. Shaw, *W. E. B. Du Bois and* The Souls of Black Folk (Chapel Hill: University of North Carolina Press, 2013); Wilson, "Towards a Discursive Theory of Racial Identity"; Robert A. Wortham, "The Sociological Souls of Black Folk," in W. E. B. Du Bois, *The Sociological Souls of Black Folk: Essays by W. E. B. Du Bois*, ed. Robert A. Wortham (Lanham, MD: Lexington Books, 2011), xiii–xlv.

35 Byerman, "W. E. B. Du Bois and the Construction of Whiteness," 161–71; Owen, "Whiteness in Du Bois's *The Souls of Black Folk*," 107–26; Yancy, "W. E. B. Du Bois on Whiteness and the Pathology of Black Double-Consciousness," 10–22.

36 Du Bois, *The Souls of Black Folk*, 1.

37 Ibid., 2.

38 Ibid., 3.

39 Ibid., 12.

40 Ibid., 58.

41 Ibid., 86.

42 Ibid., 89.

43 Blau and Brown, "Du Bois and Diasporic Identity"; Owen, "Whiteness in Du Bois's *The Souls of Black Folk*," 108–10.

44 Owen, "Whiteness in Du Bois's *The Souls of Black Folk*," 119–21.

45 Charles W. Mills, "White Supremacy," in *A Companion to African American Philosophy*, ed. Tommy L. Lott and John P. Pittman (Malden: Blackwell, 2003), 269–84; Charles W. Mills, "White Supremacy," in *The Routledge Companion to the Philosophy of Race*, ed. Paul C. Taylor, Linda Martín Alcoff, and Luvell Anderson (London: Routledge, 2018), 475–87.

46 For further discussion of white colonial and racial rule throughout Africa, see Padraig Carmody, *The New Scramble for Africa* (Cambridge: Polity, 2016); Muriel Evelyn Chamberlain, *The Scramble for Africa* (London: Routledge, 2013); John Mackenzie, *The Partition of Africa: European Imperialism, 1880–1900* (London: Routledge, 1983); Thomas Pakenham, *The Scramble for Africa: White Man's Conquest of the Dark Continent, 1876–1912* (New York: Perennial, 1991); Lee Wengraf, *Extracting Profit: Imperialism, Neoliberalism, and the New Scramble for Africa* (Chicago: Haymarket Books, 2018); Henri L. Wesseling, *Divide and Rule: The Partition of Africa, 1880–1914* (London: Praeger, 1996). For further discussion of the African diaspora, its enslavement, and endurance of racial segregation, see Michael L. Conniff and Thomas J. Davis, *Africans in the Americas: A History of the Black Diaspora* (New York: St. Martin's Press, 1994); Toyin Falola, ed., *The African Diaspora: Slavery, Modernity, and Globalization* (University of Rochester Press, 2013); Michael Angelo Gomez, *Reversing Sail: A History of the African Diaspora* (New York: Cambridge University Press, 2005); Michael Angelo Gomez, ed., *Diasporic Africa: A Reader* (New York University Press, 2006); Patrick Manning, *The African Diaspora: A History Through Culture* (New York: Columbia University Press, 2009); Ronald Segal, *The Black Diaspora: Five Centuries of the Black Experience Outside Africa* (New York: Farrar, Straus and Giroux, 1996); Ronald Segal, *Islam's Black Slaves: The Other Black Diaspora* (New York: Farrar, Straus and Giroux, 2001); John K. Thornton, *Africa and Africans in the Making of the Atlantic World, 1400–1800* (Cambridge University Press, 1998).

47 For more detailed discussion of global white supremacy, see Charles W. Mills, "Revisionist Ontologies: Theorizing White Supremacy," in Charles W. Mills, *Blackness Visible: Essays on Philosophy and Race* (Ithaca: Cornell University Press, 1998), 97–118.

48 Theodore W. Allen, *The Invention of the White Race, Volume 1* (New York: Verso, 1994); Theodore W. Allen, *The Invention of the White Race, Volume 2* (New York: Verso, 1997).

49 Du Bois, "The Souls of White Folk," 31.

50 Ibid., 29.

51 For further discussion of the "black gaze," or what bell hooks calls the "oppositional gaze," see bell hooks, "The Oppositional Gaze:

Black Female Spectators," in bell hooks, *Black Looks: Race and Representation* (Boston: South End Press, 1992), 115–31. See also bell hooks, "Representing Whiteness in the Black Imagination," in hooks, *Black Looks*, 165–78.

52 Du Bois, "The Souls of White Folk," 39–40.

53 My analysis here has been greatly influenced by Charles Mills's conception of "white ignorance," see Charles W. Mills, "White Ignorance," in Charles W. Mills, *Black Rights / White Wrongs: The Critique of Racial Liberalism* (Oxford University Press, 2017), 49–71; Charles W. Mills, "Global White Ignorance," in *Routledge International Handbook of Ignorance Studies*, ed. Matthias Gross and Linsey McGoey (New York: Routledge, 2015), 217–27.

54 W. E. B. Du Bois, *Darkwater: Voices from Within the Veil* (New York: Harcourt, Brace and Howe, 1920), 25.

55 For further discussion of white supremacy as its own morality, see Charles W. Mills, *The Racial Contract* (Ithaca: Cornell University Press, 1997), 91–119.

56 Byerman, "W. E. B. Du Bois and the Construction of Whiteness," 168.

57 For further discussion of America representing liberation for whites and symbolizing domination for blacks, see Avidit Acharya, Matthew Blackwell, and Maya Sen, "The Political Legacy of American Slavery," *Journal of Politics* 78, no. 3 (2016): 621–41; Douglas A. Blackmon, *Slavery by Another Name: The Re-Enslavement of Black Americans from the Civil War to World War II* (New York: Anchor, 2009); Tommy L. Lott, ed., *Subjugation and Bondage: Critical Essays on Slavery and Social Philosophy* (Lanham, MD: Rowman & Littlefield, 1998); Howard McGary and Bill E. Lawson, eds., *Between Slavery and Freedom: Philosophy and American Slavery* (Bloomington: Indiana University Press, 1993); Frank McGlynn and Seymour Drescher, eds., *The Meaning of Freedom: Economics, Politics, and Culture after Slavery* (University of Pittsburgh Press, 1992).

58 Du Bois, "The Souls of White Folk," 32–3.

59 For further discussion of the "Red Summer of 1919," see Barbara Foley, *Spectres of 1919: Class and Nation in the Making of the New Negro* (Urbana: University of Illinois Press, 2003); Theodore Kornweibel, *Seeing Red: Federal Campaigns against Black Militancy, 1919–1925* (Bloomington: Indiana University Press, 1998); Cameron McWhirter, *Red Summer: The Summer of 1919 and the Awakening of Black America* (New York: Henry Holt, 2011); William M. Tuttle, *Race Riot: Chicago in the Red Summer of 1919* (Urbana: University of Illinois Press, 1970); Jan Voogd, *Race Riots and Resistance: The Red Summer of 1919* (New York: Peter Lang, 2008); Robert Whitaker, *On the Laps of Gods: The Red Summer of 1919 and the Struggle for Justice that Remade a Nation* (New York: Broadway Books, 2009).

60 Du Bois, "The Souls of White Folk," 33.

61 On the fallaciousness of American democracy, see Frank Cunningham,

"Democratic Theory and Racist Ontology," *Social Identities* 6, no. 4 (2000): 463–82; Charles W. Mills, "White Supremacy as Socio-Political System: A Philosophical Perspective," in *White Out: The Continuing Significance of Racism*, ed. Ashley W. Doane and Eduardo Bonilla-Silva (New York: Routledge, 2003), 35–48.

62 Du Bois, "The Souls of White Folk," 34.

63 On white religious superiority and its anti-black racist ethics, see William R. Jones, *Is God a White Racist? A Preamble to Black Theology* (Boston: Beacon Press, 1998).

64 See Charles W. Mills, "Racial Exploitation and the Wages of Whiteness," in *What White Looks Like: African American Philosophers on the Whiteness Question*, ed. George Yancy (New York: Routledge, 2004), 25–54; Charles W. Mills, "Racial Exploitation," in Mills, *Black Rights / White Wrongs*, 113–38; Mills, "White Supremacy as Socio-Political System"; Roediger, *The Wages of Whiteness*.

65 Without in any way demonizing whites, it is important to emphasize the recurring theme of demonism that runs through European and European American Christian culture. See, for example, Peter Reginald Beardsell, *Gods and Demons, Self and Other: Images of Europe in the Cultures of Latin America* (University of Hull Press, 1994); Stuart Clark, *Thinking with Demons: The Idea of Witchcraft in Early Modern Europe* (Oxford University Press, 1999); Nathan Johnstone, *The Devil and Demonism in Early Modern England* (Cambridge University Press, 2006); Lyndal Roper, *Oedipus and the Devil: Witchcraft, Religion and Sexuality in Early Modern Europe* (London: Routledge, 1997); Charles Stewart, *Demons and the Devil: Moral Imagination in Modern Greek Culture* (Princeton University Press, 1991); Nienke Vos and Willemien Otten, eds., *Demons and the Devil in Ancient and Medieval Christianity* (Leiden: Brill, 2011).

66 Du Bois, "The Souls of White Folk," 35–6.

67 W. E. B. Du Bois, *The Negro* (New York: Henry Holt, 1915); Du Bois, *Black Reconstruction*; W. E. B. Du Bois, *Black Folk: Then and Now – An Essay in the History and Sociology of the Negro Race* (New York: Henry Holt, 1939); W. E. B. Du Bois, *Color and Democracy: Colonies and Peace* (New York: Harcourt Brace & Co., 1945); W. E. B. Du Bois, *The World and Africa* (New York: Viking Press, 1947).

68 W. E. B. Du Bois, "The African Roots of the War," *Atlantic Monthly* 115 (May 1915): 707–14. See also Mark Ellis, "'Closing Ranks' and 'Seeking Honors': W. E. B. Du Bois in World War I," *Journal of American History* 79, no. 1 (1992): 96–124; Jennifer D. Keene, "W. E. B. Du Bois and the Wounded World: Seeking Meaning in the First World War for African Americans," *Peace & Change* 26, no. 2 (2001): 135–52; Shane A. Smith, "*The Crisis* in the Great War: W. E. B. Du Bois and His Perception of African American Participation in World War I," *The Historian* 70, no. 2 (2008): 239–62; Alberto Toscano, "'America's Belgium': W. E. B.

Du Bois on Race, Class, and the Origins of World War I," in *Cataclysm 1914: The First World War and the Making of Modern World Politics*, ed. Alexander Anievas (Leiden: Brill, 2015), 236–57.

69　Du Bois, "The Souls of White Folk," 37–9.

70　See Ricky Lee Allen, "The Globalization of White Supremacy: Toward a Critical Discourse on the Racialization of the World," *Educational Theory* 51, no. 4 (2001): 467–85; Gerald Horne, *The Apocalypse of Settler Colonialism: The Roots of Slavery, White Supremacy, and Capitalism in 17th-Century North America and the Caribbean* (New York: Monthly Review Press, 2018); Gerald Horne, *The Dawning of the Apocalypse: The Roots of Slavery, White Supremacy, Settler Colonialism, and Capitalism in the Long Sixteenth Century* (New York: Monthly Review Press, 2020); Charles W. Mills, "The Racial Polity," in Mills, *Blackness Visible*, 119–37; Mills, "Revisionist Ontologies"; Mills, "White Supremacy as Socio-Political System"; Gretchen Murphy, *Shadowing the White Man's Burden: U.S. Imperialism and the Problem of the Color-Line* (New York University Press, 2010).

71　Du Bois, "The Souls of White Folk," 41.

72　W. E. B. Du Bois, "The Souls of White Folk," *The Independent* 69, August 18, 1910, 339. See also the revised 1920 *Darkwater* version of the essay, which is being used throughout this chapter: Du Bois, "The Souls of White Folk," 31. Again, all references to "The Souls of White Folk" hereafter are to the final version of the essay published in *Darkwater*.

73　See Mills, *Black Rights / White Wrongs: The Critique of Racial Liberalism*; Charles W. Mills, "White Supremacy and Racial Justice, Here and Now," in *Social and Political Philosophy: Contemporary Perspectives*, ed. James P. Sterba (New York: Routledge, 2001), 321–37.

74　Du Bois, "The Souls of White Folk," 30.

75　See Jessie Daniels, *White Lies: Race, Class, Gender and Sexuality in White Supremacist Discourse* (London: Routledge, 1997); Abby L. Ferber, *White Man Falling: Race, Gender, and White Supremacy* (Lanham, MD: Rowman & Littlefield Publishers, 1998); Abby L. Ferber, ed., *Home-Grown Hate: Gender and Organized Racism* (New York: Routledge, 2004); Glenda Elizabeth Gilmore, *Gender and Jim Crow: Women and the Politics of White Supremacy in North Carolina, 1896–1920* (Chapel Hill: University of North Carolina Press, 2019).

76　See Laura Chrisman, "Theorizing 'Race,' Racism and Culture: Pitfalls of Idealist Tendencies," *Paragraph* 16, no. 1 (1993): 78–90; Wilson J. Moses, "W. E. B. Du Bois's 'The Conservation of Races' and Its Context: Idealism, Conservatism and Hero Worship," *Massachusetts Review* 34, no. 2 (1993): 275–94.

77　See David Camfield, "Elements of a Historical Materialist Theory of Racism," *Historical Materialism* 24, no. 1 (2016): 31–70; John Gabriel and Gideon Ben-Tovim, "Marxism and the Concept of Racism," *Economy and Society* 7, no. 2 (1978): 118–54; Eugene D. Genovese, "Materialism and Idealism in the History of Negro Slavery in the Americas," *Journal of Social History* 1, no. 4 (1968): 371–94; Robert Young, "Putting Materialism Back into Race Theory: Toward a Transformative Theory of Race," in *Race and the Foundations of Knowledge: Cultural Amnesia in the Academy*, ed. Joseph Young and Jana Braziel (Urbana: University of Illinois Press, 2006), 32–45.

78 See Lee D. Baker, *From Savage to Negro: Anthropology and the Construction of Race, 1896–1954* (Berkeley: University of California Press, 1998); Ruth Frankenberg, *White Women, Race Matters: The Social Construction of Whiteness* (London: Routledge, 2005); Ian Haney-López, *White by Law: The Legal Construction of Race* (New York University Press, 2006); Stephen Middleton, David R. Roediger, and Donald M. Shaffer, eds., *The Construction of Whiteness: An Interdisciplinary Analysis of Race Formation and the Meaning of a White Identity* (Jackson: University Press of Mississippi, 2016).

79 Du Bois, "The Souls of White Folk," 29.

80 Mills, "The Racial Polity."

81 Du Bois, "The Souls of White Folk," 35.

82 Ibid., 36.

83 Du Bois, "The African Roots of the War."

84 Du Bois, "The Souls of White Folk," 40.

85 Here, I am hinting at the fact that non-whites have a long history of colonizing one another, albeit never in the worldwide imperial and white supremacist fashion of European imperialism and global domination. This, of course, is a fact that the astute historical researcher, Du Bois, did not allow to fall through the cracks in his more mature historical writing. For, perhaps, the best examples from his oeuvre, see Du Bois, *The Negro*; Du Bois, *Color and Democracy*; Du Bois, *The World and Africa*.

86 W. E. B. Du Bois, *The Conservation of Races*, The American Negro Academy Occasional Papers, no. 2 (Washington, D.C.: American Negro Academy Press, 1897), 11.

87 See W. E. B. Du Bois, *The Gift of Black Folk: The Negroes in the Making of America* (Boston: Stratford, 1924).

88 Du Bois, "The Souls of White Folk," 41.

89 For more detailed discussion of Du Bois's late-life combination of intellectual activism, insurgent internationalism, and radical humanism, and his emphasis on non-white folks' solidarity, see W. E. B. Du Bois, *W. E. B. Du Bois on Asia: Crossing the World Color-Line*, ed. Bill V. Mullen and Cathryn Watson (Jackson: University Press of Mississippi, 2005); Gerald Horne, *Black and Red: W. E. B. Du Bois and the Afro-American Response to the Cold War, 1944–1963* (Albany: State University of New York Press, 1986); Bill V. Mullen, *Un-American: W. E. B. Du Bois and the Century of World Revolution* (Philadelphia: Temple University Press, 2015); Bill V. Mullen, *W. E. B. Du Bois: Revolutionary across the Color-Line*

(London: Pluto Press, 2016); Eric Porter, *The Problem of the Future World: W. E. B. Du Bois and the Race Concept at Midcentury* (Durham: Duke University Press, 2010); Phillip Luke Sinitiere, ed., *Citizen of the World: The Late Career and Legacy of W. E. B. Du Bois* (Evanston: Northwestern University Press, 2019).

90 Du Bois, "The Souls of White Folk," 41–2.

91 Ibid., 42.

92 For more detailed discussion of the 1857 *Dred Scott v. Sandford* Supreme Court decision, see Don E. Fehrenbacher, *Slavery, Law, and Politics: The Dred Scott Case in Historical Perspective* (Oxford University Press, 1981); Don E. Fehrenbacher, *The Dred Scott Case: Its Significance in American Law and Politics* (Oxford University Press, 2001); Mark A. Graber, *Dred Scott and the Problem of Constitutional Evil* (Cambridge University Press, 2006); Earl M. Maltz, *Dred Scott and the Politics of Slavery* (Lawrence: University Press of Kansas, 2007).

93 See Mills, *Black Rights / White Wrongs*.

94 Mills, *The Racial Contract*, 58–9.

95 Du Bois, "The Souls of White Folk," 35.

96 Mills, *The Racial Contract*, 56.

97 See Du Bois, *The Gift of Black Folk*. See also Christine Di Stefano, "A Gift of the Spirit: Reading *The Souls of Black Folk*," *Perspectives on Politics* 6, no. 1 (2008): 171–2; Jane Anna Gordon, "The Gift of Double-Consciousness: Some Obstacles to Grasping the Contributions of the Colonized," in *Postcolonialism and Political Theory*, ed. Nalini Persram (Lanham, MD: Lexington Books, 2007): 143–61; Shannon Sullivan, "Remembering the Gift: W. E. B. Du Bois on the Unconscious and Economic Operations of Racism," *Transactions of the Charles S. Peirce Society* 39, no. 2 (2003): 205–25.

4 "The Damnation of Women": Critique of Patriarchy, Contributions to Black Feminism, and Early Intersectionality

1 Nagueyalti Warren, "His Deep and Abiding Love: W. E. B. Du Bois, Gender Politics, and Black Studies," *Phylon* 51, no. 1 (2014): 18–19, 23.

2 Joy A. James, *Transcending the Talented Tenth: Black Leaders and American Intellectuals* (New York: Routledge, 1997), 36–7.

3 Warren, "His Deep and Abiding Love," 19. See also James, *Transcending the Talented Tenth*, 36–9.

4 Susan Gillman and Alys E. Weinbaum, eds., *Next to the Color-Line: Gender, Sexuality, and W. E. B. Du Bois* (Minneapolis: University of Minnesota Press, 2007), 1–2.

5 Ibid., 2.

6 See Aldon Morris, *The Scholar Denied: W. E. B. Du Bois and the Birth of Modern Sociology* (Oakland: University of California Press, 2015); Aldon

Morris and Amin Ghaziani, "Du Boisian Sociology: A Watershed of Professional and Public Sociology," *Souls* 7, nos. 3–4 (2005): 47–54; Melissa F. Weiner, "Decolonial Sociology: W. E. B. Du Bois's Foundational Theoretical and Methodological Contributions," *Sociology Compass* 12, no. 8 (2018): https://doi.org/10.1111/soc4.12601.

7 Charles Lattimore Howard, "*Darkwater*: Lessons on Movement-Making from W. E. B. Du Bois," in Charles Lattimore Howard, *Black Theology as Mass Movement* (New York: Palgrave Macmillan, 2014), 81–92.

8 Gillman and Weinbaum, eds., *Next to the Color-Line*, 2–9.

9 W. E. B. Du Bois, "The Damnation of Women," in W. E. B. Du Bois, *Darkwater: Voices from Within the Veil* (New York: Harcourt, Brace and Howe, 1920), 163–86.

10 Ibid., 181.

11 Ibid., 163.

12 Barbara McCaskill, "Anna Julia Cooper, Pauline Elizabeth Hopkins, and the African American Feminization of Du Bois's Discourse," in *The Souls of Black Folk: One Hundred Years Later*, ed. Dolan Hubbard (Columbia: University of Missouri Press, 2003), 73.

13 W. E. B. Du Bois, "The Black Mother," *Crisis* 5, no. 2 (1912): 78.

14 W. E. B. Du Bois, "Woman Suffrage," *Crisis* 11, no. 1 (1915): 29–30.

15 Du Bois, "The Black Mother," 78.

16 Du Bois, "Woman Suffrage," 29–30.

17 Ibid., 29. See also Bettina Aptheker, "W. E. B. Du Bois and the Struggle for Women's Rights: 1910–1920," *San Jose Studies* 1, no. 2 (1975): 7–16; Garth E. Pauley, "W. E. B. Du Bois on Woman Suffrage: A Critical Analysis of His *Crisis* Writings," *Journal of Black Studies* 30, no. 3 (2000): 383–410; Valethia Watkins, "Votes for Women: Race, Gender, and W. E. B. Du Bois's Advocacy of Woman Suffrage," *Phylon* 53, no. 2 (2016): 3–19; Valethia Watkins, "Votes for Women: W. E. B. Du Bois and the Politics of Race in the Woman Suffrage Movement," *African Journal of Rhetoric* 8, no.1 (2016): 97–124; Jean Fagan Yellin, "Du Bois's *Crisis* and Woman's Suffrage," *Massachusetts Review* 14, no. 2 (1973): 365–75.

18 W. E. B. Du Bois, *The Autobiography of W. E. B. Du Bois: A Soliloquy on Viewing My Life from the Last Decade of Its First Century* (New York: International Publishers, 1968), 197.

19 Du Bois, "Woman Suffrage," 29.

20 See Rodney D. Coates, Sandra Lee Browning, and Moshay Beenah, "Race, Class, and Power: The Impact of Du Bois's Scholarship and Revolutionary Agenda," *Research in Race & Ethnic Relations* 9 (1996): 211–39; Ange-Marie Hancock, "W. E. B. Du Bois: Intellectual Forefather of Intersectionality?" *Souls* 7, nos. 3–4 (2005): 74–84; Angela J. Hattery and Earl Smith, "William Edward Burghardt Du Bois and the Concepts of Race, Class, and Gender," *Sociation Today* 3, no. 1 (2005): 1–35, www.ncsociology.org/sociationtoday/v31/smith.htm; Betsy Lucal, "Race, Class, and Gender in the Work of W. E. B. Du Bois: An Exploratory

Study," *Research in Race & Ethnic Relations* 9 (1996): 191–210; Assata Zerai, "Agents of Knowledge and Action: Selected Africana Scholars and their Contributions to the Understanding of Race, Class and Gender Intersectionality," *Cultural Dynamics* 12, no. 2 (2000): 182–222.

21 Frantz Fanon, *The Wretched of the Earth*, trans. Constance Farrington (New York: Grove, 1968), 147.

22 Ibid.

23 McCaskill, "Anna Julia Cooper, Pauline Elizabeth Hopkins, and the African American Feminization of Du Bois's Discourse," 75.

24 Ibid., 74.

25 Du Bois, "The Damnation of Women," 175–8.

26 Du Bois, "The Damnation of Women," 177; Frederick Douglass, *Autobiographies: Narrative of the Life, My Bondage and My Freedom, Life and Times* (New York: Library of America, 1994), 719; Nell Irvin Painter, *Sojourner Truth: A Life, A Symbol* (New York: Norton, 1996), 160–3.

27 W. E. B. Du Bois, "The Freedom of Womanhood," in W. E. B. Du Bois, *The Gift of Black Folk: The Negroes in the Making of America* (Boston: Stratford, 1924), 259–73.

28 Du Bois, "The Damnation of Women," 179, 186.

29 Hancock, "W. E. B. Du Bois," 76–9.

30 Du Bois, "The Damnation of Women," 186.

31 W. E. B. Du Bois, *The Philadelphia Negro: A Social Study* (Philadelphia: University of Pennsylvania Press, 1899), 83–286. See also Marcus Anthony Hunter, "W. E. B. Du Bois and Black Heterogeneity: How *The Philadelphia Negro* Shaped American Sociology," *American Sociologist* 46, no. 2 (2015): 219–33.

32 See Coates, Browning, and Beenah, "Race, Class, and Power"; Hancock, "W. E. B. Du Bois," 74–84; Hattery and Smith, "William Edward Burghardt Du Bois and the Concepts of Race, Class, and Gender," 1–35; Lucal, "Race, Class, and Gender in the Work of W. E. B. Du Bois"; Zerai, "Agents of Knowledge and Action."

33 W. E. B. Du Bois, *The Souls of Black Folk* (Chicago: A. C. McClurg & Co., 1903), 1.

34 Carole Pateman, *The Sexual Contract* (Palo Alto: Stanford University Press, 1988).

35 Audre Lorde, *Sister Outsider: Essays and Speeches by Audre Lorde* (Freedom, CA: The Crossing Press Feminist Series, 1984).

36 Ibid., 119.

37 See Gloria T. Hull, Patricia Bell-Scott, and Barbara Smith, eds., *All the Women Are White, All the Blacks Are Men, But Some of Us Are Brave: Black Women's Studies* (New York: Feminist Press, 1982); Stanlie Myrise James, Frances Smith Foster, and Beverly Guy-Sheftall, eds., *Still Brave: The Evolution of Black Women's Studies* (New York: Feminist Press, 2009); Barbara Smith, ed., *Home Girls: A Black Feminist Anthology* (New Brunswick: Rutgers University Press, 2000).

38 Cheryl Townsend Gilkes, "The Margin as the Center of a Theory of History: African American Women, Social Change, and the Sociology of W. E. B. Du Bois," in *W. E. B. Du Bois: On Race and Culture*, ed. Bernard W. Bell, Emily R. Grosholz, and James B. Stewart (New York: Routledge, 1996), 112, 117.

39 Betsy Lucal, "Race, Class, and Gender in the Work of W. E. B. Du Bois: An Exploratory Study," *Research in Race & Ethnic Relations* 9 (1996): 199.

40 Du Bois, "The Damnation of Women," 164–6, 169, 171. See also Lawrie Balfour, "Representative Women: Slavery, Citizenship, and Feminist Theory in Du Bois's 'Damnation of Women,'" *Hypatia* 20, no. 3 (2005): 127–48.

41 Frances M. Beal, "Double Jeopardy: To Be Black and Female," in *Sisterhood is Powerful: An Anthology of Writings from the Women's Liberation Movement*, ed. Robin Morgan (New York: Random House, 1970), 340–53; Deborah K. King, "Multiple Jeopardy, Multiple Consciousness: The Context of a Black Feminist Ideology," *Signs: Journal of Women in Culture and Society* 14, no. 1 (1988): 42–72; Third World Women's Alliance, eds., *Triple Jeopardy: Racism, Imperialism, Sexism* (New York: Third World Women's Alliance, 1971).

42 It is important to bring a couple of episodes in Du Bois's private life – or, rather, his "private affairs" – to the readers' attention. Widely considered Du Bois's "definitive" biographer, two-time Pulitzer Prize-winning historian David Levering Lewis controversially gets into the thick of things with regard to Du Bois's public male feminism and private male-chauvinism (including his "womanizing," haphazard husbandhood, and faltering fatherhood) in *W. E. B. Du Bois: Biography of a Race, 1868–1919* (New York: Henry Holt, 1993), see especially 449–65. "The episodic dalliances, the star-crossed love affair with [Jessie] Fauset, the comfortable arrangements with Georgia Johnson and Mildred Jones began to be replicated with a seeming insatiety that yielded nothing to advancing years, and may, perhaps, have been a spectacular version of the generalized male late-life crisis," announced Lewis, righteously returning to this sordid subject in the massive second volume of his Du Bois biography, *W. E. B. Du Bois: The Fight for Equality and the American Century, 1919–1963* (New York: Henry Holt, 2000), 267. If his hinting at Du Bois's adulterous behavior in the first volume shocked and awed his readers, in the second volume Lewis was surely hoping to create a *cause célèbre* by painstakingly documenting and detailing Du Bois's extramarital affairs with: novelist and poet Jessie Fauset (49–50, 188–90); schoolteacher Mildred Bryant Jones (128, 267); poet Georgia Douglas Johnson (183–5); dramatist Anne Cooke (186); his secretary Marvel Jackson Cooke (186–7); *Opportunity* secretary Ethel Ray (189, 268); sculptor Elizabeth Prophet (268–9); the infamous "other Mrs. Du Bois," white high-schoolteacher Rachel Davis Du Bois (189, 270–2); New York City white socialite Nora Waring

(272); widow Louie Shivery (382–4); Atlanta University graduate student and, later, Du Bois's research assistant Ellen Irene Diggs (305, 383–4); and, perhaps most famously, the woman to whom he dedicated *Black Reconstruction*, physician Virginia Alexander (267–74).

43 For further discussion of intersectionality – or, rather, intersectionalism – see Anna Carastathis, *Intersectionality: Origins, Contestations, Horizons* (Lincoln: University of Nebraska Press, 2016); Rodney D. Coates, Abby L. Ferber, and David L. Brunsma, *The Matrix of Race: Social Construction, Intersectionality, and Inequality* (Los Angeles: Sage, 2018); Patricia Hill Collins and Sirma Bilge, *Intersectionality* (Cambridge: Polity, 2016); Kimberlé Crenshaw, *On Intersectionality: Essential Writings* (New York: New Press, 2019); Patrick R. Grzanka, ed., *Intersectionality: A Foundations and Frontiers Reader* (New York: Routledge, 2019); Ange-Marie Hancock, *Intersectionality: An Intellectual History* (Oxford University Press, 2016); Helma Lutz, Maria Teresa Herrera Vivar, and Linda Supik, eds., *Framing Intersectionality: Debates on a Multi-Faceted Concept in Gender Studies* (London: Routledge, 2016); Nina Lykke, *Feminist Studies: A Guide to Intersectional Theory, Methodology, and Writing* (London: Routledge, 2010); Vivian M. May, *Pursuing Intersectionality, Unsettling Dominant Imaginaries* (New York: Routledge, 2015); Jennifer C. Nash, *Black Feminism Reimagined: After Intersectionality* (Durham: Duke University Press, 2019); Mary Romero, *Introducing Intersectionality* (Cambridge: Polity, 2018); Yvette Taylor, Sally Hines, and Mark E. Casey, eds., *Theorizing Intersectionality and Sexuality* (London: Palgrave MacMillan, 2011); Barbara M. Tomlinson, *Undermining Intersectionality: The Perils of Powerblind Feminism* (Philadelphia: Temple University Press, 2019); Riki Wilchins, *Gender Norms and Intersectionality: Connecting Race, Class, and Gender* (London: Rowman & Littlefield International, 2019).

44 Warren, "His Deep and Abiding Love," 24.

45 Amy Helene Kirschke, "Du Bois and *The Crisis* Magazine: Imaging Women and Family," *Source: Notes in the History of Art* 24, no. 4 (2005): 42.

46 Ibid., 40. See also W. E. B. Du Bois, "Black Folk and Birth Control," *Birth Control Review* 16, no. 6 (1932): 166–7.

47 Patricia Hill Collins, *Intersectionality as Critical Social Theory* (Durham: Duke University Press, 2019), 1–20.

48 Celena Simpson, "Du Bois's Dubious Feminism: Evaluating through *The Black Flame* Trilogy," *The Pluralist* 10, no. 1 (2015): 48–63.

49 For more on black male feminism in the late twentieth and early twenty-first centuries, see Samuel Adu-Poku, "Envisioning (Black) Male Feminism: A Cross-Cultural Perspective," *Journal of Gender Studies* 10, no. 2 (2001): 157–67; Michael Awkward, "A Black Man's Place in Black Feminist Criticism," in Michael Awkward, *Negotiating Difference: Race, Gender, and the Politics of Positionality* (University of Chicago

Press, 1995), 43–57; David Ikard, *Breaking the Silence: Toward a Black Male Feminist Criticism* (Baton Rouge: Louisiana State University Press, 2007); Gary L. Lemons, "To Be Black, Male and 'Feminist': Making Womanist Space for Black Men," *International Journal of Sociology and Social Policy* 17, nos. 1/2 (1997): 35–61; Gary L. Lemons, "'When and Where [We] Enter': In Search of a Feminist Forefather – Reclaiming the Womanist Legacy of W. E. B. Du Bois," in *Traps: African American Men on Gender and Sexuality*, ed. Rudolph P. Byrd and Beverly Guy-Sheftall (Indianapolis: Indiana University Press, 2001), 71–89; Gary L. Lemons, *Womanist Forefathers: Frederick Douglass and W. E. B. Du Bois* (Albany: State University of New York Press, 2009).

50 Du Bois, "The Damnation of Women," 185. See also W. E. B. Du Bois, "The Work of Negro Women in Society" *Spelman Messenger* 18 (1902): 1–3; Du Bois, "The Black Mother"; W. E. B. Du Bois, "Hail Columbia!" *Crisis* 5, no. 6 (1931): 289–90; Du Bois, "Woman Suffrage"; Du Bois, "The Freedom of Womanhood"; W. E. B. Du Bois, "Sex and Racism," *The Independent* (March 1957): 6–7.

51 Joy A. James and Tracy Denean Sharpley-Whiting, eds., *The Black Feminist Reader* (Malden: Blackwell, 2000), 1. See also Gilkes, "The Margin as the Center of a Theory of History," 114, 116–17.

52 For further discussion of Du Bois's conception of democracy, see Lawrie Balfour, "*Darkwater*'s Democratic Vision," *Political Theory* 38, no. 4 (2010): 537–63; Lawrie Balfour, *Democracy's Reconstruction: Thinking Politically with W. E. B. Du Bois* (Oxford University Press, 2011); Nick Bromell, "W. E. B. Du Bois and the Enlargement of Democratic Theory," *Raritan* 30, no. 4 (2011): 140–51; Kazuhisa Honda, "W. E. B. Du Bois and the Paradox of American Democracy: A Battle for World Peace," *Journal of Applied Sociology* 58 (2016): 93–104; Terrence L. Johnson, *Tragic Soul-Life: W. E. B. Du Bois and the Moral Crisis Facing American Democracy* (Oxford University Press, 2012); Manning Marable, *W. E. B. Du Bois: Black Radical Democrat* (Boston: Twayne, 1986); R. David Sumpter, "W. E. B. Du Bois: Reflections on Democracy," *Journal of Thought* 36, no. 2 (2001): 25–31.

53 Warren, "His Deep and Abiding Love," 20. See also Balfour, "*Darkwater*'s Democratic Vision"; Balfour, *Democracy's Reconstruction*, 97–114.

54 W. E. B. Du Bois, "Of the Ruling of Men," in W. E. B. Du Bois, *Darkwater: Voices from Within the Veil* (New York: Harcourt, Brace and Howe, 1920), 153–4. See also Harriet Fertik, "Hell to Pay: Aristotle and W. E. B. Du Bois's Vision of Democracy in 'Of the Ruling of Men,'" *International Journal of the Classical Tradition* 26, no. 1 (2019): 72–85.

55 Du Bois, "The Damnation of Women," 179.

56 Gilkes, "The Margin as the Center of a Theory of History," 113.

57 Ibid., 133.

58 Ibid., 114.

59 Ibid., 117.

60 bell hooks, *Black Looks: Race and Representation* (Boston: South End, 1991), 87–114; bell hooks, *We Real Cool: Black Men and Masculinity* (London: Routledge, 2004); bell hooks, *The Will to Change: Men, Masculinity, and Love* (New York: Washington Square Press, 2005).

61 Anthony Giddens, *Capitalism and Modern Social Theory: An Analysis of the Writings of Marx, Durkheim, and Max Weber* (Cambridge University Press, 1971), vii.

62 Gilkes, "The Margin as the Center of a Theory of History," 113.

63 For more detailed discussion of Du Bois's critique of capitalism and its interconnections with racism and sexism, see the next chapter, "*Black Reconstruction*: Critique of Capitalism, Contributions to Black Marxism, and Discourse on Democratic Socialism."

64 Du Bois, "The Damnation of Women," 181, emphasis added.

65 Ibid.

66 See Hancock, "W. E. B. Du Bois," 74–84; Coates, Browning, and Beenah, "Race, Class, and Power," 211–39; Lucal, "Race, Class, and Gender in the Work of W. E. B. Du Bois," 191–210; Zerai, "Agents of Knowledge and Action," 182–222.

67 Hattery and Smith, "William Edward Burghardt Du Bois and the Concepts of Race, Class, and Gender," 3, emphasis in original.

68 Patricia Hill Collins, "Du Bois's Contested Legacy," *Ethnic and Racial Studies* 39, no. 8 (2016): 1398–406.

69 See Manning Marable, "Reconstructing the Radical Du Bois," *Souls* 7, nos. 3–4 (2005): 1–25.

70 Dan S. Green and Edwin D. Driver, "W. E. B. Du Bois: A Case in the Sociology of Sociological Negation," *Phylon* 37, no. 4 (1976): 308–33.

71 Hattery and Smith, "William Edward Burghardt Du Bois and the Concepts of Race, Class, and Gender," 6.

72 King, "Multiple Jeopardy, Multiple Consciousness," 42–72.

73 Gilkes, "The Margin as the Center of a Theory of History," 132.

74 Ibid., 134.

75 Du Bois, *Darkwater*; W. E. B. Du Bois, *The Gift of Black Folk: The Negroes in the Making of America* (Boston: Stratford, 1924); W. E. B. Du Bois, *Dark Princess: A Romance* (New York: Harcourt, Brace & Co., 1928); W. E. B. Du Bois, *Black Reconstruction in America, 1860–1880* (New York: Harcourt, Brace & Co., 1935); W. E. B. Du Bois, *Black Folk: Then and Now – An Essay in the History and Sociology of the Negro Race* (New York: Henry Holt, 1939); W. E. B. Du Bois, *Color and Democracy: Colonies and Peace* (New York: Harcourt, Brace & Co., 1945); W. E. B. Du Bois, *The World and Africa* (New York: Viking Press, 1947).

76 Gilkes, "The Margin as the Center of a Theory of History," 120.

77 Balfour, "Representative Women."

78 See Patricia Hill Collins, *Fighting Words: Black Women and the Search for Social Justice* (Minneapolis: University of Minnesota Press, 1998), 95–123; Patricia Hill Collins, *Black Feminist Thought: Knowledge,*

Consciousness, and the Politics of Empowerment, Second Edition (New York: Routledge, 2000), 51–90.

79 Du Bois, "Woman Suffrage," 29.
80 Du Bois, "The Damnation of Women," 185.
81 See Du Bois, *The Gift of Black Folk*, 273.
82 Gilkes, "The Margin as the Center of a Theory of History," 115.
83 Du Bois, *Black Reconstruction*, 16.
84 Du Bois, "The Freedom of Womanhood," 261.
85 Ibid., 259–62.
86 Alexandra J. Finley, *An Intimate Economy: Enslaved Women, Work, and America's Domestic Slave Trade* (Chapel Hill: University of North Carolina Press, 2020); Daina Ramey Berry and Leslie M. Harris, eds., *Sexuality and Slavery: Reclaiming Intimate Histories in the Americas* (Athens: University of Georgia Press, 2018).
87 Bettye Collier-Thomas and V. P. Franklin, eds., *Sisters in the Struggle: African American Women in the Civil Rights / Black Power Movement* (New York University Press, 2001); Vicki L. Crawford, Jacqueline Anne Rouse, and Barbara Woods, eds., *Women in the Civil Rights Movement: Trailblazers and Torchbearers, 1941–1965* (Bloomington: Indiana University Press, 1990); Dayo F. Gore, Jeanne Theoharis, and Komozi Woodard, eds., *Want to Start a Revolution? Radical Women in the Black Freedom Struggle* (New York University Press, 2009); Davis W. Houck and David E. Dixon, eds., *Women and the Civil Rights Movement, 1954–1965* (Jackson: University Press of Mississippi, 2009).
88 Manning Marable, "Grounding with My Sisters: Patriarchy and the Exploitation of Black Women," in Manning Marable, *How Capitalism Underdeveloped Black America* (Boston: South End, 1983), 70, emphasis in original.
89 Du Bois, "The Damnation of Women," 179–80.

5 *Black Reconstruction*: Critique of Capitalism, Contributions to Black Marxism, and Discourse on Democratic Socialism

1 W. E. B. Du Bois, "Interview with Dr. W. E. B. Du Bois," in *The Seventh Son: The Thought and Writings of W. E. B. Du Bois, Volume 2*, ed. Julius Lester (New York: Vintage Books, 1971), 701.
2 Ibid., 702.
3 W. E. B. Du Bois, *Black Reconstruction in America, 1860–1880* (New York: Harcourt, Brace & Co., 1935).
4 Bill V. Mullen, *W. E. B. Du Bois: Revolutionary across the Color-Line* (London: Pluto Press, 2016), 38–53, 89–104; Eric Porter, *The Problem of the Future World: W. E. B. Du Bois and the Race Concept at Midcentury* (Durham: Duke University Press, 2010), 103–44.

5 David Levering Lewis, *W. E. B. Du Bois: Biography of a Race, 1868–1919* (New York: Henry Holt, 1993), 419–21.

6 Adolph L. Reed, *W. E. B. Du Bois and American Political Thought: Fabianism and the Color-Line* (New York: Oxford University Press, 1997), 83.

7 Francis L. Broderick, *W. E. B. Du Bois: Negro Leader in a Time of Crisis* (Palo Alto: Stanford University Press, 1959), 124.

8 Ibid., 123–4. See also W. E. B. Du Bois, "Race Relations in the United States," *Annals of the American Academy of Political and Social Science* 140, no. 1 (1928): 6–10.

9 Bill V. Mullen, *Un-American: W. E. B. Du Bois and the Century of World Revolution* (Philadelphia: Temple University Press, 2015), 19–95.

10 W. E. B. Du Bois, "A Memorial to the Legislature of Georgia on Negro Common Schools," in W. E. B. Du Bois, *Pamphlets and Leaflets*, ed. Herbert Aptheker (New York: Kraus-Thomson, 1986), 25.

11 Porter, *The Problem of the Future World*, 21–62.

12 See Kevin K. Gaines, *Uplifting the Race: Black Leadership, Politics, and Culture in the Twentieth Century* (Chapel Hill: University of North Carolina Press, 1996), 152–78; Brian Johnson, ed., *Du Bois on Reform: Periodical-based Leadership for African Americans* (Lanham, MD: Rowman & Littlefield, 2005); Raymond Wolters, *Du Bois and His Rivals* (Columbia: University of Missouri Press, 2002), 40–76.

13 Lewis, *W. E. B. Du Bois: Biography of a Race*, 143–4.

14 W. E. B. Du Bois, "The Class Struggle," *Crisis* 22, no. 4 (1921): 151.

15 A. Philip Randolph and Chandler Owen, "Du Bois Fails as a Theorist," in *Black Protest Thought in the Twentieth Century*, ed. August Meier, Elliott Rudwick, and Francis L. Broderick (New York: MacMillan, 1971), 95, 93. On *The Messenger*, see Sondra K. Wilson, ed., *The Messenger Reader: Stories, Poetry, and Essays from* The Messenger *Magazine* (New York: Modern Library, 2000).

16 For further discussion of the "New Negro" and the New Negro Movement, see Ann Elizabeth Carroll, *Word, Image, and the New Negro: Representation and Identity in the Harlem Renaissance* (Bloomington: Indiana University Press, 2005); Erin D. Chapman, *Prove It On Me: New Negroes, Sex, and Popular Culture in the 1920s* (New York: Oxford University Press, 2011); Martin J. Favor, *Authentic Blackness: The Folk in the New Negro Movement* (Durham: Duke University Press, 1999); Barbara Foley, *Spectres of 1919: Class and Nation in the Making of the New Negro* (Urbana: University of Illinois Press, 2003); Henry Louis Gates and Gene Andrew Jarrett, eds., *The New Negro: Readings in Race, Representation, and African American Culture, 1892–1938* (Princeton University Press, 2007); Caroline Goeser, *Picturing the New Negro: Harlem Renaissance Print Culture and Modern Black Identity* (Lawrence: University Press of Kansas, 2007); Daphne M. Lamothe, *Inventing the New Negro: Narrative, Culture,*

and Ethnography (Philadelphia: University of Pennsylvania Press, 2008); Alain L. Locke, ed., *The New Negro* (New York: Boni, 1925); William J. Maxwell, *New Negro, Old Left: African American Writing and Communism Between the Wars* (New York: Columbia University Press, 1999); Martha Jane Nadell, *Enter the New Negroes: Images of Race in American Culture* (Cambridge, MA: Harvard University Press, 2004); Anna Pochmara, *The Making of the New Negro: Black Authorship, Masculinity, and Sexuality in the Harlem Renaissance* (Amsterdam University Press, 2011); James Edward Smethurst, *The New Red Negro: The Literary Left and African American Poetry, 1930–1946* (New York: Oxford University Press, 1999).

17 A. Philip Randolph and Chandler Owen, "Du Bois on Revolution: A Reply," in *Voices of a Black Nation: Political Journalism in the Harlem Renaissance*, ed. Theodore G. Vincent (Trenton, NJ: Africa World Press, 1973), 88–92.

18 Randolph and Owen, "Du Bois Fails as a Theorist," 94.

19 Manning Marable, *W. E. B. Du Bois: Black Radical Democrat* (Boston: Twayne, 1986), 109.

20 Ibid., 110. It is interesting to observe that Owen's resignation from the Socialist Party mirrored Du Bois's short-lived stay in the party. According to Marable, "Du Bois became a member of the Socialist party in 1911," but his "commitment to the Socialist party lasted only one year." Du Bois "was fully aware that some of his [white socialist] comrades 'openly excluded Negroes and Asiatics' from their definition of socialism." As a consequence, in November of 1912, "he left the party." Marable quickly quipped, "Du Bois may have resigned from the Socialist party, but he remained a Socialist": Marable, *W. E. B. Du Bois*, 90. See also W. E. B. Du Bois, *Darkwater: Voices from Within the Veil* (New York: Harcourt, Brace and Howe, 1920), 138.

21 Marable, *W. E. B. Du Bois*, 110.

22 On Randolph, see Jervis Anderson, *A. Philip Randolph: A Biographical Portrait* (New York: Harcourt Brace Jovanovich, 1973); Cornelius L. Bynum, *A. Philip Randolph and the Struggle for Civil Rights* (Urbana: University of Illinois Press, 2011); Andrew Edmund Kersten, *A. Philip Randolph: A Life in the Vanguard* (Lanham, MD: Rowman & Littlefield, 2007); Andrew Edmund Kersten and Clarence Lang, eds., *Reframing Randolph: Labor, Black Freedom, and the Legacies of A. Philip Randolph* (New York University Press, 2016); A. Philip Randolph, *For Jobs and Freedom: Selected Speeches and Writings of A. Philip Randolph*, ed. Andrew Edmund Kersten and David Lucander (Amherst: University of Massachusetts Press, 2014). On Rustin, see Jervis Anderson, *Bayard Rustin: Troubles I've Seen* (Berkeley: University of California Press, 1998); John D'Emilio, *Lost Prophet: The Life and Times of Bayard Rustin* (University of Chicago Press, 2004); Bayard Rustin, *Time on Two*

Crosses: The Collected Writings of Bayard Rustin, ed. Devon W. Carbado and Donald Weise (New York: Cleis Press, 2015).

23 Paula F. Pfeffer, *A. Philip Randolph, Pioneer of the Civil Rights Movement* (Baton Rouge: Louisiana State University Press, 1990), 256.

24 Marable, *W. E. B. Du Bois*, 90.

25 Wilson Jeremiah Moses, *The Golden Age of Black Nationalism, 1850–1925* (New York: Oxford University Press, 1978), 139.

26 Marable, *W. E. B. Du Bois*, 109, 112; Moses, *Golden Age*, 140; Reed, *W. E. B. Du Bois and American Political Thought*, 83–89.

27 Zhang Juguo, *W. E. B. Du Bois: Quest for the Abolition of the Color-Line* (New York: Routledge, 2001), 137. See also, Mullen, *W. E. B. Du Bois*, 57–72.

28 W. E. B. Du Bois, "Application for Membership in the Communist Party of the United States of America," in *W. E. B. Du Bois: A Reader*, ed. David Levering Lewis (New York: Henry Holt, 1995), 632.

29 For further discussion of Du Bois's inauguration of an anti-racist Marxist critique of capitalism, see Gerald Horne, *Black and Red: W. E. B. Du Bois and the Afro-American Response to the Cold War, 1944–1963* (Albany: State University of New York Press, 1986).

30 For further discussion of a "racial polity," see Charles W. Mills, *Blackness Visible: Essays on Philosophy and Race* (Ithaca: Cornell University Press, 1998), and Charles W. Mills, "The Racial Polity," in Susan E. Babbitt and Sue Campbell, eds., *Racism and Philosophy* (Ithaca: Cornell University Press, 1999), 13–31.

31 Dan S. Green and Earl Smith, "W. E. B. Du Bois and the Concepts of Race and Class," *Phylon* 44, no. 4 (1983): 262–72; Mullen, *W. E. B. Du Bois*, 73–88; Joe William Trotter, "W. E. B. Du Bois: Ambiguous Journey to the Black Working-Class," in *Reading Southern History: Essays on Interpreters and Interpretations*, ed. Glenn Feldman (Tuscaloosa: University of Alabama Press, 2001), 61–75.

32 Du Bois, *Black Reconstruction*, 15.

33 Ibid., 3.

34 Karl Marx, "Marx to Pavel Vasilyevich Annenkov, December 28, 1846," in *Marx & Engels Collected Works, Volume 38: Letters 1844–1851* (London: Lawrence & Wishart, 2010), 101–2.

35 Cedric Robinson, *Black Marxism: The Making of the Black Radical Tradition* (Chapel Hill: University of North Carolina Press, 2000).

36 Du Bois, *Black Reconstruction*, 5.

37 Patrick Anderson, "Pan-Africanism and Economic Nationalism: W. E. B. Du Bois's *Black Reconstruction* and the Failings of the 'Black Marxism' Thesis," *Journal of Black Studies* 48, no. 8 (2017): 732–57; David Levering Lewis, *W. E. B. Du Bois: The Fight for Equality and the American Century, 1919–1963* (New York: Henry Holt, 2000), 302–87; Marable, *W. E. B. Du Bois*, 99–120; Reed, *W. E. B. Du Bois and American Political Thought*, 71–89; Robinson, *Black Marxism*, 212–40.

38 Du Bois, *Black Reconstruction*, 67.
39 Guy Emerson Mount, "When Slaves Go On Strike: W. E. B. Du Bois's *Black Reconstruction* 80 Years Later," *Black Perspectives*, December 28, 2015, www.aaihs.org/when-slaves-go-on-strike.
40 Du Bois, *Black Reconstruction*, 358.
41 Robinson, *Black Marxism*, 236. See also Du Bois, *Black Reconstruction*, 708.
42 Robinson, *Black Marxism*, 235–6.
43 Eric Foner, *Reconstruction: America's Unfinished Revolution, 1863–1877* (New York: Harper Perennial, 2002), 512–63.
44 Du Bois, *Black Reconstruction*, 708.
45 Ibid., 15–16.
46 Karl Marx, *Capital, Volume I: A Critique of Political Economy* (New York: Penguin, 1992), 873–6.
47 Du Bois, *Black Reconstruction*, 16. Du Bois's mention of "Surplus Value" is a reference to Karl Marx, *Theories of Surplus Value, Part 1* (London: Lawrence & Wishart, 1969); Karl Marx, *Theories of Surplus Value, Part 2* (London: Lawrence & Wishart, 1969); Karl Marx, *Theories of Surplus Value, Part 3* (London: Lawrence & Wishart, 1969).
48 Marx, *Capital*, 414.
49 David R. Roediger, *The Wages of Whiteness: Race and the Making of the American Working-Class* (London: Verso, 1991).
50 Du Bois, *Black Reconstruction*, 700–1.
51 Ibid., 300.
52 Ibid., 12.
53 Karl Marx and Frederick Engels, *The Civil War in the United States, Second Edition*, ed. Andrew Zimmerman (New York: International Publishers, 2017).
54 Hal Draper, *Socialism from Below* (Chicago: Haymarket Books, 2019).
55 Karl Marx and Frederick Engels, *The German Ideology: Critique of Modern German Philosophy*, in *Marx & Engels Collected Works, Volume 5: 1845–1847* (London: Lawrence & Wishart, 2010), 819.
56 Mount, "When Slaves Go On Strike," 3.
57 Ibid.
58 Du Bois, *Black Reconstruction*, 708.
59 Oscar Berland, "The Emergence of the Communist Perspective on the 'Negro Question' in America, 1919–1931, Part One," *Science & Society* 63, no. 4 (1999): 411–32; Oscar Berland, "The Emergence of the Communist Perspective on the 'Negro Question' in America, 1919–1931, Part Two," *Science & Society* 64, no. 2 (2000): 194–217; Susan Campbell, "'Black Bolsheviks' and Recognition of African America's Right to Self-Determination by the Communist Party USA," *Science & Society* 58, no. 4 (1994): 440–70; Harvey Klehr and William Tompson, "Self-Determination in the Black Belt: Origins of a Communist Policy," *Labor History* 30, no. 3 (1989): 354–66; Beverly Tomek, "The

Communist International and the Dilemma of the American 'Negro Problem': Limitations of the Black Belt Self-Determination Thesis," *WorkingUSA* 15, no. 4 (2012): 549–76.

60 Denise Lynn, "The Marxist Proposition, Claudia Jones, and Black Nationalism," *Black Perspectives*, November 1, 2017, www.aaihs.org/the-marxist-proposition-claudia-jones-and-black-nationalism.

61 Ibid.

62 On Du Bois's "Talented Tenth" theory, see W. E. B. Du Bois, "The Talented Tenth," in *The Negro Problem: A Series of Articles by Representative American Negroes of Today*, ed. Booker T. Washington (New York: J. Pott & Company, 1903), 33–75. On Du Bois's Marxist-influenced radicalization of his "Talented Tenth" thesis, see W. E. B. Du Bois, "The Talented Tenth Memorial Address," *The Boulé Journal* 15, no. 1 (1948): 3–13.

63 W. E. B. Du Bois, *W. E. B. Du Bois on Africa*, ed. Eugene F. Provenzo and Edmund Abaka (Walnut Creek, CA: Left Coast Press, 2012); W. E. B. Du Bois, *W. E. B. Du Bois on Asia: Crossing the World Color-Line*, ed. Bill V. Mullen and Cathryn Watson (Jackson: University Press of Mississippi, 2005).

64 W. E. B. Du Bois, "Colonialism, Democracy, and Peace after the War," in W. E. B. Du Bois, *Against Racism: Unpublished Essays, Papers, Addresses, 1887–1961*, ed. Herbert Aptheker (Amherst: University of Massachusetts Press, 1985), 232–3. In "India, the 'Indian Ideology,' and the World Revolution," Bill Mullen asserted that "Even more than in his support for the Russian Revolution, Du Bois's dedication to India's twentieth-century struggle for independence bespeaks the widest field of his ideational attachment to the World Revolution concept." See Mullen, *Un-American*, 96. Mullen argued that, as indicated in Du Bois's quotation above, India's colonial history and the Indian Revolution played a pivotal role in Du Bois's conception of revolution. Indeed, Mullen's work in *Un-American* deftly demonstrates that, by his later years, Du Bois was a student of "World Revolution," not merely revolutionary struggles in Europe and North America. For further discussion, see Mullen's "The East is Red: Supporting Revolutions in Asia," in Mullen, *W. E. B. Du Bois*, 123–35; Kate A. Baldwin, *Beyond the Color-Line and the Iron Curtain: Reading Encounters between Black and Red, 1922–1963* (Durham: Duke University Press, 2002), 149–201; Du Bois, *W. E. B. Du Bois on Asia*; Robeson Taj Frazier, *The East Is Black: Cold War China in the Black Radical Imagination* (Durham: Duke University Press, 2014), 1–107; Bill V. Mullen, *Afro-Orientalism* (Minneapolis: University of Minnesota Press, 2004), 1–41; Nikhil Pal Singh, *Black Is a Country: Race and the Unfinished Struggle for Democracy* (Cambridge, MA: Harvard University Press, 2005); Nico Slate, *Colored Cosmopolitanism: The Shared Struggle for Freedom in the*

United States and India (Cambridge, MA: Harvard University Press, 2012).

65 Karl Marx and Friedrich Engels, *The Marx–Engels Reader, 2nd Edition*, ed. Robert C. Tucker (New York: Norton, 1978), 489.

66 Robinson, *Black Marxism*, 9–28.

67 Marx and Engels, *The Marx–Engels Reader*, 489.

68 Ibid., 476–7.

69 Cornel West, *Keeping Faith: Philosophy and Race in America* (New York: Routledge, 1993), 258, 267.

70 See Rosemary Cowan, *Cornel West: The Politics of Redemption* (Cambridge: Polity, 2003), 79–101; Floyd Hayes, "Cornel West and Afro-Nihilism: A Reconsideration," in *Cornel West: A Critical Reader*, ed. George Yancy (Malden: Blackwell, 2002), 245–60; Clarence Sholé Johnson, *Cornel West and Philosophy: The Quest for Social Justice* (New York: Routledge, 2003), 61–92, 121–46; John P. Pittman, "'Radical Historicism,' Antiphilosophy, and Marxism," in *Cornel West: A Critical Reader*, ed. George Yancy (Malden: Blackwell, 2002), 224–44; Mark David Wood, *Cornel West and the Politics of Prophetic Pragmatism* (Urbana: University of Illinois Press, 2000), 41–86.

71 Cornel West, "Black Strivings in a Twilight Civilization," in Henry Louis Gates and Cornel West, *The Future of the Race* (New York: Alfred A. Knopf, 1996), 55, emphasis added.

72 Cornel West, "W. E. B. Du Bois: The Jamesian Organic Intellectual," in *The American Evasion of Philosophy: A Genealogy of Pragmatism* (Madison: University of Wisconsin Press, 1989), 145–50.

73 Horne, *Black and Red*.

74 W. E. B. Du Bois, "The Negro and Radical Thought," *Crisis* 22, no. 3 (1921): 104.

75 Robinson, *Black Marxism*, 196.

76 Ibid., 228.

77 Moses, *Golden Age*, 140.

78 W. E. B. Du Bois, "Negro and Socialism," in W. E. B. Du Bois, *Selections from The Horizon*, ed. Herbert Aptheker (White Plains, NY: Kraus-Thomson, 1985), 6.

79 In "The Socialist Analysis of W. E. B. Du Bois" (Ph.D. dissertation, State University of New York at Buffalo, 1985), William Wright declared, "Simply put, Du Bois, in many ways, just went beyond the thinking of his socialist contemporaries, not only in America, but also in Europe, that simply made it difficult for them to follow much of his socialistic thinking or to appreciate it." For instance, Wright continued, "Du Bois was virtually the only American socialist in his day, and one of the few in the Western world, who took a strong analytical interest in the impact that Western expansion, in the form of racism, capitalism, colonialism, and imperialism had on the histories and lives of people in non-Western areas of the world" (ix–x). See,

also, W. E. B. Du Bois, *Color and Democracy: Colonies and Peace* (New York: Harcourt, Brace & Co., 1945); and W. E. B. Du Bois, "The World Problem of the Color-Line" (35–6), "The Negro and Imperialism" (37–47), and "The American Negro and the Darker World" (48–55), in W. E. B. Du Bois, *W. E. B. Du Bois on Asia: Crossing the World Color-Line*, ed. Bill V. Mullen and Cathryn Watson (Jackson: University Press of Mississippi, 2005).

80 W. E. B. Du Bois, *In Battle for Peace: The Story of My 83rd Birthday* (New York: Masses & Mainstream, 1952); Horne, *Black and Red*; Marable, *W. E. B. Du Bois*, 99–189; Mullen, *Un-American*, 56–95; Mullen, *W. E. B. Du Bois*, 57–104; Robinson, *Black Marxism*, 185–240; Wright, "The Socialist Analysis of W. E. B. Du Bois," 280–466.

81 W. E. B. Du Bois, "The Salvation of the American Negro Lies in Socialism," in *Let Nobody Turn Us Around: Voices of Resistance, Reform, and Renewal, An African American Anthology*, ed. Manning Marable and Leith Mullings (Lanham, MD: Rowman and Littlefield, 2000), 410. Originally published as W. E. B. Du Bois, "The Negro and Socialism," in *Toward a Socialist America: A Symposium of Essays*, ed. Helen L. Alfred (New York: Peace Publications, 1958), 179–91.

82 Du Bois, "The Salvation of the American Negro Lies in Socialism," 410.

83 Ibid.

84 Du Bois, "Colonialism, Democracy, and Peace after the War," 230.

85 W. E. B. Du Bois, "On Being Ashamed of Oneself: An Essay on Race Pride," *Crisis* 40 no. 9 (1933): 200.

86 W. E. B. Du Bois, "The Negro and Communism," *Crisis* 38, no. 9 (1931): 313–15, 318–20; W. E. B. Du Bois, "Karl Marx and the Negro," *Crisis* 40, no. 2 (1933): 55–6; W. E. B. Du Bois, "Marxism and the Negro Problem," *Crisis* 40, no. 5 (1933): 103–4, 118; W. E. B. Du Bois, "Our Class Struggle," *Crisis* 40, no. 7 (1933): 164–5; W. E. B. Du Bois, "Negroes and the Crisis of Capitalism in the United States," *Monthly Review* 4 (April 1953): 478–85.

87 Du Bois, "The Salvation of the American Negro Lies in Socialism," 414.

88 W. E. B. Du Bois, "My Evolving Program for Negro Freedom," in *What the Negro Wants*, ed. Rayford W. Logan (Chapel Hill: University of North Carolina Press, 1944), 65, all emphasis in original.

89 W. E. B. Du Bois, "Socialism and the American Negro," in Du Bois, *Against Racism*, 304.

90 W. E. B. Du Bois, "A Social Program for Black and White Americans," in Du Bois, *Against Racism*, 218.

91 Ibid.; W. E. B. Du Bois, "The Future of Europe in Africa," in Du Bois, *Against Racism*, 184.

92 Du Bois, "Colonialism, Democracy, and Peace after the War," 237.

93 Du Bois, "A Social Program for Black and White Americans," 215.

94 Du Bois, "Colonialism, Democracy, and Peace after the War," 231. See also Du Bois, *Color and Democracy*, 73–99.

95 Du Bois, "Colonialism, Democracy, and Peace after the War," 242–3.

96 Du Bois, "The Future of Europe in Africa," 184.

97 Du Bois, "Colonialism, Democracy, and Peace after the War," 230.

98 Du Bois, "The Salvation of the American Negro Lies in Socialism," 417; Du Bois, "My Evolving Program for Negro Freedom," 616; Du Bois, "A Social Program for Black and White Americans," 216.

99 Du Bois, "The Future of Europe in Africa," 196. See also Du Bois, *Darkwater*; Du Bois, *Color and Democracy*; Du Bois, *W. E. B. Du Bois on Asia*.

100 Du Bois, "Socialism and the American Negro," 303; Du Bois, "A Social Program for Black and White Americans," 218.

101 Du Bois, "My Evolving Program for Negro Freedom," 69.

102 Ibid.

103 Ibid., 69–70.

104 Moses, *Golden Age*, 138. See Du Bois, "The Talented Tenth." See also Du Bois, "The Talented Tenth Memorial Address."

105 Du Bois, *Darkwater*; Du Bois, *Color and Democracy*; W. E. B. Du Bois, *Africa in Battle against Colonialism, Racism, and Imperialism* (Chicago: Afro-American Heritage Association, 1960).

106 W. E. B. Du Bois, "The Future of Africa in America," in Du Bois, *Against Racism*, 183, 181; Du Bois, "A Social Program for Black and White Americans," 206.

107 Frantz Fanon, *The Wretched of the Earth*, trans. Constance Farrington (New York: Grove, 1968), 36.

108 W. E. B. Du Bois, "Socialism and Democracy," *American Socialist* 4, no. 1 (1957): 6–9.

109 Du Bois, "My Evolving Program for Negro Freedom," 68.

110 Ibid., 70.

111 Fanon, *The Wretched of the Earth*, 315.

112 Du Bois, "My Evolving Program for Negro Freedom," 70. See also Du Bois, "The Negro and Imperialism," 37–47; W. E. B. Du Bois, "We Fight for a Free World ... This or Nothing!" *Chicago Defender*, September 26, 1942, 4; W. E. B. Du Bois, "Prospect of a World Without Race Conflict," *American Journal of Sociology* 49, no. 5 (1944): 450–6.

113 Du Bois, "The Future of Europe in Africa," 197–8.

114 Gerald Horne, "Du Bois and the Socialist Countries," in Horne, *Black and Red*, 313–30.

115 Lewis, *W. E. B. Du Bois: The Fight for Equality and the American Century*, 556.

116 Karl Marx and Friedrich Engels, *The Communist Manifesto* (New York: International Publishers, 1948).

117 Lewis, *W. E. B. Du Bois: The Fight for Equality and the American Century*, 556.

118 Ibid., 260–1, emphasis in original. See also Gerald Horne, "Du Bois and the Communists," in Horne, *Black and Red*, 289–312.
119 W. E. B. Du Bois, "Russia and America: An Interpretation, 1950" (W. E. B. Du Bois Papers, MS 312, Special Collections and University Archives, University of Massachusetts Amherst Libraries). See also Kate A. Baldwin, "Du Bois, Russia, and the 'Refusal to Be White,'" in Baldwin, *Beyond the Color-Line and the Iron Curtain*, 149–201; Horne, *Black and Red*, 266–8; Lewis, *W. E. B. Du Bois: The Fight for Equality and the American Century*, 557; Mullen, *W. E. B. Du Bois*, 57–72.
120 Horne, *Black and Red*, 255–88.
121 Lewis, *W. E. B. Du Bois: The Fight for Equality and the American Century*, 407–9.
122 C. L. R. James, *State Capitalism and World Revolution*, with Raya Dunayevskaya and Grace Lee Boggs (Oakland, CA: PM Press, 2013).
123 Lewis, *W. E. B. Du Bois: The Fight for Equality and the American Century*, 563.
124 Robeson Taj Frazier, "Ruminations on Eastern Passage," in Frazier, *The East Is Black*, 37–71; Marable, *W. E. B. Du Bois*, 205.
125 Mullen, *W. E. B. Du Bois*, 135. See also Mullen, *Un-American*, 1–12.
126 Baldwin, *Beyond the Color-Line and the Iron Curtain*, 153.
127 Du Bois, "Russia and America," 247.
128 Porter, *The Problem of the Future World*, 10, 154.
129 Gary Wilder, "Reading Du Bois's Revelation: Radical Humanism and Black Atlantic Criticism," in *The Postcolonial Contemporary: Political Imaginaries for the Global Present*, ed. Jini Kim Watson and Gary Wilder (New York: Fordham University Press, 2018), 95–125.
130 Lewis, *W. E. B. Du Bois: The Fight for Equality and the American Century*, 196.
131 W. E. B. Du Bois, "The Independocrat at the Dinner Table," in W. E. B. Du Bois, *The Seventh Son: The Thought and Writings of W. E. B. Du Bois, Volume 2*, ed. Julius Lester (New York: Vintage Books, 1971), 655.
132 W. E. B. Du Bois, *The Philadelphia Negro: A Social Study* (Philadelphia: University of Pennsylvania Press, 1899); W. E. B. Du Bois, *The Souls of Black Folk: Essays and Sketches* (Chicago: A. C. McClurg & Co., 1903); Du Bois, "The Talented Tenth."

Conclusion: Du Bois's Legacy

1 Robert Gooding-Williams and Lawrie Balfour, "W. E. B. Du Bois as Political Philosopher," *Du Bois Review: Social Science Research on Race* 8, no. 2 (2011): 379–82; Lewis R. Gordon, "Du Bois's Humanistic Philosophy of Human Sciences," *Annals of the American Academy of Political and Social Science* 568, no. 1 (2000): 265–80; Michael B. Katz and Thomas J. Sugrue, eds., *W. E. B. Du Bois, Race, and the City:*

The Philadelphia Negro *and Its Legacy* (Philadelphia: University of Pennsylvania Press, 1998); Lawrence J. Oliver, "W. E. B. Du Bois and the Dismal Science: Economic Theory and Social Justice," *American Studies* 53, no. 2 (2014): 49–70; Robert E. Prasch, "W. E. B. Du Bois's Contributions to U.S. Economics (1893–1910)," *Du Bois Review: Social Science Research on Race* 5, no. 2 (2008): 309–24; Robert W. Williams, "The Early Social Science of W. E. B. Du Bois," *Du Bois Review: Social Science Research on Race* 3, no. 2 (2006): 365–94.

2 Bill V. Mullen, *Un-American: W. E. B. Du Bois and the Century of World Revolution* (Philadelphia: Temple University Press, 2015), 19–95.

3 Ronald Aronson, *After Marxism* (New York: Guilford, 1995), 161–80.

4 W. E. B. Du Bois, "Last Message," in W. E. B. Du Bois, *The Seventh Son: The Thought and Writings of W. E. B. Du Bois, Volume 2*, ed. Julius Lester (New York: Vintage Books, 1971), 736.

Index